W9-BDQ-086

GILL LIBRARY

THIS VOLUME IS THE GIFT OF

Joan Kelly SAS '76

in honor of

Ruth Mitchell Kelly

CNR Wisdom for life.

The College of New Rochelle

Criminal Justice
Recent Scholarship

Edited by
Marilyn McShane and Frank P. Williams III

A Series from LFB Scholarly

Race, Gender, and Mental Illness in the Criminal Justice System

Melissa Thompson

LFB Scholarly Publishing LLC
New York 2005

Copyright © 2005 by LFB Scholarly Publishing LLC

All rights reserved.

Library of Congress Cataloging-in-Publication Data

Thompson, Melissa, 1973-
    Race, gender, and mental illness in the criminal justice system /
Melissa Thompson.
        p. cm. -- (Criminal justice : recent scholarship)
    Includes bibliographical references and index.
    ISBN 1-59332-129-5 (alk. paper)
    1. Discrimination in criminal justice administration--United States. 2.
Crime and race--United States. 3. Crime--United States--Sex
differences. 4. Criminals--Mental health--United States. I. Title. II.
Series: Criminal justice (LFB Scholarly Publishing LLC)
    HV9950.T48 2005
    364.3'0973--dc22

2005022451

ISBN 1-59332-129-5

Printed on acid-free 250-year-life paper.

Manufactured in the United States of America.

CONTENTS

ACKNOWLEDGEMENTS

I owe a huge thanks to the many people at Hennepin County who facilitated access to my data and improved my research: Lawrence Panciera, Roberta Ellis, Rita Erickson, Carol Skradski, Marcy Podkopacz, Deb Eckberg, and Nancy Skilling were all invaluable and went above and beyond the call of duty and I am indebted to each of them.

This book has benefited greatly from thoughtful comments and vast amounts of encouragement provided by Candace Kruttschnitt. Her guidance and suggestions greatly enhanced the overall quality and relevance of this work and it would be incomplete without her. Joel Samaha, Nicki Crick, Carl Malmquist, Joachim, Salvesberg, and Liz Boyle were all invaluable in providing support, encouragement, and knowledge throughout this research. Others to whom I owe a debt include Deb Dragseth, Sheryl Trittin, Sara Wakefield, Amy Blackstone, Angie Behrens, Janna Cheney, Jessica Huiras, Mayra Gómez, and Andrew Odubote.

My family has always supported me and was hugely important throughout this process. I am especially thankful for my sister, Sarah Thompson, my parents, Phil and Judy Thompson, my sister and her family: Teresa, Dave, Dan, Chris and Maranda Beyer and my brother and his family: Mark, Laura, and Aria Thompson.

Finally, I would like to thank Chris Uggen for taking an interest in my professional development; over the past several years, Chris has given a great deal of his time in providing me with invaluable professional and substantive advice. I can honestly say that this work would not exist without his encouragement and support.

## CHAPTER 1

OVERVIEW OF THE RESEARCH

The relationship between the criminal justice and mental health systems is complex but essentially reciprocal, with increased hospital admissions in times of fewer jail admissions and decreased hospital admissions when jail populations increase (Rothman 1980; Hochstedler 1986; Cirincione et al. 1992; Torrey et al. 1992; Miller 1993; Cirincione, Steadman, and Monahan 1994; Teplin and Voit 1996; Hiday 1999; Liska et al. 1999). As a general rule, if prison populations are large, the asylum populations are relatively small; the reverse also tends to be true (Steadman et al. 1984; U.S. Department of Justice 1997a; Kupers 1999; Liska et al. 1999). Mentally ill criminal offenders are in a unique position at the intersection of both the mental health and legal systems (Freeman and Roesch 1989), often resulting in debates over which system should control mentally ill offenders. Consequently, involuntary civil commitment laws have changed dramatically, with patients' rights emphasized from the 1960s through approximately 1980; since then, the law has emphasized community security (LaFond 1994).

At the level of the individual, our knowledge of where decision-makers (primarily attorneys and judges) direct potentially mentally ill criminal offenders—whether into mental health or criminal justice—is scant. In contrast, analysis of the criminal justice system and the role of legal and extralegal factors in processing decisions is an important and well-established area of study in the sociology of law and criminology. This literature suggests that official responses of the criminal justice

1

system to offenders are based on many factors, such as evidence, individual biographies, situational factors, cultural expectations, and prior legal events, all of which intersect (Farrell and Swigert 1986; Reskin and Visher 1986; Steffensmeier and Allen 1986; Wooldredge 1998). The research in this area has also suggested that decision-makers' expectations about criminal defendants and their typical crimes affect criminal justice outcomes (Sudnow 1965; Bridges and Steen 1998). This set of expectations is developed through social interaction and results in at least two socially constructed sets of assumptions: one based on gender and another based on race.

The first set of expectations held by the criminal justice system is based on gender, where assumptions about normative male and female behavior may influence criminal justice decision-making. Stereotypes of feminine behavior include passivity, dependence, and submissiveness, whereas masculine stereotypes include dominance, assertiveness, and independence (Baskin et al. 1989; Chesney-Lind and Shelden 1998). Criminal behavior may be interpreted in light of these gendered expectations so that women who engage in non-normative criminal behavior—particularly violent crimes—are thought to violate these stereotypes (Baskin et al. 1989). Because of this, feminists have asserted that the criminal justice system is more likely to label female criminal offenders as mentally ill while treating male offenders as "rational" and therefore more responsible for their actions (Smart 1995); this process is termed "the medicalization of female deviance" (Offen 1986).

Supporters of the medicalization of female deviance hypothesis point out that 24 percent of female prisoners have been identified as mentally ill compared to 16 percent of the male prison population (U.S. Department of Justice 1999a), suggesting that mental disorders are over-diagnosed in female prisoners. The alternative hypothesis, however, is that female offenders are labeled mentally ill at a higher rate due to greater levels of actual mental illness in the female inmate population.

The second set of expectations criminal justice officials hold are related to the race of the defendant. While violent women might be considered incomprehensible or mentally ill, stereotypes of African Americans frequently focus on criminality and violence (Smith 1991; Sniderman and Piazza 1993; Emerson, Yancey, and Chai 2001; Quillian and Pager 2001). This stereotype of African Americans as criminal is deeply embedded in Americans' collective consciousness and may be used by decision-makers who must make choices based on incomplete information (Devine and Elliot 1995; Emerson et al. 2001; Quillian and Pager 2001; Pager 2004). This argument is postulated by economic theories of statistical discrimination. Statistical discrimination refers to the use of information concerning groups, rather than individuals, in decision-making. These uses of group norms in decision-making often occur in the absence of scientific data—and may in fact be contrary to these data—yet are used in the pursuit of expedience (Phelps 1972).

Sociologists have similarly argued that individuals use stereotypes about racial minorities in their perceptions of neighborhood crime rates and the stigma of incarceration (Emerson et al. 2001; Quillian and Pager 2001; Western 2002). Applying this perspective to the legal system, the use of group norms is efficient in screening cases to decide which type of punishment is fair and appropriate. Group variables such as race, age, or gender are therefore assumed to provide information regarding an individual's expected criminality or insanity[1] (Becker 1985; Kennedy 1997; Konrad and Cannings 1997). Therefore, it is expected that stereotypically "normal" offenders will be less likely than other defendants to be referred for a psychiatric evaluation to determine criminal responsibility. The average criminal defendant, who is young, African American, and male (Steffensmeier, Ulmer, and Kramer 1998; U.S. Department of Justice 1999b), will be less likely to be psychiatrically evaluated since he is not viewed as an abnormal criminal defendant. In fact, some have argued that behavior indicating severe mental pathology in minority groups is often ignored or considered to be criminal behavior rather than mental illness (Kutchins and Kirk 1997:225).

To this point, the available literature in this area has been speculative, with little empirical evidence. Thus, the extent to which female and non-African American deviance is attributed to mental illness in the criminal justice system is unclear. This limitation in the literature stems from the difficulty associated with disentangling gender and race from other issues legitimately tied to medical and psychiatric labels, such as poverty or "real" mental disorder. In this research, this concern is addressed by using unique data and methods to isolate the effects of race and gender on medicalization in the criminal justice system. The purposes of this project, therefore, are to systematically test the medicalization of female deviance hypothesis and to determine the effect of race on medicalization; this project also seeks to determine how medicalization alters case outcomes.

RESEARCH QUESTIONS

The primary interest in of this research is criminal responsibility and how it is attributed to criminal defendants. The question that is addressed is: *What effects do racial and gendered expectations have on criminal justice processing?* More specifically: *Are women labeled "mad" while men are labeled "bad?" Are African American defendants "criminal" while non-African Americans are "ill?"* The primary objectives in this project include determining:

1. What are the characteristics of defendants who are evaluated to determine their mental state at the time of a criminal offense?
2. What is the role of race and gendered expectations[2] in predicting psychiatric evaluations for felony defendants? More specifically:
    a. Are female offenders medicalized by being more likely to receive a psychiatric evaluation than similar male offenders?
    b. Are there race-specific expectations of "normal" behavior that govern perceptions of the appropriateness or rationality of criminal actions?
3. How does receipt of a psychiatric evaluation alter final case outcomes?

To meet these objectives, demographic, criminal, familial, and psychiatric data were gathered for felony defendants in Hennepin County, Minnesota. Data for the cases came from case files for defendants referred by lawyers or judges for a psychiatric evaluation to determine mental status at the time of the offense. The research involved reviewing the psychiatric records of all felony defendants referred between 1993 and 2001 (N = 412). These cases were compared to a matching control group of felony defendants who did not receive a psychiatric evaluation. Data for this comparison group came from pre-sentence investigative reports (N = 517).

The primary threat to this analysis would come from a comparison of two groups that differ due to some unknown factor. The sampling strategy, which is based on a case-control methodology, is designed to address this concern by randomly sampling a control group from the entire population at risk for an evaluation: felony defendants in Hennepin County. By using this methodology, estimates are obtained of the relative risk of a psychiatric referral for male, female, African American, and non-African American defendants. Thus, the main benefit of this methodology is its ability to isolate the effects of race and gender by statistically controlling for other factors also associated with psychiatric referral, such as mental illness and socioeconomic status.

Using logistic regression, this research models predictors of psychiatric evaluation. With a series of nested models, it ascertains the extent to which the differential treatment of offenders is due to medicalization. The primary findings include the following:

1. After statistically controlling for psychiatric disorder, criminal history, and the current offense type, the analysis determines whether female offenders are significantly more likely than male offenders to receive a psychiatric evaluation. The results demonstrate that in the bivariate analysis, women are actually *less* likely than men to receive psychiatric evaluations. This is not, however, entirely unexpected since women tend to commit more non-violent offenses than men, and violent offenses are positively correlated with psychiatric evaluations. Under other specifications, which statistically control for violent offense, gender either has no effect or increases the likelihood of a psychiatric evaluation.

2. To determine whether sex-specific expectations of "normal" behavior govern perceptions of the appropriateness or rationality of criminal actions, this project tests whether the type of crime alters the likelihood of a psychiatric referral and case outcome. For example, if females charged with a more typical female crime (such as theft) are medicalized at a

different rate than females charged with a less typical female crime (such as robbery), this would provide some evidence that gendered expectations are influencing case outcome. In the first few models, this project finds that women who committed violent offenses were significantly more likely to receive psychiatric evaluations than non-violent women or all men. Once controls are included for psychiatric history, however, the significance of the violent-by-female interaction effect disappears, indicating that these violent women actually *are* more mentally ill—or at least had received psychiatric treatment and diagnosis in the past.

3. This project demonstrates a strong, robust race effect indicating that African Americans are significantly less likely than non-African Americans to receive psychiatric evaluations to determine mental status at the time of the offense. This implies that criminal justice decision-makers have expectations about the "normal" or typical offender—based on race—and that the typical offender (perceived to be African American) is held fully responsible for criminal offenses, while the non-typical offender (non-African American) is thought to be less responsible for criminal offenses.

Using both probit and tobit estimation, this project determines the effects of psychiatric evaluations on case outcomes; it tests whether receipt of an evaluation increases or decreases the severity of case outcomes. Specifically, this project finds:

4. Defendants who receive a psychiatric evaluation to determine mental status are significantly less likely than those not evaluated to have their case dismissed; those evaluated are also more likely to be found guilty, to receive a prison sentence, and to receive longer sentences. These results imply that mental health and legal agents might work together—rather than in opposition—to determine the best outcome for potentially mentally ill individuals. Consequently, decision-makers in the criminal justice system may inadvertently be causing differential treatment on the basis of a perceived mental illness.

Overall, this research indicates that most female deviance is *not* medicalized, notwithstanding compelling arguments made by feminist scholars. Despite the inconsistent effect of gender, this lack of support for the medicalization of female deviance hypothesis is an important finding with two primary implications. First, the results indicate that the feminist view that female deviance is labeled "mad not bad" should be reconsidered. Many feminists contend that gender inequalities should be expected since the legal system reflects the masculine perspective and views women the way men view women. Since this research fails to support this point of view, it may be that recent changes in the legal system—reflecting the presence of more women— have altered the legal system's perception of women.[3] Thus, feminist assertions may need to be modified to reflect changes in social expectations and their reflections in criminal justice processing. Second, since female defendants do not appear to be funneled into mental health treatment at a greater rate than males, the criminal justice system should re-examine gendered differences in mental health treatment in the nation's prisons. Female mentally ill offenders are significantly more likely than similar males to report receiving mental health treatment while incarcerated (U.S. Department of Justice 1999a). Further research is needed to determine why mentally ill women are more likely than mentally ill men to receive treatment. This treatment difference in prisons may have long-term consequences, particularly for those with untreated mental disorders.[4]

While this project focused initially on gendered constructions of "normal" behavior and how they might alter the path a defendant takes through the criminal justice system, these results point to perhaps a more interesting story about race. In their 1998 *American Sociological Review* article, Bridges and Steen explain that "officials may have different theories about the causes of crimes for blacks and whites and perceive minority youths as more threatening than white youths" (1998:568). They state that this "indicates that a perceptual logic of explanation and assessment directs the disposition of offenders" (1998:568). This book contends that this assessment of offenders also occurs in the context of appraising mental health and defining criminal responsibility. By deeming some offenders to be ill, or not culpable, criminal justice officials make decisions based on limited knowledge. Criminal justice decision-makers are likely making judgments based on past experiences and stereotypes, which are socially constructed in the course of their work. These judgments about which defendants to hold criminally responsible for their behavior and which ones to treat medically are meaningful avenues for research and will yield important information about the social control of female and African American offenders.

The following chapters focus on the predictors of psychiatric evaluations for felony defendants and the effects of these evaluations on case outcomes. This study aims to contribute to the state of sociological and criminological knowledge in four ways: (1) by using a sampling strategy that isolates the effects of race and gender on attributions of mental illness, (2) by testing feminist, labeling, and social control theories about attributions of mental illness, (3) by applying logistic regression to determine the relative effect of race and gender on mental illness evaluations, and (4) by determining the effect mental illness attributions have on final case outcomes.

To explore the relationships between race, gender, crime, and mental illness, this book begins by reviewing the relevant literature and by explaining the theoretical perspective taken, that of differential labeling based on racial/gendered assumptions or expectations. The following six chapters of this book lay out the theoretical perspective, research design, results, and conclusions in greater detail. Chapter Two is an in-depth discussion of the relevant literature on race, gender, mental illness, and crime. It also considers the current state of knowledge along with the limitations of this literature.

Chapter Three lays out the theoretical perspective, focusing on feminist, labeling, and social control theories and how these theories relate to gender and race differences in attributions of mental illness. This chapter ends by proposing a theory of mental illness labeling in the criminal justice system and by stating the relevant hypotheses.

Chapter Four documents the data, measures, and methods; in this chapter the data sources, maintained by Hennepin County, are described. Chapter Four also describes case-control methods and the procedure used for sampling. This chapter also includes a discussion of the generalizability of these data.

Chapter Five presents the first stage of the data analysis, which examines the predictors of psychiatric evaluations, determining the set of factors that best explains which defendants will be evaluated. This chapter presents descriptive data and compares the demographic characteristics of the cases and controls. Later in Chapter Five, the results of a series of logistic regression models are presented, which identify the predictors of receipt of a psychiatric evaluation.

Chapter Six presents the next stage of the analysis, examining the effect of these psychiatric evaluations on various case outcomes. This chapter presents descriptive statistics and then presents an analysis of the effect of evaluations on various case outcomes. It also explores the possibility of sample selection bias affecting these results.

In the final chapter, Chapter Seven, the key findings of this project are summarized and discuss the implications and limitations of this research are discussed. This chapter explains how race and gender impact criminal justice processing and attributions of mental illness; it also discusses both the theoretical and policy implications of the results. Finally, this chapter concludes by pointing to avenues for future research.

NOTES

[1] The term "insanity" is used throughout this book to refer to the use of a defense of mental disease or defect. Although the actual term "insanity" is not typically used in the statutory language of mental illness defenses, this term is nevertheless used because of its ease of use – it is significantly simpler to refer to an insanity defense than to repeatedly say "defense of mental disease or defect" (which is the actual statutory language).

[2] This project uses *gendered expectations* and *gender roles* in reference to stereotypical conceptions of women as nurturing caretakers who are economically dependent and men as self-reliant and economically independent.

[3] This possible change in the legal system's perception of women might be especially apparent in the state of Minnesota, which tends to be more progressive on gender issues than other states. For example, Minnesota ranks in the top seven states in women's median earnings (U.S. Department of Labor 2002).

[4] While most people would expect negative effects of untreated mental illness, labeling theory emphasizes the negative effect of psychiatric labels; those labeled mentally ill who are not "objectively" mentally ill might similarly face long-term negative consequences.

## CHAPTER 2

THE STUDY OF GENDER, RACE, MENTAL ILLNESS, AND CRIME

GENDER, RACE, AND CRIMINAL JUSTICE PROCESSING

Trends in Crime

Gender. Together with age, gender is one of the most consistent predictors of crime (Hagan, Gillis and Simpson 1985; Farnworth and Teske 1995); men are more involved than women in criminal activity "always and everywhere" (Gottfredson and Hirschi 1990:145). With recent increases in the female percentage of arrests (Steffensmeier and Allan 1996), convictions (Nagal and Johnson 1994), and incarcerations (U.S. Department of Justice 1998b), a great deal of attention has focused on the "new" type of criminal: women. The most important gender differences in arrests, however, involve the proportionately greater female involvement in minor property crimes. The gender gap continues to be greatest for crimes against persons and for major property crimes (Steffensmeier and Allan 1996).

Historical research demonstrates that the current slight increase in female criminality is relatively small compared to earlier levels of female crime. According to Feeley and Little (1991), women constituted a "substantial portion" of felony indictments (ranging from larceny to murder) in much of the 18th century. While the female share of indictments declined thereafter, it appears that other methods of social control picked up the slack (Feeley and Little 1991; see also Boritch and Hagan 1990). Changing economic structures removed women from the formal economy and placed them under the supervision of their husbands (Feeley and Little 1991). At the same time, women increasingly became subject to the control of insane asylums, with women viewed as "not bad but mad" (Zedner 1991:264). This "new" conception of female offenders as "feeble-minded" resulted in a significant decline in the female prison population in the early 20th century (Zedner 1991).[1] To some extent, this portrayal of women criminals as mentally deficient has endured into contemporary criminal justice (Worrall 1990; Zedner 1991:296).

Women, both historically and currently, are most likely to be involved in property offenses, especially larceny or fraud. Men are more likely than women to be involved in more aggressive crimes, such as assault or robbery (Worrall 1990; Feeley and Little 1991; Zedner 1991; Steffensmeier and Allan 1996; U.S. Department of Justice 1998a). The recent gains that have occurred in female criminality have primarily been within a category of relatively minor property and drug offenses (Steffensmeier and Allan 1996; U.S. Department of Justice 1998c). Although the same criminal activity may have similar social causes for both men and women, the reactions of the criminal justice system may not be uniform across the sexes (see Boritch and Hagan 1990; Worrall 1990; Zedner 1991).

The current knowledge about differences in criminal justice responses to male and female criminals is based primarily on female offenders who fulfill gender stereotypes by committing less physically aggressive crimes—such as theft and drug smuggling. It is unknown, however, if violations of gender stereotypes alter punishment. For example, what effect does committing a crime against a family member have on case processing? Do women who kill their batterers receive harsher or more lenient punishment than males who kill their spouses? In one study, a majority of female-perpetrated homicides involved family members as victims (48 percent were domestic partners; 11 percent children) (Mann 1996:69). Since this type of crime violates two expectations by revealing (1) violence by a woman and (2) a non-nurturing mother or wife, how does the official response to violence differ for males and females? One study of official reactions to spousal murder is presented by the U.S. Department of Justice (DOJ) (1994), using 1988 data. According to the DOJ, there are significant differences in case outcomes when a woman is accused of killing her husband compared to when a man is accused of killing his wife (1994:6). Women facing these charges are more likely than men to have charges dismissed or be acquitted. Of those convicted, women are less likely to receive a prison sentence, and among those who are sentenced to prison, men's sentences are longer than women's sentences (DOJ 1994).

While these data from the DOJ are significant and provide important information about how gender and violence interact with social expectations of family, they are limited. These statistics fail to adjust for the different criminal history of men and women. Compared to women without a criminal history, men with a lengthy criminal history should be less likely to have their cases dismissed and should also expect a lengthier prison sentence. This study also uses data several years old (from 1988), which is problematic because social expectations of women may have changed significantly in the last 15 years. Because this single limited study is insufficient to determine how official responses to violent crime differ for men and women, further investigation of gendered attributions of criminal responsibility is necessary.

Race. African Americans are over-represented in all stages of the criminal justice system. For example, 57 percent of felony defendants in large urban counties in the U.S. are black, whereas 41 percent are white (U.S. Department of Justice 2001a); in comparison, African Americans comprise approximately 13 percent of the U.S. population and whites approximately 81 percent (U.S. Bureau of the Census 2003a). Black males comprise the largest proportion of felony defendants, with white males second; black females are third and comprise a slightly higher percentage than white females (U.S. Department of Justice 2001a). In addition to being overrepresented in the felony population, African Americans have the highest likelihood of being imprisoned. According to the DOJ, African Americans have a 16.2 percent lifetime chance of going to prison while the chance of imprisonment is lowest for whites at 2.5 percent (1997b).

Consequently, at year-end 2003, there were 3,405 sentenced black male inmates per 100,000 black males in the United States and 465 white male inmates per 100,000 white males (U.S. Department of Justice 2004). These race differences are also apparent among women; at year-end 2003, there were 185 sentenced black female inmates per 100,000 black females in the United States and 38 white female inmates per 100,000 white females (U.S. Department of Justice 2004).

There are two primary explanations for the disproportionate representation of African Americans in U.S. correctional populations. The first is that African Americans are overrepresented in the criminal justice system simply because they commit more severe crimes and have a longer criminal history than non-African Americans. This perspective tends to argue that effectively controlling for all legally relevant variables, such as criminal history and offense severity, eliminates racial differences (Blumstein 1982; Petersilia and Turner 1998). In general, the body of research on unwarranted disparity demonstrates large effects of legally relevant variables on case outcome, and there is little evidence of direct racial discrimination once these legal factors are appropriately included in statistical analysis (Myers and Talarico 1987; Wilbanks 1987; Klein, Petersilia, and Turner 1988; Engen and Gainey 2000). This evidence led Sampson and Lauritsen to conclude that "there is little evidence that racial disparities reflect systematic, overt bias on the part of criminal justice decision makers (as a whole)" (1997:362).

The second explanation for racial differences is discrimination on the part of decision-makers in the criminal justice system. In response to the literature suggesting little or no racial discrimination, some have argued that modeling discrimination requires greater statistical rigor than has previously been used (Miethe and Moore 1986; Albonetti 1997; Steffensmeier et al. 1998). For example, when analyzing the length of prison sentences, models that exclude offenders who received other sentences, such as probation, fail to account for racial differences that may have occurred earlier in the justice process. To solve this problem, most researchers use techniques that control for this sample-selection bias (see Bushway and Piehl 2001). When such analytical techniques are implemented, there is some evidence of harsher treatment within the criminal justice system for African American defendants in comparison to non-African American (especially white) defendants (Spohn and Holleran 2000; Steffensmeier and DeMuth 2000; Bushway and Piehl 2001).

Criminal Justice Processing, Determinate Sentencing, and Extralegal Factors

How does the criminal justice system respond to criminal defendants? Are male and female and African American and non-African American offenders treated similarly or have stereotypes of "normal" behavior influenced the processing of "abnormal" behavior (see Worrall 1990; Zedner 1991)? This section focuses on answering these and other questions about how the justice system responds to defendants based on their gender and race.

In 1984 the United States Congress adopted the Sentencing Reform Act. This Act created the United States Sentencing Commission, whose purpose was to implement "facially neutral sentencing guidelines, in order to reduce unwarranted sentencing disparity and eliminate the sentencing impact of extralegal factors such as the offender's race, gender, and socioeconomic status" (Nagel and Johnson 1994: 183). While this Act took place on the federal level, many states made similar changes in their sentencing practices, with the goal of reducing the amount of discretion a judge has in determining a sentence for a convicted offender. While other criminal justice practices, such as pretrial release, conviction, and incarceration, were not officially affected by this Act, it is believed that many practices that occurred in the court tended to follow the same pattern as that for sentencing (Nagel and Johnson 1994).

The idea behind determinate sentencing is that by reducing the amount of judicial discretion, fewer extralegal factors will influence the criminal justice process. There are three primary schools of thought, however, that argue determinate sentencing fails to reduce sentencing disparities based on extralegal factors. First, some argue that instead of reducing gender and racial disparity in treatment, determinate sentencing systems have instead heightened the discretionary impact of decisions made at other points in the system (Wonders 1996). Since police officers have discretion in making arrests, for example, use of number of prior arrests or convictions under a determinate sentencing scheme ignores the fact that police behavior is discretionary and therefore subject to its own form of discrimination. Wonders (1996) also suggests that using prior arrests as a legal variable fails to account for that fact that poverty areas are over-enforced by the police, and that different jurisdictions may develop "drug courier profiles" or "gang lists," which are used to stop suspicious persons (p. 630). If an African American male offender is more likely to be arrested than a white female, he would probably have more convictions, which might bump him up into the next level of sentencing severity.

Second, within determinate sentencing schemes, courts are allowed the discretion to deviate from guidelines in atypical situations. These deviations also appear to be the "locus of significant extralegal differences" involving both gender and race (Kramer and Ulmer 1996:81). While it is often asserted that differences in sentencing male and female offenders are due to greater involvement in serious and violent crime among men, Bridges and Beretta argue that gender differences in criminal behavior contribute "substantially less to disparities in imprisonment than suggested or implied by many previous writers" (1994:173). Under determinate sentencing schemes, judges have ranges that determine the high and low end of appropriate sentences, but allowances are made for some judicial discretion. Judges are still allowed to consider mitigating and aggravating factors that influence the final sentence imposed. Nagal and Johnson argue that

> female offenders benefit disproportionately from each of the principal discretionary components in the guidelines scheme: downward departure for substantial assistance to authorities; downward departure due to atypical facts or circumstances; and selection of a sentence from within the low end of the applicable sentencing range (1994:216).

For example, in drug cases, if a woman agrees to testify against others involved in a smuggling operation, she will receive a lighter sentence than one based strictly on the guidelines. Nagel and Johnson report that almost 45 percent of female drug offenders received downward departures in 1992 compared to just 28 percent of male drug offenders. While the research is not clear enough to conclude that equally cooperative male and female offenders are treated dissimilarly, these results are notable since a majority of female offenders tend to play minor roles in drug offenses. As a result, female drug offenders tend to "lack sufficient information to provide legally adequate substantial assistance" (Nagal and Johnson 1994:218).

Third, since we often attribute certain personal characteristics to perpetrators of certain classes of crime (Sudnow 1965; Farrell and Swigert 1986), the legislative determination of appropriate sentence lengths may also conceal discrimination. With stereotypes of the "typical" drug offender, for example, drug laws are subject to a "social construction of seriousness," which results in enormous differences in sentencing for crack and powder cocaine (Wonders 1996:628). By "legislating justice from a distance" (Daly and Tonry 1997:243), these determinate policies may have unwittingly removed the positive effects of judicial discretion and concealed the continuing effects of extralegal variables such as race and gender in criminal justice processing.

Therefore, despite the presence of structural factors meant to eliminate the effects of extralegal factors on criminal justice outcomes, there is evidence that race and gender still affect legal decision-making. For example, many believe that for women, social status is significant in determining the type of criminal court disposition she receives. Variables that contribute to this notion of respectability or social position include age, health status, whether she receives welfare, marital status, if she has family responsibilities, prior arrests, previous psychiatric care, drug/alcohol abuse, the extent of peer deviance, and whether she is a student or unemployed (Black 1976; Kruttschnitt 1980-81; Kruttschnitt 1982; Simpson 1989). While some of these variables are legal factors, which are appropriate for determining criminal justice responses (e.g., prior arrests), others are extralegal factors (e.g., prior psychiatric care) and are not explicitly thought to play a role in institutional responses.[2] These social characteristics are believed to predict the nature and extent of offenders' sentences and criminal court dispositions for women (Kruttschnitt 1980-81; 1982; Simpson 1989; Kruttschnitt 1996).

Among adults, women are treated more severely in the decision to prosecute but they are more likely than men to enter guilty pleas, which are traditionally thought to ensure lighter sentences (Daly 1989; Daly 1994; Engen et al. 2003). Additionally, women are treated less severely in pretrial release decisions (Boritch 1992; Farnworth and Teske 1995; Daly and Tonry 1997:229), which may similarly alter sentencing severity. Within homicide cases, some evidence suggests that the sex of the defendant, the race, sex, and occupational prestige of victims, and the interaction of defendant's and victims' occupational prestige (Farrell and Swigert 1986; Hanke 1995) affect adjudication decisions. In general, males and defendants of lower status receive harsher sentences. Since the concept of femininity is incongruent with violence, women in court processing are generally not perceived as provoking their victimization (Farrell and Swigert 1986). This appears to result in harsher treatment for defendants with female victims (Farrell and Swigert 1986; but see Hanke 1995).

Steffensmeier, Kramer, and Streifel conclude, "when men and women appear in (contemporary) criminal court in similar circumstances and are charged with similar offenses, they receive similar treatment" (1993:439). They find this after arguing that the sentencing practices of judges are driven by (1) blameworthiness (prior record, type of involvement, and remorse) and (2) practicality (childcare responsibilities, pregnancy, emotional or physical problems, and availability of adequate jail space) (Steffensmeier, Kramer, and Streifel 1993; Steffensmeier, Ulmer, and Kramer 1998). They acknowledge an important policy question arising from their findings: is disparate treatment warranted when it is due to issues such as pregnancy or emotional problems (Steffensmeier, Kramer, and Streifel 1993)? These differences may actually reflect social expectations that benefit some women, leaving others to be treated more harshly for their "failure" to meet social expectations; it is therefore doubtful that a consensus can be reached as to what is a warranted source of gender disparity.[3] For example, a defendant's race may alter decision-makers' perceptions of appropriate family ties and responsibilities (Bickle and Peterson 1991; Daly and Bordt 1995; Steffensmeier, Ulmer, and Kramer 1998). Race and gender may interact so that the "mother" role of staying at home and taking care of children is considered appropriate for white women but is viewed as laziness (or taking advantage of public assistance such as Temporary Assistance for Needy Families [TANF]) on the part of African American women (Collins 2000; Roberts 2002; see also Hudson 2002:40).

The most consistent criminal justice gender difference is the decision to imprison offenders (Steffensmeier et al. 1993; Daly and Bordt 1995), with females less likely to be imprisoned; gender does not appear to affect the length of the sentence, however. Once on probation or parole, other gender differences appear. While probation and parole officers perceive men with emotional instability as "needy," they do not appear to view emotionality as significant for women (Erez 1989; 1992). Erez explains that the message sent by the correctional system to its clients is that "the only acceptable mode of reintegration into society is through conformity to gender stereotypes and traditional sex-roles" (1989:323).

While it is relatively simple to focus only on a dichotomous gender variable when analyzing the role of women in the criminal justice system, this approach has serious limitations in that it disregards variability due to multiple group memberships (Simpson 1989; Menkel-Meadow and Diamond 1991; Collins 1998; Frazier and Hunt 1998; Collins 2000). The race of the defendant, victim, lawyer, and judge are important avenues for research. When race *has* been addressed in previous research, it tends to fall into the "essentialism trap," by equating *all* women with white women or *all* minorities with black women (Harris 1990; Omi and Winant 1994; Alcoff 1988; Narayan 1997; Goodkind 2005). Differences in the response of the criminal justice system are not based solely on gender, but particularly on cultural and social differences within groups of women. Some authors, for example, assert that the institutional responses are "selectively chivalrous" (Nagel and Johnson 1994), only benefiting certain groups of women—such as white women (Hudson 2002).

There is some evidence suggesting that both the defendant's race and the victim's race affect sentencing. Hanke, for example, analyzed sentencing of violent women offenders based on their race and that of their victims in Alabama (1995). She noted that the lightest sentences (1-5 years) were given for whites who murdered blacks and for blacks who murdered other blacks. Moderate to heavy sentences (6-20 years) were given to whites murdering whites, while the most severe sentences (life in prison) were received by black women who murdered white women.[4] Hanke suggests that these findings indicate that stereotypes of appropriate behavior may be an important factor in sentence severity. She offers the explanation that African Americans are perceived to be violent (1995:294) and if they direct this violence against other African Americans, sanctions do not need to be severe. Her explanation for the moderate sentences of white-on-white homicide is that murder violates stereotypes of "lady-like" behavior. Hanke's results clarify the limitations of corrections research based solely on gender or race. The *interaction* of race and gender is therefore an important area for research (see Crew 1991; Horowitz and Pottieger 1991; Steffensmeier, Ulmer, and Kramer 1998).

Family Factors

Some have argued that the social reactions to gender and race are conditioned on other factors, including the defendant's family status. For example, Daly (1989; 1994) contends that gender differences in criminal justice processing are actually the result of differences in the social location of women compared to men. She explains that it is clear that many gender differences in sentencing may be the result of judges taking family factors into account. This stems from concern that when mothers are locked up, children also suffer (see Steffensmeier, Kramer, and Streifel 1993). When men are imprisoned, there is usually another parental figure to assume responsibility for children. Since many women are the sole support for their children, any punishment directed at these women would also punish children. This perspective also contends that it is more costly (impractical) to imprison women with families than men with families since wage-earner support (provided by men) is more readily replaced (through public assistance, TANF) than care-taking labor (foster or institutional care) (Daly 1987:281). As a result, Daly (1989; 1994) argues that gender differences are simply a reflection of judges working to ensure that parental supervision will remain for children in the future.

Research does not consistently support Daly's contention, however. Crew (1991), for example, did find that economic support was important for men's sentencing and family roles were important determinants of women's, but Bickle and Peterson (1991) found that economic support had little influence on decisions to incarcerate. Race appears to further condition the effect of family factors on court outcomes (Daly 1989; Bickle and Peterson 1991; Crew 1991). While the use of gender-based family factors provides an important conceptual framework for decision-making, these studies fail to account for the traditional gender-based leniency and often ignore the role of legal variables in sentencing decisions.

Methodological Issues in Previous Research

In addition to understanding the effect of discretion on race, gender, and criminal justice processing, it is important to note the effect of legal variables in altering case outcomes. In testing the arguments that white and female criminals receive preferential treatment within the criminal justice system, several factors may pose difficulties for direct comparison of criminal defendants. One major criticism of early research on gender differences in sentencing is that gender role stereotypes were considered while ignoring important legal variables (Kruttschnitt 1996). This concern is significant since structural factors, including the sentencing guidelines, emphasize legally relevant factors such as previous criminal activity in sentencing decisions (Wonders 1996).

An additional criticism of previous sentencing disparity research is that examiners occasionally fail to control in their statistical analyses for the type of crime committed, which obviously has a tremendous impact on sentencing decisions (Crew 1991; Daly and Tonry 1997). Therefore, since both African American and male defendants tend to have more prior contacts with the criminal justice system and since they tend to engage in much more violent behavior (Daly and Wilson 1988; Boritch and Hagan 1990; Worrall 1990; Feeley and Little 1991; Zedner 1991; Kruttschnitt 1996; Steffensmeier and Allan 1996; U.S. Department of Justice 1998a), any differences attributed to race or gender may, in fact, be the result of criminological variables which are central to sentencing decision-making.

Early research on the effect of extralegal factors on criminal processing was characterized by its failure to control for important legal variables such as prior record and seriousness of offense (Steffensmeier et al. 1993; Daly and Bordt 1995). More recent work has largely addressed these issues and provided adequate controls. Once these control variables are added, however, the pattern of more lenient treatment of women and the harsher treatment of African Americans remains (Steffensmeier et al. 1992; Spohn and Spears 1997; Steffensmeier and DeMuth 2000; Bushway and Piehl 2001). For women lenient treatment is especially apparent in the decision to incarcerate (Steffensmeier et al. 1993; Daly and Bordt 1995; Spohn and Spears 1997). For African Americans, harsher treatment is especially apparent when examining the actions of one set of actors (e.g., lawyers and judges) rather than the actions of the justice system as a whole (Bushway and Piehl 2001). While researchers have made methodological advances in their use of controls for prior record and current charges, the choice of measures for these factors can vary, often influencing the results (Daly and Bordt 1995; Wooldredge 1998). For example, Wooldredge (1998) explains that when predicting sentence severity, "whether a person has *ever* been arrested...may be a more reliable measure of prior record than number of arrests" (p. 158). This is because the *exact* number of arrests may be distorted by other social statuses; Wooldredge (1998) explains that certain age and race groups are more geographically mobile, resulting in underestimates in the number of prior arrests (p. 158).

Much of the literature on gender and criminal justice processing is limited by focusing solely on "normal" feminine criminal behaviors, such as shoplifting and forgery. Focusing on activities that are routinely associated with females limits understanding of the effect of gender-role expectations. Since comparatively few physically aggressive women appear in the legal system, there is little research addressing how the legal system responds in such situations.[5] Instead, most studies tend to examine criminal behavior that happens more frequently for women, such as theft and forgery. As a result, much of the literature in this area is limited by failing to address behaviors that most radically violate gender-role expectations. From the few limited examinations of serious person offenses, it appears that differences between male and female criminal justice processing may either be insignificant (Farnworth and Teske 1995), or less severe for women (Spohn and Spears 1997). While expectations of feminine weakness and passivity date at least to the Victorian Era (Zedner 1991), their impact in criminal justice processing remains relatively unknown.

Conflicting studies of gender differences in criminal court outcomes may reflect different sample types and different control variables (Horowitz and Pottieger 1991). In addition, there may be serious methodological limitations in the data sources used, often official arrest or court records, which may not accurately reflect actual crimes committed. These sources reflect only one stage of criminal justice processing, when gender bias or racial bias may occur at many stages and the cumulative effect may be greatly different than that portrayed in official statistics (see Wonders 1996). These official data often refer to sentencing, which falls late in criminal justice processing. Rather than presenting all offenses, official statistics often reflect only the most serious final charge, which may be significantly altered through the process of plea-bargaining (see Crew 1991). Finally, by restricting analysis to official records, studies frequently result in far too few female observations to effectively compare males with females (Horowitz and Pottieger 1991).

GENDER, RACE, AND MENTAL ILLNESS

Gender and Race Differences in the Prevalence and Types of Mental Illness

Gender. While there appear to be no gender differences in the overall *rates* of mental disorder, men and women do differ in the *type* of disorder experienced (Dohrenwend and Dohrenwend 1976; Kessler and McLeod 1984; Hankin 1990; Aneshensel, Rutter, and Lachenbruch 1991; Rosenfield 1999).[6] With respect to gender differences for specific diagnoses, women have higher rates of depression and anxiety disorder (referred to as "internalizing" disorders), and men have higher rates of substance abuse and antisocial disorders (also called "externalizing" disorders) (Robins et al. 1981; 1991; Potts, Burnam, and Wells 1991; Bourdon et al. 1992; APA 1994:341, 647; Kessler and Shanyang 1999; Rosenfield 1999; Sharp, Brewster, and Love 2005).[7] Taking all psychological disorders together, however, most studies show that there are no differences overall in men's and women's rates of mental disorder, which also holds for some of the more severe disorders such as schizophrenia (Kessler et al. 1993; APA 1994:281; Kessler et al. 1994; Rosenfield 1999).[8]

The explanations for the gender differences that do exist (internalizing versus externalizing disorders) refer to divisions in power and responsibilities—women earn less than men, tend to have jobs with less power and autonomy, and are more responsive to the problems of people in their social networks—all of which contribute to psychological distress on the part of women (Kessler and McLeod 1984; Mowbray and Chamberlain 1986; Brown and Harris 1989;

Rosenfield 1989; Aneshensel et al. 1991; Horwitz, McLaughlin, and White 1998; Rosenfield 1999; Thoits 1999; Turner and Lloyd 1999). While women are encouraged to act out their distress in an emotional or dependent manner, men are socialized into acting out, or externalizing their distress, through substance abuse or antisocial behavior. Although these studies point to the comparative presence of labeled mental disorder, some argue that psychiatric labels are subject to gendered expectations, similar to the criminal labeling process.

Race. Although there has not been a great deal of research on racial differences in mental illness, most available evidence points to higher rates of psychological distress and mental illness among African Americans compared to whites (Tausig et al. 1999; Williams and Harris-Reid 1999; Cockerham 2000; Schultz et al. 2000; Gallagher 2002). For example, using Epidemiologic Catchment Area (ECA) data, Williams and Harris-Reid report lifetime prevalence rates for any mental disorder of 38 percent for African Americans and 32 percent for whites (1999:299).

There have been two primary explanations for the racial differences in mental disorder. The first is essentially that mental illness is the result of racism. In comparison to whites, African Americans are exposed to additional stressors based on their racial identity, even when matched on the basis of education, income, and occupation (Tausig et al. 1999). This perspective asserts that because African Americans are at a disadvantage when compared to whites with similar educational and employment histories (Pager 2004), they experience additional psychological stressors which may lead to higher levels of mental disorder (Tausig et al. 1999; Cockerham 2000; Schultz et al. 2000; Gallagher 2002). Some support has been found for this perspective. Analysis of data from several prior U.S. mental health surveys found that among those in the lowest social class, African Americans showed more psychological distress than whites (Kessler and Neighbors 1986). Some suggest that the combined effects of poverty and racial discrimination produce greater distress for poor blacks in comparison to poor whites (Kessler and Neighbors 1986). Others, however, find that this higher level of psychological distress among lower-class African Americans does not necessarily lead to higher levels of mental illness when compared to lower-class whites (Cockerham 1990; Williams et al. 1992). Consequently, there is insufficient evidence to indicate that racism leads to greater levels of mental disorder in African Americans.

The second explanation for racial differences in mental illness is social class. Because low socioeconomic status is one of the most consistent predictors of mental illness (Faris and Dunham 1939; Hollingshead and Redlich 1953; Link, Dohrenwend, and Skodol 1986; Mirowsky and Ross 1989a; Ortega and Corzine 1990; Turner, Wheaton, and Lloyd 1995), the higher rate of mental disorder found among African Americans may simply be the result of the lower SES position of African Americans. In fact, most research that finds a significant racial difference in rates of mental illness also finds that adequately controlling for SES causes the race effect to disappear (Dohrenwend and Dohrenwend 1969; 1974; Warheit et al. 1973; Warheit Holzer, and Avery 1975; Kessler 1979; Frerichs, Aneshensel, and Clark 1981; Kessler et al. 1994; Schultz et al. 2000). Thus, despite the few studies that appear to demonstrate a difference between whites and African Americans in psychological stressors, a majority of research studies indicate that racial differences in psychological disorder can be attributed to social class differences rather than race itself (Kutchins and Kirk 1997; Tausig et al. 1999; Cockerham 2000; Gallagher 2002).

Critiques of Psychiatric Labeling

Mirowsky and Ross (1989b) are quite critical of psychiatric labeling. Their major criticism is that psychological problems are *not* discrete entities. A mental illness is not entirely present or entirely absent— there are gradations in between that the DSM (*Diagnostic and Statistical Manual of Mental Disorders*) fails to convey. Mirowsky and Ross question the validity of the DSM, since the diagnosis of all disorders is reduced to a dichotomy, ignoring subtle variations. They are also concerned because disorders are listed in the DSM through the consensus of a committee of psychiatrists, making it "informed but not *formed* by research" (Mirowsky and Ross 1989b:13). This argument contends that people are pigeonholed into slots that may not be valid, but are instead based on the experiences of a few individuals (see also Conrad 1975; Eaton, Ritter, and Brown 1990).

Rogler (1997) summarizes the historical changes in the DSM, explaining that while it has dramatically increased in both size and number of disorders, it has also collapsed many disorders with subtle variation into one overarching disorder. This was implemented with the goal of increasing reliability, but raises the question introduced by Mirowsky and Ross (1989b) of whether these changes had the effect of obliterating important differences, resulting in reduced validity in diagnosis. These and other critics of psychiatric labeling assert that in an effort to provide social control over the mentally disordered, an increasing number of behaviors are being medicalized[9] (Szasz 1961; Conrad 1975; Eaton, Ritter, and Brown 1990; Greeley 1990). With increased medicalization comes increased psychiatric control over drugs, electroshock therapy, insurance reimbursement, and power to declare mental or legal incompetence (Szasz 1961; Light 1982; Kutchins and Kirk 1997). Finally, by giving such power to psychiatry, these critics argue that we hand over the power of determining what is "normal" to a small group of relatively homogeneous individuals (Szasz 1961; Eaton, Ritter, and Brown 1990).

Gender. Specific to gender differences, Potts, Burnam, and Wells (1991) explore the extent to which medical and mental health clinicians[10] tend to diagnose depression differentially on the basis of the gender of their patients. This is assessed using independent measures of depression: (a) the clinician's diagnosis of clinically meaningful depression and (b) standardized assessment of depressive disorder using the Diagnostic Interview Schedule (DIS). They note that among patients who met DIS criteria for depressive disorder, medical practitioners were significantly more likely to identify depression in women than in men; among patients who did *not* meet DIS criteria for depression, mental health specialists were significantly more likely to identify depression in women than in men. These findings remained after adjustment for patient demographic and other clinically relevant factors, including depression severity (Potts, Burnam, and Wells 1991). These researchers attribute their results to several factors related to gender role socialization, including that clinicians may expect women to discuss symptoms and men to refrain from doing so. Clinicians may therefore be less likely to ask men about their symptoms, decreasing the likelihood the depression will be identified (Potts, Burnam, and Wells 1991).

Although the DSM cautions against over-diagnosing or under-diagnosing certain disorders in males or females due to social stereotypes about typical gender roles and behaviors (APA 1994:632), about 75 percent of individuals diagnosed with Borderline Personality Disorder (BPD) are female (APA 1994:652) whereas Antisocial Personality Disorder (APD) is much more common in males than females (APA 1994:647). While both of these disorders are characterized by manipulative behaviors, individuals with APD are considered manipulative to gain profit or some other material gratification, whereas the goal in BPD is directed more toward gaining the concern of caretakers (APA 1994:653). This distinction may reflect some type of expectation or interpretation of behavior due to stereotypes of male and female behavior.

Baskin et al. (1989) explored differences in gender role expectations and their effects on prison inmates. They found that when prisoners demonstrate problematic behavior, the responses of the correctional administrators vary depending on gender role expectations. Beyond the traditional gender roles there are also norms that define appropriate *deviant* behaviors for men and women. "Deviant behavior that is passive or submissive (e.g., shoplifting or certain types of mental illness) is viewed as congruent with female gender roles. Deviant behavior of the acting-out or aggressive variety is regarded as more consistent with the male role" (Baskin et al. 1989:306). Using this understanding of the expected gender roles, Baskin et al. examined placement decisions for those exhibiting problem behaviors within correctional facilities. Their findings indicated that even when controlling for the level of psychiatric need (the women in this study scored higher on measures of mental health need), women were still more likely than men to be placed in a mental health unit. Additionally, the likelihood of mental health placement significantly increased if female inmates engaged in prison violence and/or aggressive behavior (role-incongruent acts). In contrast, male inmates who participated in similar acts (but ones that were role-congruent) were placed in disciplinary confinement (Baskin et al. 1989). While this study focused on female inmates, the authors also note "males were more likely to be placed in mental health service units for "female" psychiatric disorders (e.g., depression) than were women with the same type and level of symptomatology" (p. 312).

Rosenfield (1982) also researched gender roles and the effects of rejecting them. She studied patients entering a New York City emergency room and found that men and women exhibiting "'deviant' deviance" were more likely to be admitted to the hospital for psychiatric evaluations. She concluded that both males and females are more likely to be hospitalized for disorders that are incompatible with traditional gender roles. For example, men with anxiety disorders or women displaying violent behavior are more likely to violate gender role norms and therefore be hospitalized for psychiatric treatment (Rosenfield 1982).

Race. Specific to race, Kirk and Kutchins contend that in the DSM there is an "implicit assumption that the clinician is from the dominant culture" (1997:233). Consequently, when clients are not members of the "dominant culture," they are at risk for receiving diagnoses based on cultural stereotypes and assumptions. The introduction to the DSM explains that "Diagnostic assessment can be especially challenging when a clinician from one ethnic or cultural group uses the DSM-IV Classification to evaluate an individual from a different ethnic or cultural group" (APA 1994: xxiv). For example, the DSM's discussion of Paranoid Personality Disorder includes the following discussion of "Specific Culture, Age, and Gender Features":

> Some behaviors that are influenced by sociocultural contexts or specific life circumstances may be erroneously labeled paranoid and may even be reinforced by the process of clinical evaluation. Members of minority groups...or individuals of different ethnic backgrounds may display guarded or defensive behaviors due to unfamiliarity...or in response to the perceived neglect or indifference of the majority society. These behaviors can, in turn, generate anger and frustration in those who deal with these individuals, thus setting up a vicious cycle of mistrust, which should not be confused with Paranoid Personality Disorder (APA 1994:636).

Kirk and Kutchins use this description to explain that appropriate and understandable behavior is often misconstrued by suspicious clinicians who are fearful of their clients and unable to understand their behavior (1997:234). Thus, due to the cultural differences, psychiatrists may be more likely to label those who suffer actual social exclusion— including African Americans—as paranoid (Gallagher 2002). Another criticism of psychiatric labeling with respect to race is that when African American behavior is *not* considered to be the product of paranoia, it is often assumed to be criminal behavior rather than mental illness (Kirk and Kutchins 1997:225).

In studying the effect of race and gender on psychiatric diagnosis, Loring and Powell (1988) used a vignette approach; they sent descriptions of clients to 290 psychiatrists.[11] Each vignette was exactly the same with the exception of the gender and race of the individual being studied. The significant results indicated that the sex and race of the client *and* psychiatrist influenced the diagnosis, even with a relatively straightforward diagnosis. For example, black male and black female psychiatrists tended to give white males the least serious diagnosis, as compared to the diagnoses given to females and black males with identical descriptions. Further, clinicians appear to "ascribe violence, suspiciousness, and dangerousness to black clients" (Loring and Powell 1988). Male psychiatrists were also more inclined to diagnose women with a depressive disorder, while female psychiatrists were reluctant to use this category. Loring and Powell attribute this to male psychiatrists accepting the stereotypical conception of females as emotional; consequently, male psychiatrists might be quick to assume depression for female clients. Female psychiatrists were apparently hesitant to do this, indicating that behavior seemingly too emotional for male psychiatrists may be more understandable to women.

GENDER, RACE, AND PSYCHIATRIC EVALUATIONS

When these race and gender differences in criminal and psychiatric labeling converge in the criminal justice system, they may result in a psychiatric evaluation and a possible insanity plea. There is a general lack of sociological research on the insanity defense (although considering its infrequent use, it has received perhaps disproportionate attention from psychological researchers and legal commentators). This project is an attempt to address this limitation and apply a sociological perspective to the study of mental illness attributions in the criminal justice system.

Insanity: Applications and Assumptions

The criminal law assumes that persons act with "free will" and that they should be held responsible for their own behavior (Perlin 1994; Borum and Fulero 1999). The insanity defense, however, exempts from criminal responsibility and accountability a narrow class of persons who commit offenses while experiencing mental impairment (Morse 1985; Palermo and Knudten 1994; Elliott 1996; Borum and Fulero 1999). Since criminal intent, or *mens rea*, is a principal component of establishing guilt, it is important to determine a defendant's mental state before assigning criminal responsibility (Slovenko 1995). As Minnesota's Supreme Court stated in *Anderson v. Grasberg*,

> Insanity has been recognized in all civilized countries as a defense against punishment for crime, and this has been so because, if the perpetrator is so mentally diseased that he does not have the intent or animus in the commission of the crime, the act lacks the elements which constitute the crime the law seeks to punish.

Palermo and Knudten explain that "vengeance is not a sign of personal or social maturity. Insane offenders should be treated with compassion, not branded as criminals" (1994:4). The insanity defense is viewed as an excuse rather than a justification; insane people are acquitted not because they did nothing wrong, but because they are considered morally blameless for their wrongful conduct (Smith 1985; Palermo and Knudten 1994; Finkel and Slobogin 1995). Through the insanity process, the criminal justice system determines whether to attribute responsibility to the defendant. The law deems the necessary criminal mental state absent in children below a certain age, in extreme drunkenness or automatism, in certain stages of mental disorder, and even (in the past) in wives committing certain crimes accompanied by their husbands (Smith 1985). For example, historically wives who helped their husbands commit an offense were viewed as pawns of their husbands and therefore less culpable for the crime.

The first legal standard for insanity[12]—and the standard currently used in Minnesota—is the M'Naghten Rule.[13] The M'Naghten Rule demonstrates the prevailing understanding in the legal system that everyone is to be considered a rational individual, capable of weighing their choices and deciding what type of behavior is appropriate. The basic assumption about the human mind (using M'Naghten) is that "every man is...sane, and possess[es] a sufficient degree of reason to be responsible for his crimes." Additionally, the M'Naghten Rules make it clear that the only exceptions to this assumption are when one of two things occurs, given a mental disorder: that the defendant: (1) "did not know the nature and quality of the act" or (2) "did not know...[it] was wrong." Since neither the lawyer nor the judge is trained in uncovering the mental state of the defendant, the legal system typically uses psychiatrists in making this determination.

Despite state-to-state differences in insanity standards across the country, all current expectations require the presence of a "mental disease or defect" that is severe enough to impair responsible behavior (Roberts and Goulding 1991). Because the meaning of this "mental disease or defect" is not precisely defined, the ultimate decision is subject to some interpretation. Since the DSM was prepared for clinical rather than legal purposes, labels given out using psychiatric techniques do not necessarily imply legal labels as well (Smith 1985; Freeman and Roesch 1989; APA 1994:xxvii; Slovenko 1995). In fact, profound differences exist between clinical insanity and state-law definitions of criminal insanity: "It is by now well-established that insanity as defined by the criminal law has no direct analog in medicine or science." (Blakey 1996:227). With this caveat in mind, however, the role of psychiatric expertise is enormous in any insanity decision and is typically the single most important determinant of this plea's success (Steadman et al. 1983; 1993). At minimum, to qualify for a defense of insanity, the accused must suffer from a mental disease or defect that is distinguishable from the general population of criminal offenders (Slovenko 1995). Attorneys, judges, and mental health professionals work together to determine whether this is the case.

Attorneys. In studying the decision of whether to raise a defense of insanity, Bonnie et al. (1996) conducted 139 telephone interviews with attorneys. All of these attorneys had clients who were examined by Michigan psychiatrists and had a diagnosis supportive of the insanity defense. The interviewers found that 10 percent of the defendants, when approached with the idea of a defense of insanity, resisted the plea. Another 15 percent were unreceptive to the attribution of mental illness. These researchers found that when the decision was made to pursue the defense, the attorneys pre-empted their clients' participation in the decision-making process in 36 percent of the cases—acting in the absence of consultation. Even when the client was consulted, the degree of participation was relatively low. Bonnie et al. attribute this behavior to "a distinct tendency toward paternalistic decision-making in cases involving defendants with documented histories of serious mental illness" (Bonnie et al. 1996). With 35 percent of U.S. jurisdictions permitting the insanity defense to be imposed on an unwilling defendant, even defendants who are competent to make an informed decision regarding whether they wish to utilize the insanity defense are not always free to choose (Miller et al. 1996). This implies that attorneys—and especially defense attorneys—have enormous power in determining who receives a psychiatric evaluation and who proceeds with an insanity plea in a criminal trial.

Judges. Boehnert found that the decision-maker in insanity defense cases is quite significant for determining its success (1989). Judges (as compared to juries) made the decision in 96 percent of the successful cases. Callahan et al. (1991) also noted that it was quite rare for a jury to acquit based on insanity; in all but seven percent of their successful Not Guilty by Reason of Insanity (NGRI) pleas, the decision to acquit was made by other key players in the criminal justice system, including the judge, prosecutor, and defense attorney. Cirincione (1996), however, reports that the high conviction rate for jury trials may be at least partially attributed to the fact that jury trials are more commonly used in contentious cases involving severe crimes and less mental disorder. Cirincione speculates that bench trials are more likely to occur when the prosecution agrees to the insanity verdict and/or the judge is more likely to be swayed by the defense's arguments (1996).

Mental Health Professionals. The legal system uses psychiatry in a variety of ways depending on the desired outcome. Despite the absence of precise knowledge concerning mental illness and its effect in determining behavior, courts and community agencies must make important decisions regarding mental states. Psychiatrists are used in court to determine an individual's competency to stand trial, an individual's mental state at the time of a criminal offense (for insanity defense purposes), and whether an individual is mentally ill and dangerous, which is necessary to involuntarily commit individuals to a psychiatric hospital.[14]

If an individual has been successful with an insanity plea, the criminal justice system must decide what to do with this acquittee. Public opinion of the insanity defense is negative, partly due to inaccurate perceptions that acquittees are immediately set free (Hans 1986). The legal system, however, faces a contradiction in wanting to automatically commit these individuals to a psychiatric institution, since they have been deemed "not guilty," and any commitment would appear to violate due process (Rogers, Bloom, and Manson 1986). To compromise, the courts tend to require a short period of detention to determine current psychiatric status. During this time, psychiatrists are charged with determining the acquittee's current mental state.[15]

Various studies have suggested that psychiatric testimony plays an enormous role in legal determinations of mental states (Ewing 1983; Dahl 1985; LaFond 1994). Indeed, psychiatrists "'take the weight' on difficult decisions involving commitment or release, especially in the cases of individuals hospitalized following insanity acquittals" (Perlin 1989-90: 675). Wasyliw et al. agree, stating that these insanity decisions "are often so close to impossible that those charged with making them are more than anxious to pass their burdens to unwitting experts" (1985:152). Dahl (1985) explains that "in many cases, the lives or liberty of criminal defendants seeking to invoke the insanity defense rest largely on the medical opinions of their psychiatrists" (p. 717). In *Youngberg v. Romeo* the Supreme Court recognized that judges give substantial deference to professional judgment. Judges tend to consider physicians experts in an area (mental illness) that the judge is at best only an amateur. As a result, judges are reluctant to reject any opinion offered by a psychiatrist (Mechanic 1969; Ewing 1983; Dahl 1985; LaFond 1994).

Insanity Defendants and Insanity Pleas

Frequency and success of the insanity plea. Public opinion data show that the most commonly expressed concern is that the insanity defense is a loophole through which many would-be criminals escape punishment for illegal acts (Jeffrey and Pasewark 1983; Hans 1986; Rice and Harris 1990; Callahan et al. 1991; Steadman et al. 1993). This notion tends to be based on inaccurate perceptions, since the defense is actually quite rare and those successful with this plea are rarely set free (Jeffrey and Pasewark 1983; Hans 1986; Rice and Harris 1990; Callahan et al. 1991; Steadman et al. 1993; Palermo and Knudten 1994; Silver, Cirincione, and Steadman 1994; Janofsky et al. 1996). Callahan et al. (1991), in examining the frequency and rate of insanity pleas and acquittals in eight states, found that overall, the insanity defense was raised in one percent of all felony cases. Further, only 26 percent of those raising the insanity defense were actually acquitted NGRI (Callahan et al. 1991; Steadman et al. 1993; Hiday 1999). The public also underestimates the extent to which insanity acquittees are confined upon acquittal (Silver, Cirincione, and Steadman 1994).

Characteristics of insanity defendants. Very few researchers have presented the characteristics of insanity defendants. Primarily for data access reasons, most studies have focused on the successful insanity cases only. As a result, very little aggregate information exists about individuals who unsuccessfully raise this defense, or individuals who consider this defense, only to drop it later in justice processing (see Steadman et al. 1993). Due to this lack of evidence, one of the goals of this project is to address this current limitation in the literature.

There are a few studies that do provide comparisons between insanity defendants and the remainder of the criminal justice population. The first such study was part of a psychology dissertation by Morris (1992) who found that in Hawaii, in the years 1970 until 1982, insanity defendants were likely to be: Caucasian, unmarried, generally older than typical criminal defendants, in possession of a history of prior arrests and drug and alcohol abuse, and almost exclusively male. Female insanity defendants were significantly older and had significantly more education than male insanity defendants. Female insanity defendants were also more likely to have their charges dismissed than male defendants. Of defendants with a history of previous inpatient treatment, females had more prior hospitalizations, and were more likely to have been hospitalized for extensive periods of time, than their male counterparts (Morris 1992).

Callahan et al. (1991), in examining the volume and characteristics of insanity pleas in eight states (California, Georgia, Montana, New Jersey, New York, Ohio, Washington, and Wisconsin), found few differences in the sociodemographic characteristics of persons pleading insanity and those acquitted NGRI. The differences between these two groups on diagnosis, target offense, prior history, and type of trial were more significant, however. The group unsuccessfully pleading NGRI was less likely to have a diagnosis of schizophrenia or another major mental disorder (55 percent) than the group successful with this plea (84 percent). Unsuccessful insanity pleaders were similarly less likely to be charged with murder, physical assault, or other violent offenses (50 percent) as compared to those successful (65 percent). Finally, insanity acquittees were more likely to have had a prior hospitalization and to have been adjudicated by bench trial rather than by a jury or plea bargain than defendants unsuccessfully raising the defense (Callahan et al. 1991).

Boehnert (1989) compared 30 male insanity acquittees with 30 male insanity defendants who had unsuccessfully attempted an insanity defense. Subjects were matched on type of crime as well as length of confinement in either the state hospital or the prison system. Both groups were mostly white, unskilled or semi-skilled laborers, with a record of prior arrests, and both groups primarily had public defenders. The significant differences between successful and unsuccessful insanity attempts included a finding of incompetency to stand trial (80 percent of successful pleaders versus 33 percent of unsuccessful pleaders) and trial by judge instead of jury (96 percent of successful pleaders versus 24 percent of unsuccessful pleaders relied on a bench trial) (Boehnert 1989).

Characteristics of insanity acquittees. The more numerous studies that present demographic characteristics of successful insanity defendants tend to paint a fairly consistent portrait. The average insanity acquittee is male, between the ages of 20 and 29, unmarried, unemployed, and minimally educated (Steadman et al. 1993; Lymburner and Roesch 1999). He has been acquitted for a violent offense, has had prior contact with both the criminal and mental health systems, and suffers from a severe psychiatric illness or sub-average intellectual ability (Rice and Harris 1990; Callahan et al. 1991; Bloom and Williams 1994; Cirincione et al. 1995; Slovenko 1995; Roesch et al. 1997; Lymburner and Roesch 1999). In fact, one of the most significant and consistent correlates of an insanity acquittal is a diagnosis of a psychotic disorder (Rice and Harris 1990; Morris 1992; Warren, Rosenfeld, and Fitch 1994; Cirincione et al. 1995; Slovenko 1995; Janofsky et al. 1996; Lymburner and Roesch 1999). Eighty-nine percent of insanity acquittees have been diagnosed as schizophrenic or mentally retarded while 82 percent have been hospitalized at least once (Slovenko 1995). This tends to be interpreted that criminal justice officials reserve insanity acquittals—or only provide insanity acquittals—for the most seriously disturbed defendants (Callahan et al. 1991). Nevertheless, research has also consistently demonstrated that a small number of individuals who are not diagnosed with a psychiatric disorder are acquitted by reason of insanity (Callahan et al. 1991; Cirincione et al. 1995; Lymburner and Roesch 1999).

Morris noted that insanity acquittees are commonly given psychotic diagnoses (with schizophrenic disorder comprising the bulk of those); are older and more likely to be white; and are likely to be charged with a crime of violence or potential violence against persons as opposed to property offenses (1992). Morris also explained that these defendants typically know their victims, and that the NGRI offenses of males who are adjudicated insane seem to range across the continuum of criminal behavior, while the crimes of females tend to cluster at either end of that range. More than twice as many NGRI men (60 percent) as women (27 percent) have incurred prior arrests and none of the females in Morris's study have been hospitalized previously, in contrast to 24 percent of the males (Morris 1992). As compared to those convicted, NGRI acquittees tend to have fewer prior convictions and are less likely to have been previously imprisoned (Hodgins 1993; Cirincione et al. 1995). For psychiatric diagnosis, female acquittees are more likely to receive either a personality disorder or a non-psychotic diagnosis, which Morris suggests may lend itself to speculation about potential gender bias in the subjective diagnosis process (1992).

Since women make up approximately 22 percent of all arrestees, 16 percent of the correctional population, and 14 percent of violent offenders in the United States (U.S. Department of Justice 1999b), it is probably not surprising that research on the insanity defense has consistently demonstrated that male insanity acquittees outnumber female acquittees by a ratio of about 10:1 (Callahan et al. 1991; Cirincione et al. 1995; Roesch et al. 1997; Callahan and Silver 1998; Lymburner and Roesch 1999). Despite the many studies describing the characteristics of insanity acquittees, few have explored the role of gender, primarily due to the paucity of women in the role of criminal defendant. While most empirical studies of insanity do find women significantly more likely than men to be acquitted (Callahan et al. 1991;

Cirincione et al. 1995; Lymburner and Roesch 1999), to date, few empirical investigations have examined what differences might exist between the men and women who consider a defense of insanity.

Although gender is frequently included as a variable in research on the insanity defense, very few studies have set out to comprehensively compare male and female insanity defendants and acquittees. Seig, Ball, and Menninger (1995) conducted the most recent investigation comparing male and female acquittees committed to a mental health institution in Colorado. Their research revealed significant differences in terms of mental and criminal history as well as demographic variables. Generally, females were likely to be older at the time of commitment, were more likely to be diagnosed with mood disorders or borderline personality disorder, and were less likely to receive diagnoses of antisocial personality disorder or substance abuse; these diagnoses for female acquittees are also consistent with mental health populations outside the criminal justice system. Further, significantly more women then men were married at the time of the offense (65 percent of women versus 46 percent of men) and women had a less stable work history than men (55 percent of females held their longest job for less than one year versus 32 percent of males). Females were also less likely to have a history of violent crime and tended to start their criminal activity at a later age; on the other hand, the crime for which they were acquitted was more likely to be a serious offense (43 percent of women were acquitted of murder versus 19 percent of men). Despite this, the length of detention was significantly shorter for females than for males, a finding that is supported by other studies (Morris 1992; Callahan and Silver 1998; Lymburner and Roesch 1999). In fact, Callahan and Silver (1998) note that their data from New York present a rather disturbing pattern. Diagnosis and dangerousness (i.e., crime seriousness) do not even enter into the decision model as significant factors predicting release from involuntary hospitalization. Instead, gender proves to be the best predictor, followed by educational attainment, race, and prior forensic hospitalizations (Callahan and Silver 1998).[16]

These findings, while based on bivariate relationships, still raise questions with respect to differential treatment of males and females under the insanity defense. To the extent that such differences reflect true gender differences in mental disorder as well as variability in the circumstances under which males and females come into contact with the legal system, variability is to be expected and is acceptable. However, the possibility that such differences may arise from gender biases cannot be eliminated without further research (Morris 1992; Lymburner and Roesch 1999). We also cannot know whether these gender differences would still be observed if the authors had used a multivariate, more analytically rigorous study, controlling for important legal variables such as prior convictions and crime seriousness.

While the role of gender in psychiatric evaluations and case outcomes has been partially explored, for the most part the role of race has been ignored. In the handful of studies that mention race, it is primarily used as a control variable and is not tested very systematically or extensively. Among the few mentions of race, Morris (1992) noted that in comparison to those unsuccessful with an NGRI plea, NGRI acquittees are more likely to be white. Callahan and Silver (1998) find that for successful NGRI pleaders, white defendants spend the least amount of time in psychiatric hospitals.

CONCLUSION

A review of the relevant sociological, criminological, psychological, and legal literature related to gender, race, crime, mental illness, and psychiatric evaluations demonstrates that women are underrepresented while African Americans (and especially African American men) are overrepresented in the criminal justice system. Much research has demonstrated that the response of corrections officials has altered case outcomes for women and African Americans.

Examining the literature with respect to mental illness and psychiatric labeling demonstrates how research has failed to find significant race or gender differences in the prevalence of psychiatric disorders. Among the important findings of the mental illness literature is the high likelihood of women receiving "internalizing" diagnoses while men receive "externalizing" diagnoses. African Americans may be more likely to be labeled paranoid, particularly when receiving this label from non-African Americans. African Americans also appear to have higher lifetime prevalence rates of mental illness, but this difference tends to disappear when adequate controls for socioeconomic status are included.

· Finally, the current state of the literature on psychiatric evaluations in the criminal justice system is limited by problematic statistical techniques; the evidence that is available appears to indicate that women are more successful than men with an insanity defense. This research also suggests that whites might also be more successful than non-whites, but this information is limited to a single study which did not focus on race. Thus, there is currently a significant gap in the knowledge regarding the relationship between the extralegal factors of race and gender and criminal justice processing of mentally ill offenders, which is met in part by the current research.

NOTES

[1] While many find evidence for lenient treatment of females in much of the 20th century, Boritch (1992) points to historical evidence suggesting the opposite pattern. During the Urban Reform Era (1871-1920) in Ontario, "women were more likely to receive prison dispositions and to incur longer sentences than men" (p. 316).

[2] This means that psychiatric diagnosis and other extralegal factors are not typically considered in the sentencing guidelines to alter presumptive sentence. Mental disorder may, however, be used in downward departures as a mitigating factor.

[3] The question of whether it is better to have equality of treatment or for women to receive lenient treatment in the criminal justice system is hotly debated by feminists (see Carlen 2002a). On one hand, arguments made promoting equality of treatment for men and women in the criminal justice system ignore important gender differences that might affect responsibility. For example, some women with dependent children might commit crime out of economic need whereas some men might commit the same economic offense out of greed. By strictly treating men and women as equals, we ignore economic need as a potential mitigating circumstance, one that might be particularly relevant for women with dependent children (Carlen 2002; Hudson 2002:36). On the other hand, arguments that women should be treated more leniently than men are also controversial. If feminists argue that women's economic position, relative to men's, disadvantages women and should be remedied through lenient criminal justice processing, this implies that women — constructed as less responsible — are also less rational. "Being seen as less culpable means being seen as less possessed of agency: women are less culpable if they are sick, dominated, or mentally unstable, in other words if their capacity to act is seen as less than 'normal.'" (Hudson 2002:41). Consequently, leniency comes at the price of being perceived as having lesser rationality. Thus, while this preferential treatment benefits a few individual women, the result has a negative impact on all women. This is not the case for men, however. According to Hudson, the criminal justice system constructs circumstances that affect male offenders — such as loss of employment and problems with alcohol — as emanating from outside the individual, making him

act out of character and which do not diminish his essential rationality or the rationality of men in general (2002:41).

[4] As is true with most analyses of gender and violence, the number of cases in Hanke's study is relatively small. This is particularly a concern when she discusses white women in prison for the murder of a black victim; in this analysis, Hanke is only referring to eight women. This is also a limitation when Hanke refers to African American inmates with white victims—she had only twelve cases. The numbers of women in the other categories were significantly larger: she reported 136 white offenders with white victims and 518 black offenders with black victims. Consequently, Hanke's racial differences in punitiveness may be less attributable to racial dynamics than to the rarity of these victim/offender combinations.

[5] Farnworth and Teske (1995) did explore the relationship between gender and type of charge (whether it was consistent or inconsistent with stereotypes of female offenders). They noted no gender difference due to the type of crime with which the offender is charged. However, these authors do not account for the possibility of additional charges and/or plea agreements. In addition, this research uses assault as the atypical female offense. Since the severity of assaults can vary enormously, one could argue that the authors' scale of offense severity fails to account for these large differences.

[6] One of the few studies with contradictory results is an older study by Gove and Tudor (1973). They argue that women tend to be more frustrated by the status differentials between men and women in society, leading to higher rates of mental illness for women. In order to support this, Gove and Tudor analyze people in psychiatric treatment and find that women are, in fact, represented in greater numbers among those receiving psychiatric treatment. This conclusion is problematic, however, since help-seeking behavior is different for men and women, with women more likely to seek psychiatric help for their difficulties (Horwitz 1977; Thoits 1985; Greeley and Mullen 1990; Hankin 1990).

[7] One difficulty with a discussion of rates of mental illness is that data tend to come from public clinics, rather than private hospitals where privacy is ensured. These studies therefore tend to provide only a partial picture of

mentally disordered individuals, primarily representing mental illnesses in the lower classes.

[8] According to the APA, while men and women are affected by schizophrenia in roughly equal numbers, women are more likely to have a later onset, more prominent mood symptoms, and a better prognosis. Estimates of the sex ratio are confounded, however, by issues of ascertainment and definition; hospital-based studies suggest a higher rate in males, whereas community-based surveys tend to suggest an equal sex ratio (APA 1994:281-2).

[9] These critics argue that along with medicalization (and the application of a DSM diagnosis) comes money, whether in the form of pharmaceutical payoffs (Szasz 1961; Conrad 1975) or research funding (Eaton, Ritter, and Brown 1990).

[10] The medical and mental health clinicians in this study consisted of a representative sample of clinicians across systems of care, including health maintenance organizations; large multispeciality groups; and predominately fee-for-service, single-speciality, solo, or small group practices. Most of the participants in the study were from HMOs and large multispeciality groups.

[11] The case sent had previously received a diagnosis of undifferentiated schizophrenic disorder (Axis I) with a dependent personality disorder (Axis II).

[12] One of the earliest definitions of insanity in England was the wild beast test, formulated in the 13th century by a judge in King Edward's court. Using this test, a criminal defendant was found to be insane once he/she demonstrated that his or her mental abilities "were no greater than that of a brute, wild beast or lunatic" (Robin 1997:225). In the early 18th century, the terminology adopted was whether the accused "does not know what he is doing, no more than a wild beast" (Washington v. U.S., 1967). While this is test is obviously vague, it was assumed that judges and juries had a "commonsense understanding of the mentality of a wild beast and did not need to hear and evaluate a complex body of evidence bearing on the issue" (Robin 1997:226).

There are various insanity standards across the U.S. For additional information on these standards see (Robin 1997; Plaut 1983; Reisner and Slobogin 1995). Whenever insanity outcomes appear problematic, invoking public outcry, the remedy of choice is to change the legal definition of insanity, this despite empirical studies showing no significant differences among tests (Finkel 1991; Ogloff 1991; Borum and Fulero 1999). Writing in *California Law Review*, Dahl (1985) explains that the major concerns of the legal system with respect to insanity are that (1) psychiatrists will have increasing influence on ultimate legal determinations, and (2) the law will become dependent on concepts that belong to an outside discipline (p. 411).

[13] There is no consistency in the spelling of "M'Naghten" (it has been spelled at least twelve different ways according to Moran [1981]); this book uses the spelling provided by the Minnesota Supreme Court. This rule (dating back to 1843) states:

> The jurors ought to be told in all cases that every man is to be presumed to be sane, and to possess a sufficient degree of reason to be responsible for his crimes, until the contrary be proved to their satisfaction; and that to establish a defense on the grounds of insanity, it must be conclusively proved that, at the time of committing the act, the party accused was laboring under such a defect of reason, from the disease of the mind, as not to know the nature and quality of the act he was doing; or if he did know it, that he did not know what he was doing was wrong.

(For more information on the M'Naghten case and the history of insanity see Caesar 1982; Gallo 1982; Walker 1968; Walker 1968; Pasework 1986; Robin 1997; Eigen 1999).

[14] It is necessary to determine whether defendants are competent to stand trial because if defendants are legally insane at the time of the trial, they would be unable to contribute to their own defense. *Dusky v. United States* (1960) set forth the standard that defendants need a factual and rational understanding of the charges and proceedings against them before proceeding with a trial. The U.S. Supreme Court has viewed the fact that an incompetent defendant cannot be tried as "fundamental to an adversary system of justice" (*Drope v. Missouri*). A criminal defendant may not plead guilty or waive the right to counsel unless the waiver is voluntary, knowing, and intelligent (Weiss 1997). Criminal defendants who *are* deemed incompetent to stand trial are typically committed to a psychiatric hospital until competence has been restored

(Berberoglu, Conroy, and Schaefer 1998). (In Minnesota, when the offense is a misdemeanor, the charge is dropped upon a finding of incompetence to stand trial.) This poses an additional dilemma; as the U.S. Supreme Court held in *Jackson v. Indiana* (1972), those found incompetent to stand trial could not be detained indefinitely solely on the basis of incompetence. The *Jackson* court also held that these individuals had the right to relevant treatment while they were committed.

[15] Involuntary civil commitment of the mentally ill is intended not as a punishment for past acts, but to prevent future ones (Reisner and Slobogin 1990). The Supreme Court has ruled that mentally ill individuals cannot be held for custodial purposes on the basis of "intolerance or animosity" (*O'Connor v. Donaldson*), but only when there is a showing of insanity and dangerousness to self or others by clear and convincing evidence (*Addington v. Texas*). Even when an involuntary confinement is considered constitutional, this confinement period must be of a reasonable duration (*Jackson v. Indiana*).

[16] Callahan and Silver examined conditional release in three additional states (Maryland, Connecticut, and Ohio) and found different patterns, with clinical outlook and the nature of the crime better predictors than gender.

## CHAPTER 3

EXTENDING SOCIOLOGICAL THEORY

Theories of Gender, Race, Mental Illness, and Criminal Labeling

As discussed in Chapter Two, race and gender both affect criminal justice processing. Racial minorities are disproportionately represented in the criminal justice system; this has often been attributed to systematic discrimination in each stage of justice processing (Spohn and Holleran 2000; Steffensmeier and DeMuth 2000; Bushway and Piechl 2001). Many researchers also argue that when decision-makers are free to exercise discretion, they systematically favor female offenders over similarly situated male offenders (Farrell and Swigert 1986; Simon and Landis 1991; Boritch 1992; Nagel and Johnson 1994; Daly and Bordt 1995; Katz and Spohn 1995; Kruttschnitt 1996; Steffensmeier et al. 1998).

While most gender roles are unwritten, Schur (1984) contends that gender norms work as a "mechanism for the social control of women" (p. 52). He explains that women are doubly stigmatized, since behavioral extremes are not tolerated, and instead are labeled. For example, women who show too little emotion are labeled "cold," "calculating," or "masculine." Conversely, if they demonstrate too much emotion, they are "hysterical" (Schur 1984:53; see Freud (1963) for one such example). Therefore, women suffer from a double bind in

45

which they are always labeled unless they act within narrowly defined limits. For example, explanations for different criminal justice responses to male and female criminals typically fall into one of two categories, based on whether the defendant's behavior is considered a violation of gendered expectations.

First, many gendered explanations are based on the chivalry or paternalism thesis; while *paternalism* is considered more pejorative than *chivalry*, these terms tend to be used interchangeably. This concept is not always precisely defined, but generally refers to a protective attitude toward women that is linked to gender stereotypes of women as (1) weaker and more passive than men, and therefore not proper subjects for imprisonment, and (2) more submissive and dependent than men, and therefore less responsible for their crimes. Judges might also regard women as more easily manipulated than men, and therefore more receptive to rehabilitative efforts (Nagal and Johnson 1994).

Second is a corollary to the chivalry/paternalism thesis: the "evil woman" thesis. This thesis hypothesizes that women whose criminal behavior violates gendered assumptions about the proper role of women are treated more harshly than their male counterparts. In other words, not only do certain types of female offenders fail to benefit from paternalistic treatment, they are actually subject to heightened social control for their choice of an "unladylike" offense (Crew 1991; Boritch 1992; Nagel and Johnson 1994). Thus, the criminal justice system may punish women harshly only when they fail to live up to their expected role (Simpson 1989; Worrall 1990; Kruttschnitt 1996). When women are fulfilling their gender roles (by marrying and taking care of their children), they are treated in a paternalistic manner, with more lenient treatment. When women fail to fulfill prescribed gender roles, however, social control is increased—more so then for men—in an attempt to bring the behavior back into line with what is expected of women (see Schur 1984; Horwitz 1990:113-114).

While women might be expected to act in a "feminine" manner, expectations of African Americans include criminality and violence (Smith 1991; Sniderman and Piazza 1993; Quillian and Pager 2001). This stereotype of African Americans as criminal is deeply embedded in Americans' expectations (Devine and Elliot 1995; Emerson et al. 2001; Quillian and Pager 2001). For example, individuals have used stereotypes about racial minorities in their perceptions of neighborhood crime rates, in support for punitive crime policies, and the stigma of incarceration (Chiricos et al. 2001; Emerson et al. 2001; Quillian and Pager 2001; Western 2002; Chiricos, Welch, and Gertz 2004). This perception of racial minorities as criminal is so strong and so deeply embedded that some have argued that behavior that actually reflects severe mental pathology in minority groups is often ignored or considered to be criminal behavior rather than mental illness (Kutchins and Kirk 1997:225).

Statistical Discrimination

To explain how the number of women and racial minorities in the criminal justice system affects criminal justice treatment, this project first draws on Gary Becker and the economics of statistical discrimination (Becker 1971). Statistical discrimination refers to the use of information concerning groups, rather than individuals, in decision-making. These uses of group means in decision-making often occur in the absence of scientific data (and may in fact be contrary to these data), yet are used in the pursuit of expedience (Phelps 1972). Maitzen (1991) explains that a group characteristic (characteristic A) correlates positively but imperfectly with some other characteristic (characteristic B) that is undesirable. We would prefer to make decisions based on characteristic B, but for reasons of convenience, we substitute A as a surrogate or proxy for B. Economists explain that "we need groups to make efficient decisions. At the same time, what is "efficient" for the economy or the criminal justice system is always "unfair" to some individuals. The problem is how to balance the gains from efficiency against the losses from unfairness" (Thurow 1980). Applying this perspective to the legal process, the legal system's use of group norms is efficient in screening cases to decide which type of punishment is fair and appropriate. Group variables such as race, age, or sex are therefore assumed to provide information regarding an individual's expected criminality or insanity (Becker 1971; 1985; Kennedy 1997; Konrad and Cannings 1997). This screening process on the part of decision-makers may be perceived as an efficient use of court time, conserving resources to deal with those perceived to need the court's attention.

Decision-makers in the criminal justice system—just as workers in other fields—develop routines and patterns in the course of their work experience. These reflexes or habits that determine what can be seen may limit the range of choices decision-makers have. The uncertainty avoidance perspective, for example, explains that decision-makers operate from limited knowledge of both the alternatives available and the consequences of particular decisions (Albonetti and Hepburn 1996). Confronting the uncertainty derived from incomplete knowledge, decision-makers achieve a "bounded rationality" (March and Simon 1965) by relying on patterned responses that have worked in the past to absorb uncertainty (Albonetti and Hepburn 1996). According to these theorists, decision-makers within organizations rely on "past experiences, stereotypes, prejudices, and highly particularized views of present stimuli" (Clegg and Dunkerley 1980:265). The literature in this area contends that simplifying attributions are made to groups of persons in an attempt to reduce the uncertainty of making an incorrect decision. Defendant characteristics culturally perceived to be linked with deviant behavior define a person as a "type," whereas characteristics associated with conforming behavior define the person as the "countertype" (Hill et al. 1985). As Hill et al. argue, "the rational decision making model cannot work without simplifying heuristics, and the constructs of perceived risk are based on the defendant's location in the stratification structure" (1985:138). Social and moral judgments regarding criminalization, mental illness, or legal insanity may therefore be portrayed as the end result of a social construction process in which the individual is "cognitively appraised and categorized in reference to individualized schemata" (Roberts and Golding 1991). Consequently, criminal justice decision-makers weigh defendants based on past experiences; these experiences indicate that the "typical" (i.e. overrepresented) defendant is a racial minority and/or male. Using statistical discrimination, these decision-makers make judgments about the rationality or "normality" of offenders based—at least in part—on the defendant's race and/or gender.

A model demonstrating how statistical discrimination relates to gender, race, mental illness, and crime is presented in Figure 3.1. In this figure, legal agents want to make decisions about the mental status of African Americans and men based on "objective" mental illness. In most situations, legal agents have incomplete information about the mental status of offenders, especially since they are not typically trained in psychology. Because this information is unavailable, decision-makers instead rely on information that *is* available: the relationships between race, gender, and crime. Since the legal system assumes sanity, and African Americans and men are overrepresented in this criminal justice system, these legal agents assume rationality for all such defendants. This assumption of sanity is at odds with a mental illness attribution, so groups of individuals who are under-represented in the criminal justice system are more likely to receive this attribution of mental illness.

Labeling Theory

This process of applying a criminal or mental illness label is central to labeling theory. Most studies of the labeling process have explored how a deviant label influences the behavior of those to whom the label has been applied. This reflects the influence of Edwin Lemert's (1951; 1972) formulation of labeling theory, with its emphasis on secondary deviance produced by societal reaction and the internalization of cultural stereotypes surrounding the labeled behavior. In this sense, the label of mental illness and the expectations attached to it perpetuate the mental illness (Scheff 1966; 1974). The proposition that such labeling causes deviance has been harshly criticized by those who view mental illness as a form of individual pathology, wherein the fate of the mentally ill depends primarily on the severity of their illnesses and their treatments, rather than extra-illness factors such as labels (Gove 1970; Kirk 1974; Schwartz, Myers, and Astrachan 1974; Huffine and Clausen 1979; Gove 1980; 1982; Lehman, Possidente, and Hawker 1986). This criticism effected a modification of labeling theory, to claim that instead of *creating* deviance, the devaluation and discrimination associated with a label interfere with "a broad range of life areas, including access to social and economic resources and general feelings of well-being" (Rosenfield 1997:660; also see Link 1982; 1987; Link et al. 1987; Link et al. 1989).

Labels can therefore have effects other than the creation or maintenance of deviance, and an emphasis on the consequences of a label for subsequent deviation has led researchers to ignore the effects of such labeling on other areas of a person's life (Link 1982:202;

Walsh 1990; Rosenfield 1997). More recent research has shown that negative labeling (such as a psychiatric diagnosis) can have other powerful short-term and long-term consequences (Rosenhan 1973; Link 1987; Link et al. 1989; Burton 1990; Link and Cullen 1990; Walsh 1990; Silver 1995; Rosenfield 1997; Lymburner and Roesch 1999). These consequences include the loss of voting rights, professional licenses, and parental rights, and also a reduction in the perceived quality of life (Link 1987; Link et al. 1989; Burton 1990; Rosenfield 1992; 1997).

While this body of research points to the negative impact of labels, it also needs to acknowledge how these labels are differently attached to distinct groups within the mentally ill or criminal justice populations. This aspect of the labeling process requires elaboration on how decision-makers within the legal system make determinations about individuals. Specific to the criminalization process, the paramount role of law enforcement officials is summarized by Becker's classic assertion that "deviance is *not* a quality of the act the person commits, but rather a consequence of the application by others of rules and sanctions to an 'offender.' The deviant is one to whom that label has successfully been applied; deviant behavior is behavior that people label" (1963:9, emphasis in original). The subjective nature of this criminalization process is emphasized by conflict, labeling, and feminist theorists (see Albonetti and Hepburn 1996).

Similar to statistical discrimination, labeling theory suggests that informal rules exist for organizational processing and that the deviant is processed according to certain routine types (e.g., Sudnow 1965; Hawkins and Tiedeman 1975; Rubington and Weinberg 1987; Albonetti and Hepburn 1996). These processing types, which are based on assessments of the individual's moral character, motivation, and behavior, are simplified images used to categorize deviants into meaningful categories (Sudnow 1965; Farrell and Swigert 1977; 1978; Albonetti and Hepburn 1996; Bridges and Steen 1998). Spohn (1990) explains that the courtroom workgroup tends to adhere to prevailing norms, working together to process cases as efficiently as possible. She states, "to expedite sentencing, for example, members of the courtroom workgroup may informally establish a range of 'normal penalties'" (p. 97; see Sudnow 1965). This perspective further implies that those who are close to (or similar to) the person who exhibits unusual behavior are less likely to label that behavior as mental illness or crime. This is true since behavior is more likely to be viewed as deviant when the observer is relationally and culturally different from the person displaying the behavior (Loring and Powell 1988; Horwitz 1990:81-82; Phelan and Link 1999).

Social "type-scripts," or the everyday assumptions about who does what, help explain gender- or race-based variations in crime (Harris 1977). Harris argues that these type-scripts are so deeply embedded in society that they impact motivations for, and attributions of, crime and deviance. These type-scripts serve to maintain order by specifying what types of actors are expected to commit what types of deviance and what types of deviance are seen as unlikely or "impossible" for other types of actors to commit (Harris 1977:12). Crime is therefore perceived as being reserved for racial minorities and males, and mental illness for females (Cloward and Piven 1979; Quillian and Pager 2001). Much of what we know about criminal behavior and psychopathology is influenced by gender and race stereotypes, and expectations about appropriate gender role behavior and typical African American behavior influence the labeling and diagnosis of deviant acts (Widom 1984; see also Schur 1984; Quillian and Pager 2001).

Labeling theory contends that individuals with lower status and less power are more likely to have their deviance detected, labeled, and sanctioned (Becker 1963; Corley, Cernkovich, and Giordano 1989). Since women and racial minorities generally have less power and fewer resources to mobilize in resisting a label, their risk of being labeled is greater than that of males and whites (Corley et al. 1989). If the "moral entrepreneurs" who initiate and enforce rules (Becker 1963) respond differently to female and African American crime, it has consequences both in criminal justice processing and in perceptions of self (Goffman 1963; Scheff 1966). Schur (1984) states that deviance is "not simply a function of a person's problematic behavior; rather, it emerges as other people define and react to a behavior as being problematic" (p. 187). In addition, "the person's sex—much like her or his social class membership and race or ethnicity—may significantly affect what these other people do" (p. 187). Since our responses to persons are often based on official labels (Goffman 1963; Scheff 1966; Schur 1984; Burton 1990; Rosenfield 1997), differential labeling of men and women would seriously alter the trajectory of African American and female offenders.

Figure 3.2 models labeling (adapted from Pescosolido, McLeod, and Alegría 2000). Labeling theory explains that neither the number of objectionable behaviors (such as indicators of mental illness) nor the number of people displaying these behaviors corresponds to who gets labeled. Instead, "type-scripts" are developed in the criminal justice system to determine which offenders will be labeled mentally ill and which ones will not (the "labeled" offender in Figure 3.2 is the circled X). The vast majority of offenders in the criminal justice system fall into the "normal" range of behavior. These "normals" or "typifications" are the racial minorities and men who comprise the bulk of the criminal justice population; they are also the women who commit typical female offenses such as minor property and drug offenses. These individuals rarely commit "offensive" acts, or acts that require additional explanation and investigation. Instead, social constructions of the causes of these behaviors include the desire for immediate gratification and economic need. While rare, there may be a few behaviors that are universally agreed upon as mental disorder. For example, a mentally retarded individual with the IQ of a 2-year-old would almost universally be deemed mentally unfit and consequently not responsible for criminal behavior. Where labeling theory may show its greatest power is in the middle "gray" area (Pescosolido et al. 2000), where the frequency of "odd" behavior does not fit our agreed-upon standard for mental illness, nor does it appear to conform to societal norms represented by the "typical" offender. This labeled group represents the social construction of a dichotomous point at which "mental disorder" is considered to be present. This social construction is influenced by larger societal stereotypes of African Americans as violent and criminal and women as weak, passive, and in need of protection.

Feminist Theory

Feminists in the U.S. have long understood that their gender has affected, and sometimes defined, their interactions with legal institutions (MacKinnon 1987; 1989; Smart 1995; Resnik 1996; Hudson 2002). Resnik cites a founding document of the gender bias task force movement: "as long as judges adhere to gender based myths, biases and stereotypes, the intent of the laws can be compromised or subverted through the exercise of judicial discretion" (1996:953). Catherine MacKinnon (1987; 1989) has similarly insisted on the maleness of the law and the completeness of male power within it, such that the male point of view is taken to be objectivity and neutrality (see also Smart 1995; Hudson 2002). MacKinnon asserts that the male point of view is: (1) the standard for point-of-viewlessness (1989:116-7), and (2) fundamental to male power (1989:174). In our society, according to MacKinnon (1989), men are considered objective, while women are the polar opposite, or subjective; "truth" and "objectivity" are produced in the interest of those with the power to shape reality. MacKinnon argues that the state and the law see women the way men see women (1989:161-2) and that the "normal" behaviors that society attributes to women become a means of controlling the actions of women even without their knowledge. "This social meaning, which is unattached to any actual anatomical differences between the sexes, or to any realities of women's response to it, pervades everyday routine to the point that it becomes a reflex, a habit" (MacKinnon 1989:90). Once developed, this notion of male superiority tends to determine what can be seen as well as what can be accomplished, therefore reaffirming the superiority (MacKinnon 1989:99).

Feminist researchers have expressed concern over the seeming inability of psychiatry to recognize gendered behavior and gender role expectations (Holstein 1987; Busfield 1988; Baskin et al. 1989).[1] This perspective contends that social expectations of "normal" behavior determine the amount and types of behavior that are appropriate for members of certain groups. In other words, psychiatric labeling is based on notions of what constitutes appropriate behavior (Baskin et al. 1989). In this sense, psychiatric diagnosis is not an objective, value-free science,[2] but one colored by gendered perceptions of appropriate behavior (see Johnson and Kandrack 1995).

Feminists therefore contend that psychiatry, and the legal system along with it, are simply pathologizing certain behaviors that are more socially accepted or even expected for certain individuals, while being incomprehensible to others (Phelan and Link 1999). For example, "defining excess fear as pathological is not neutral as to gender in a culture where expressions of fearfulness are more acceptable amongst women than men, since women are more likely to manifest all degrees of fearfulness" (Busfield 1988). Simply by acting in ways considered more appropriate to their gender, women are in more danger of being labeled phobic. The same is also true of depression and anxiety, since expressing emotion is considered to be a feminine behavior. Alternatively, certain types of mental illness are constructed in such a way as to lead to the labeling of more men than women. "In as far as alcoholism and drug taking have come to be viewed as pathological, then given present, though changing, gender constructions, these mental illnesses are biased towards men rather than women" (Busfield 1988:534). Research into gender differences in mental disorder tends to support these contentions (see Dohrenwend and Dohrenwend 1976; Hankin 1990); rates of neurosis and affective disorders are consistently higher for women while men consistently have higher rates of personality disorders and alcohol or drug related problems. While women are therefore socialized into more passive behaviors, men are expected to bear their problems with greater self-control and a reluctance to admit to symptoms of distress (Horwitz 1977; see Sharp, Brewster, and Love 2005). While it is not clear that these expectations lead to differences in the "true" prevalence of mental disorder, the social expectation remains that women are more passive and emotional and men more self-reliant.

The basic perspectives of feminist theory used in this project are displayed in Figure 3.3. In the legal system, which is a representation of a masculine perspective, women are perceived to be "emotional" and "irrational," which results in attributions of mental illness. Conversely, men are perceived to be "rational" and therefore fully responsible for their behavior, which results in a criminal (rather than a mental illness) label.

Social Control Theory

Differences in official responses to crime are particularly relevant to Horwitz's notion that social control is based on informal norms that govern relationships (1990:5; 2002a; 2002b). Since all social groups feature norms regarding the gender-related appropriateness of behavior, even deviant behavior, the degree of tolerance for male and female deviance should be related to gender role expectations (Horwitz 1990:113). Both men and women are therefore treated more harshly for behaviors that do not conform to gender specific norms (Horwitz 1990:120). When confronted with a non-normative (i.e., violent) female offender, the legal system's decision-makers may fall back on their "type-scripts," or typifications, that portray women as less responsible and therefore more amenable to psychiatric counseling to "rehabilitate" rather than "punish."

In his theory of law, Black explains that law and psychiatry represent formal social control whereas control is also exerted informally through children and marriage (1976). Black states that both the law and the treatment of mental illness vary inversely with other social control (1976:107, 119). If informal social control—including family—is strong, the offender is less subject to formal controls, including legal and psychiatric control. Horwitz (1990) asserts that the status of women, for example, alters the tolerance for female deviance; women's status tends to be derived from relationships with male relatives since the degree of tolerance for female deviance is shaped by the extent of informal social control over women. When this control is strong, female deviance is accorded higher tolerance, but when not subject to male control, there is less tolerance for women's behavior (Horwitz 1990:115-116). Further, if the formal social control of mental health treatment is strong, legal control will be diminished, and vice versa. Consequently, in the criminal justice system, Black's theory of law suggests that defendants who are treated psychiatrically (formal social control) and those with spouses and/or children (informal social control) will be subject to less law since these controls vary inversely with legal control.

Black also states that the amount of social control to which individuals have been subjected defines their level of respectability, and that law varies inversely with the respectability of the offender (1976:117). Those who have incurred much prior social control (such as ex-convicts or former mental hospital patients) have little respectability and in the future are more likely to be harshly punished by the legal system (Black 1976:112; Kruttschnitt 1982). According to Black, to be subject to law—especially criminal law—is more unrespectable than to be subject to other kinds of social control (1976:111). As a result, Black's theory explains that offenders with a criminal history are less respectable and will therefore receive harsher treatment in the legal system than those without this history. Similarly, those with a history of mental health treatment will be less respectable and will therefore receive more severe legal sanctions than those without this history.

At first glance, Black's predictions about the relationship between psychiatric and legal control appear contradictory. First, Black predicts an inverse relationship, with psychiatric control reducing legal control. This implies that legal sanctions are less severe in the presence of psychiatric treatment. In contrast, Black predicts that the presence of more social control decreases respectability, which increases legal control. This implies that legal sanctions are more severe for those with psychiatric treatment. This apparent contradiction signals the need to distinguish between past and current psychiatric care (see e.g., Kruttschnitt 1982). Since respectability refers to the amount of prior social control to which individuals are subject, those with a past history of psychiatric care should be expected to receive harsher treatment in the legal system due to their reduced respectability. Conversely, those currently receiving psychiatric treatment, along with those currently subject to informal social controls, should be expected to receive more lenient treatment because these controls reduce the need for legal control (Kruttschnitt 1982).

A competing perspective to Black's theory that law varies inversely with other social control comes from labeling theory, with its emphasis on the negative consequences of labels. Despite compelling evidence of a mental disorder, defense attorneys frequently avoid pursuing mental illness defenses in the criminal justice system because of the negative perceptions and potential negative case outcomes that come along with such a defense (Laberge and Morin 2001). Prior research found that for defendants who *unsuccessfully* attempted an insanity defense, the length of confinement was 22 percent longer than that of convicted felons who never raised the plea (Braff, Arvinites, and Steadman 1983). While public perception of the insanity defense is that it is positive for the defendants, that they "get away with murder," studies of length of confinement (prison or mental hospital) demonstrate a punishment philosophy, where the punishment fits the crime, regardless of whether the defendant is considered responsible (Silver 1995; Callahan and Silver 1998; Lymburner and Roesch 1999). It therefore appears that this defense may not actually be a lenient response to defendants since, similar to a prison sentence, crime severity determines length of confinement rather than mental state

(Silver 1995; Callahan and Silver 1998; Lymburner and Roesch 1999). These and other findings from his own research lead Menzies to conclude that mental health clinicians in the criminal justice system actually tailor their analysis so it fits into a punishment framework, often supporting dispositions that require punishment (1989:xvii). Perlin explains that defendants who plead insanity and are ultimately found guilty of their charges serve *longer* sentences than defendants who do not assert an insanity defense (2000).

Social control theory is depicted in Figure 3.4. Agents of social control, including spouses, children, and current psychiatric treatment, all exert control on criminal defendants. When these social controls are not present, the legal system will step in and take control. Thus, offenders without these current social controls will be subject to greater levels of legal control. Conversely, when these social controls are present, legal control will step back and allow other agents of social control to assume responsibility; this might result in psychiatric controls. If the offender has many prior social controls, however, this reduces respectability and will increase legal control.

Once psychiatric controls are present—via psychiatric evaluations—the effect on case outcome could proceed in two different directions. Psychiatric evaluations could result in negative consequences for the defendant, such as longer sentences and more severe punishment; this is the contention of labeling theory. Alternatively, social control theory asserts that the presence of this current psychiatric control will lead to reduced legal control, with shorter sentences and less severe punishment.

TOWARD A SOCIOLOGICAL THEORY OF MENTAL ILLNESS ATTRIBUTIONS

Studies of insanity are rarely concerned with developing or testing theory, and they usually report only basic demographic characteristics and bivariate relationships. To develop a sociological theory of insanity, this project draws on the statistical discrimination, feminist, labeling, and social control perspectives previously discussed, specifically in terms of criminal justice and mental illness labeling; but first the question of whether the psychiatric evaluation and (possible) insanity outcome is beneficial or detrimental to defendants needs to be addressed.

The Psychiatric Evaluation as Benefit or Detriment

Basic assumptions of labeling and feminist theories include the notion that those without the power to resist a label—including racial minorites and women—are more likely to be labeled *and* that this label is detrimental to the individual who is labeled. This assumption, however, may not be appropriate in the application of labeling and feminist theories to psychiatric labeling and criminal justice processing.

To develop an adequate labeling theory of insanity, the question of whether a successful insanity plea is ultimately better or worse for the defendant (compared to not raising the defense) needs to be addressed. This is necessary since the labeling perspective makes it clear that those most subject to labels are those with the least power to resist them (Becker 1963). Since a central argument of feminist theory is that the legal system views men as the standard for rationality (Rubin 1975; Hartmann 1981; Gilligan 1982; MacKinnon 1987; Alcoff 1988; MacKinnon 1989; Nicholson 1997), feminists contend that women are more likely to receive an insanity label (Edwards 1986; Kendall 1991; Ussher 1991; Wilczynski 1991; Burns 1992; Chan 1994; Nicolson 1995; Smart 1995; Chan 1999; Kendall 1999a; Kendall 1999b; Umphrey 1999). Indeed, there is some evidence that courts take a condescending view of women's "emotionalism" while attributing the emotions of men to "passionate conviction rather than a disordered mind" (Miles and August 1990:88). The common perception of insanity, however, is that the successful defendant is, in essence, "getting away with murder" (Jeffrey and Pasewark 1983; Hans 1986; Callahan et al. 1991; Palermo and Knudten 1994; Silver, Cirincione, and Steadman 1994; Janofsky et al. 1996). If this is in fact the case, one might argue that men, being the more dominant, powerful group, would achieve more success with such a defense. This apparent contradiction requires further investigation of whether such a defense is ultimately beneficial to the claimant.

Within the sociology of mental illness, some researchers emphasize the positive consequences of psychiatric labeling (Link and Cullen 1990; Link and Phelan 1999). These benefits include psychotherapy (although its therapeutic effectiveness is in question); drug treatment, which may reduce some adverse symptoms; and the haven that the hospital provides from the difficulties of life (see Link and Phelan 1999). Rosenfield (1997) finds both positive and negative effects of labeling in her face-to-face interviews with residents in a mental health center. Her results demonstrate that both access to services and perceived stigma influence life satisfaction, but in opposite directions; life satisfaction is highest for those with access to services, while satisfaction is at its lowest for those perceiving high levels of stigma (Rosenfield 1992; 1997).

Similarly, within the criminal justice system, it is a matter of debate whether the insanity defense is beneficial for criminal defendants (Lymburner and Roesch 1999). On the side of insanity as beneficial, some argue that an insanity acquittal allows defendants to access needed treatment (Neumann et al. 1996). Raising insanity questions can also help with criminal justice processing; a survey of attorneys conducted by Blau and McGinley (1995) indicated that lawyers (particularly defense lawyers) perceived some benefit to defendants from using the insanity defense, particularly when it is raised prior to the preliminary hearing: it can be used in a negotiated disposition. This finding should be interpreted with caution, however, since the authors also report that lawyers tend to have a generally poor understanding of the defense and its consequences. From the available evidence, it is unclear what effect NGRI acquittal and subsequent mental health treatment has on defendants, although most assume that psychiatric treatment is more beneficial for mentally ill individuals than time in prison or jail, which is where many mentally ill offenders are housed (Torrey et al. 1992; Hodgins 1993; U.S. Department of Justice 1997a; see Kupers 1999 for a discussion of the sanity of specific prison conditions and practices).

This psychiatric treatment, however, may also be filling the need of providing punishment, even for these individuals deemed "not guilty" (by reason of insanity) (Silver 1995). For example, on the side of insanity as detrimental to defendants, is research that insanity acquittees are confined for longer periods than if they had been found guilty of the same offense (although this is not a consistent finding). For example, Silver (1995) reported that, with respect to length of confinement, some jurisdictions hold insanity acquittees for longer than convicts, while others show the reverse trend or no differences in length of confinement. Nonetheless, it is evident that at least some insanity acquittees are being held for disproportionately long periods of time.[3] Research has also consistently demonstrated that the length of detention for insanity acquittees is related to the seriousness of the offense, seeming to reflect an underlying punishment model (Kahn and Raifman 1981; Braff et al. 1983; Clark et al. 1993; Hodgins 1993; Shah, Greenberg, and Convit 1994; Silver 1995; Callahan and Silver 1998; Lymburner and Roesch 1999).[4]

An additional consequence of an insanity label is that once the label of a mental illness has been placed on an individual, it can be almost impossible to eliminate (Link 1982; 1987; Link et al. 1987). Scheff argues that "labeled deviants are punished when they attempt to return to conventional roles" (Scheff 1963:61). He also explains that society punishes ex-mental patients if they attempt to return to "normal" society and conform to its rules. The result of this is that the ex-mental patient is taught to continue in the patient role, even if it no longer fits (Link and Phelan 1999). The fear that this status will be revealed is significant, especially since a "former mental patient" label may carry greater stigma in some situations than "former convicted felon" (see Goffman 1963; Scheff 1963; Sacks 1996).

These results question whether the successful defense of insanity benefits the defendant. Public perception of insanity is that it is positive for the defendant, who "gets away with murder." However, when looking at length of confinement and other consequences of an insanity label, it appears that this defense may not be as beneficial to defendants as is commonly believed.

Since it is unclear whether this status is ultimately "good" or "bad" for the defendant, it seems unlikely that women and African Americans today are routinely treated differently in insanity cases based solely on their race and gender and a desire to punish or treat leniently. Instead, decision-makers may use "simplifying heuristics" (Hill et al. 1985:138) and rely on patterned responses based on stereotypes and expectations of certain types of individuals (March and Simon 1965; Sudnow 1965; Hawkins and Tiedeman 1975; Farrell and Swigert 1977; 1978; Clegg and Dunkerley 1980; Rubington and Weinberg 1987; Spohn 1990;

Albonetti and Hepburn 1996; Bridges and Steen 1998), including the expectation that violence is abnormal for women and must be a result of mental illness. Violence is constructed as "normal" for African Americans, however, and is therefore not viewed as an indication of mental illness. Social and moral judgments regarding legal insanity may therefore be the end result of a social construction process in which the defendant is appraised and categorized in reference to a range of "normal penalties" established by the courtroom workgroup (Spohn 1990; Roberts and Golding 1991), with race and gender examples of many factors used in this social construction process. As a result, differences in official responses may be dependent on the type of crime committed, whether it fulfills traditional gender role stereotypes, and the characteristics of the offender, including race, SES, and family status (see Rosenfield 1982; Baskin et al. 1989; Hanke 1995; Johnson and Kandrack 1995; Lee 1998).

"Normal" Offenders and Typifications

Since the socially constructed view of "normal" crimes (Sudnow 1965) is likely to vary by race and gender (Farrell and Swigert 1986; Boritch 1992), much of what we know about criminal behavior and mental disorder is influenced by racial and gender role stereotypes, which may further influence the labeling and diagnosis of deviant acts (Cloward and Piven 1979; Schur 1984; Widom 1984). In the criminal justice system, women appear to benefit from more lenient treatment, especially in pretrial release and the decision to incarcerate. African Americans tend to receive harsher treatment, especially when examining the actions of one set of actors (e.g., lawyers and judges) rather than the actions of the justice system as a whole (Bushway and Piehl 2001).

Criminal justice officials, dealing with limited resources, must make relatively quick decisions about how cases should be processed and how scarce resources should be allocated. Labeling theory asserts that these decisions are based less on actual behavior than on definitions constructed through social interactions (LaFree 1989). Philosopher Alfred Schultz calls these definitions *typifications* (1970). Schultz argues that people process new information by comparing it to previously processed information and uncovering similarities between the two. As Schultz explains: "What is newly experienced is already known in the sense that it recalls similar or equal things formerly perceived" (1970:116). Thus, when people encounter a familiar entity (e.g., racial minorities in the criminal justice system), they also anticipate certain behavior on the part of this entity (e.g., racial minorities are "normal" offenders and should not be considered mentally ill) (LaFree 1989; see also Chiricos and Eschholz 2002; Chiricos, Welch, and Gertz 2004).

Gary LaFree argues that this ability to typify is one of the most important aspects of human development because it means that we can learn from our experiences and those of others (1989). Rather than facing the burden of constantly redefining every situation and every individual we encounter, typifications enable us to make our world more predictable, understandable, and manageable, despite the fact that these typifications are sometimes completely wrong (LaFree 1989).

Conceptual Model

This typification perspective is applied to mental illness labeling in the criminal justice system and modeled in Figure 3.5. This theory is based on statistical discrimination, feminist, labeling, and social control theories. The primary component of this theory is that psychiatric attributions in the criminal justice system are the result of social constructions of "normal" offenders. Social construction studies in criminology are concerned with documenting and analyzing the ways that the criminal justice system (along with other mass institutions such as the political system and the media) helps produce and reproduce public order and social control. From this perspective, typifications of race and gender shape and influence common images of crime, criminals, and mental illness and define the appropriate social reactions to such behaviors. These perceptions of criminals determine the appropriate labels for their behavior.

These perceptions tend to become social stereotypes, or typifications applied to classes of people (LaFree 1989). Thus, social constructions are based at least in part on typifications. Feminist theory highlights the patriarchal attitudes both in society as a whole and within the legal system. These patriarchal attitudes result in typifications of women as weak and feminine and men as rational and capable decision-makers. Racial typifications are also present in American society, with African Americans typified as violent criminals (Chiricos and Eschholz 2002; Dixon, Azocar, and Cases 2003; Chiricos, Welch, and Gertz 2004; Meyers 2004; Oliver 2004).

Legal agents are subject to the same types of social processes that affect others (see Sudnow 1965). Consequently, in the course of their daily work experience these legal agents develop typifications of the "normal" offender. These typifications make note of the overrepresentation of African Americans and the under-representation of women in the justice system, and especially in the felon population. These decision-makers are also burdened with a large number of cases needing resolution in a short period of time. Thus, they seek group characteristics that can provide important information about the appropriate disposition of cases.

When the typifications of individual decision-makers are combined with the social stereotypes present in American society, legal actors develop a set of racial and gendered expectations. These typifications of offenders influence the social reaction to criminal behavior. When criminal behavior violates these typifications (for example, women who are violent), this behavior will be attributed to mental illness. Conversely, when behavior corresponds to these expectations, the assumption of mental health will be made (as the criminal justice system assumes rationality unless evidence to the contrary is available). These attributions of either mental health or mental illness feed back into racial and gendered expectations, further strengthening these typifications of the "normal" offender. For those with the attribution of mental illness, theory suggests two competing perspectives. First, labeling theory suggests that there are negative consequences associated with a label, so a psychiatric label should result in harsher treatment for defendants. In contrast, social control theory suggests that when psychiatric controls are present, other systems of social control will be reduced. Thus when defendants are psychiatrically labeled, they will receive more lenient treatment by the legal system.

HYPOTHESES

From the theoretical model displayed in Figure 3.5 and previously discussed, 14 hypotheses of how typifications of criminal offenders are developed to explain the psychiatric evaluation process. The first ten hypotheses are tested and discussed in Chapter Five; the final four hypotheses are tested and discussed in Chapter Six.

Hypotheses Tested in Chapter Five

The severity of the symptoms of mental illness has a strong impact on whether one receives a psychiatric label (Phelan and Link 1999). If mental illness is the only requirement for receiving a psychiatric evaluation, one would expect psychiatric status or need to be the only significant predictor. This is an "objectivist" perspective, stating that only "objective" or "real" mental illness determines psychiatric labeling. Phelan and Link, however, suggest that because "the symptoms of mental illness cannot fully explain official labeling, ...[researchers should]...allow the possibility that factors identified by labeling theory are important" (1999:144). If race, gender, and other social factors influence psychiatric labeling, criminal responsibility and the need for psychiatric evaluations may be the result of a social construction process. Consequently, this project begins with two competing hypotheses:

Hypothesis 1A: *Psychiatric status will be the only significant determinant of psychiatric evaluations in the criminal justice system (objectivist account).*

Hypothesis 1B: *Social factors, in addition to psychiatric status, will predict which defendants receive psychiatric evaluations (social constructionist account).*

Most theorists expect that women are more likely to be viewed as mentally ill and that they are more likely than men to have criminal behavior attributed to a mental disorder (Edwards 1986; Ussher 1991; Wilczynski 1991; Burns 1992; Chan 1994; Nicolson 1995; Smart 1995;

Chan 1999; Kendall 1999a; Kendall 1999b; Umphrey 1999). As Zedner (1991) explains, in the 19th Century women increasingly became subject to the control of insane asylums, with women viewed as "not bad but mad" (Zedner 1991:264). This portrayal of women criminals as mentally deficient has endured into contemporary criminal justice (Worrall 1990; Zedner 1991:296).

Hypothesis 2: *Female felony defendants will be more likely than male felony defendants to receive a psychiatric evaluation (social constructionist account).*

Hypothesis 2 refers at least in part to the under-representation of women in the criminal justice system. The relative scarcity of female defendants (U.S. Department of Justice 1999a), contributes to the idea that females who *are* arrested and charged will be viewed as abnormal or ill. While criminal women might be considered abnormal, stereotypes of African Americans frequently focus on criminality and violence (Smith 1991; Sniderman and Piazza 1993; Quillian and Pager 2001). This stereotype of African Americans as criminal is deeply embedded in Americans' collective consciousness and may be used by decision-makers who must make choices based on incomplete information (Devine and Elliot 1995; Quillian and Pager 2001). Since a disproportionate number of criminal defendants are young and African American (Steffensmeier, Ulmer, and Kramer 1998; U.S. Department of Justice 1999b), they will be less likely to be psychiatrically evaluated since they are not viewed as abnormal criminal defendants.

Hypothesis 3: *African Americans will be less likely than non-African Americans to receive a psychiatric evaluation (social constructionist account).*

Hypothesis 4: *Older defendants will be more likely to receive a psychiatric evaluation (social constructionist account).*

Some feminists—in particular those from the "first wave" of feminism—focus on all women, arguing that white, Asian, and African American women all have more in common with each other than they do with men of any race (Nicholson 1997). In contrast, others assert that while women do share common experiences, these experiences are not generally the same as those affecting racial and ethnic groups (Collins 1997:248). Thus, lenient treatment of women in the legal system may be available only to white women (Carlen 2002b). Legal outcomes may also depend on constructions of culpability, on how much offenders are held responsible for their crimes (Carlen 2002b; Hudson 2002). Hudson, for example, contends that constructions of culpability are part of a continuum of blameworthiness, with black men at one end—constructed as wholly to blame for their crimes—and white women at the other end of the continuum, with white men and black women in between (2002:39).

Hypothesis 5: *Black men will be less likely to be psychiatrically evaluated than white men and black women will be less likely to be psychiatrically evaluated than white women (intersectionality account).*

In addition to race and gender expectations, there are also norms that define appropriate *deviant* behaviors for African Americans and non-African Americans and for men and women. Acting out may be considered violence or crime for African Americans rather than evidence of mental disorder (Kirk and Kutchings 1997). For women, deviant behavior that is passive or submissive (e.g., hiding stolen property for a boyfriend or certain types of mental illness) is viewed as congruent with female gender roles. Deviant behavior of the acting-out or aggressive variety is regarded as more consistent with the male role (Baskin et al. 1989:306). Similarly, Baskin et al. (1989) note that the likelihood of mental health placement in prison is significantly increased if female inmates engaged in prison violence and/or aggressive behavior (role-incongruent acts). In contrast, male inmates who participated in similar acts (but ones that were role-congruent) were placed in disciplinary confinement (Baskin et al. 1989).

Because decision-makers learn in the course of their daily work experiences that women rarely appear in court charged with violent offenses (Worrall 1990; Feeley and Little 1991; Zedner 1991; Steffensmeier and Allan 1996; U.S. Department of Justice 1998a; U.S. Department of Justice 1998c), the courtroom workgroup may view violent offenders as so abnormal that they require further investigation to determine psychological status.

Hypothesis 6: *Female defendants charged with a violent offense (role-incongruent act) will be more likely to receive a psychiatric evaluation than men who engage in violence (role-congruent).*

Because an insanity defense requires a significant amount of time and attention on the part of state actors, it is expected that these psychiatric evaluations will most frequently be given to the most serious offenders who face the longest prison sentences. In addition, the motive for violent offenses may the least apparent. While property offenses appear to be motivated by financial needs or desires, the motivation for violent offenses may be less clear, leaving decision-makers to seek alternative, including psychiatric, explanations.

Hypothesis 7: *Violent offenders will be more likely to receive a psychiatric evaluation than non-violent offenders.*

Differences in gender role expectations are very important for determining what types of behavior are considered deviant and how the criminal justice system responds. Women who violate their expected care-taking role by engaging in violence may be viewed as *so* abnormal that a psychiatric explanation is expected. According to Kirwin, a forensic psychologist in New York City, only two of the last decade's 231 trials involving infanticide in New York have resulted in verdicts of guilty (1997:34). She explains that these cases are the single most successful use of the insanity defense since "it seems incomprehensible to a jury that any mother would deliberately take the life of her own child" (1997:75). Family roles, including marital status, number of children, and primary caretaker roles, are important in affecting criminal case outcomes (see Steffensmeier, Kramer, and Streifel 1993; Daly 1987; 1994), and might also alter insanity decision-making. Since decision-makers will not want to punish defendants' children, they may seek to funnel women with children and married women onto the most beneficial path, the route with the fewest perceived repercussions (Blau and McGinley 1995). The question, however, is whether psychiatric evaluations are more or less harmful to the recipients. One might argue that seeking out an evaluation is beneficial to these women because it allows for a possible not guilty verdict (because of mental disease or defect). Conversely, the imposition of an additional label may stigmatize and ultimately harm these women relative to those who do not receive the evaluation. Therefore, two sets of competing hypotheses with respect to gender and family status are proposed:

Hypothesis 8A: *Women who fulfill their expected familial role by providing care for their children will be **less** likely to receive a psychiatric evaluation than women who are not parents.*

Hypothesis 8B: *Women who fulfill their expected familial role by providing care for their children will be **more** likely to receive a psychiatric evaluation than women who are not parents.*

Hypothesis 9A: *Women who fulfill their expected familial role by being married will be **less** likely to receive a psychiatric evaluation than women who are not married.*

Hypothesis 9B: *Women who fulfill their expected familial role by being married will be **more** likely to receive a psychiatric evaluation than women who are not married.*

Finally, women who significantly violate gendered norms by committing offenses against intimates, including children and/or significant others, may be especially likely to receive an evaluation.

Hypothesis 10: *Women charged with crimes against their intimates (children and significant others) will be more likely to receive a psychiatric evaluation compared to other women and men charged with any crime.*

Hypotheses Tested in Chapter Six

Consistent with previous research, the largest racial and gender differences in case processing are expected to appear in the earliest stage, the decision of whether to evaluate the defendant for a psychiatric disorder.[5] This is because lawyers and judges, who are not trained in evaluating mental states, play a pivotal role in determining who will be evaluated (see Bonnie et al. 1996). As a result, these legal actors are the most free to incorporate prejudice or typifications of "normal" offenders.

Hypothesis 11: *The greatest gender disparity will be found in the earliest stage, the decision to request a psychiatric evaluation.*

Hypothesis 12: *The greatest racial disparity will be found in the earliest stage, the decision to request a psychiatric evaluation.*

On the level of individual decision-making, defense attorneys may advocate for a mental illness defense in an attempt to obtain immediate mental health treatment for their clients (Perlin 2000). From this perspective, as part of their legal strategy defense attorneys will advocate for a psychiatric defense in an attempt to force prosecutors to negotiate a plea disposition that includes limited criminal justice penalties in favor of mental health treatment (Blau and McGinley 1995; Laberge and Morin 2001). From a social control perspective, defendants subject to psychiatric controls are less subject to legal controls. Consequently, the evaluation results in less severe legal sanctions.

Hypothesis 13: *Defendants in the criminal justice system who receive psychiatric evaluations will receive less severe sanctions than those who do not receive evaluations.*

Conversely, consistent with labeling theory's prediction about the negative impact of labels, there may be negative consequences to receiving a mental health evaluation. Previous research found that for defendants who *unsuccessfully* attempted an insanity defense, the length of confinement was 22 percent longer than for convicted felons who never raised the plea (Braff, Arvinites, and Steadman 1983). While public perception of the insanity defense is that it is beneficial for defendants, that they "get away with murder," studies of length of confinement (prison or mental hospital) demonstrate a punishment philosophy, where the punishment fits the crime, regardless of whether the defendant is considered responsible (Silver 1995; Callahan and Silver 1998; Lymburner and Roesch 1999). It therefore appears that this defense may not be as positive as first believed, since similar to a prison sentence, crime severity rather than mental state determines the length of confinement (Silver 1995; Callahan and Silver 1998; Lymburner and Roesch 1999). It may be that defendants who plead insanity and are ultimately found guilty of their charges serve *longer* sentences than defendants who do not assert an insanity defense (Menzies 1989; Perlin 2000). This suggests the following hypothesis, which is a competing hypothesis to number 13.

Hypothesis 14: Defendants in the criminal justice system who receive mental health evaluations will receive more severe sanctions than those who do not receive evaluations.

CONCLUSION

The theoretical argument promoted in this research is that insanity in the criminal justice system is influenced by social constructions of "normal" or expected behavior. Behavior that may be healthy or normal for men might be diagnosed and labeled insane for women (Holstein 1993), and what might be normal for an African American defendant might be perceived as abnormal for a white defendant. Crimes that are more typical among men and African Americans may be viewed as abnormal among women and whites. While there are few racial and gender differences in terms of diagnosed major psychotic disorders, expectations may, however, influence insanity case processing and outcome.

NOTES

[1] There has historically been concern that the relative lack of female psychiatric "experts" plays a role in legal decisions regarding mental states (see Walters 1994). It was believed that this relative dearth of female expert witnesses could influence the type of diagnosis received (see Loring and Powell 1988), which ultimately influenced mental health case outcomes.

[2] While this research singles out psychiatry, obviously other scientific disciplines are similarly limited by failures to be objective and value-free. Differential psychiatric labeling based on social expectations, however, is important because by naming an illness and placing it within a classification system of diseases, psychiatry makes claims about what is normal and has significant power to respond to this illness, via drug treatment or institutionalization (see Light 1982; Kutchins and Kirk 1997).

[3] It must be noted that some authors (e.g., Hodgins 1993) argue that the lengthy confinement arising from a verdict of insanity may be beneficial to the defendant, allowing him/her the opportunity to receive needed treatment.

[4] Furthermore, there appear to be some negative consequences in simply raising an insanity defense. Braff, Arvinites, and Steadman (1983) found that for the *unsuccessful* insanity defendant, the length of confinement was 22 percent longer than that of convicted felons who never raised the plea. Whereas 11 percent of all felony arrests resulted in imprisonment, 67 percent of the unsuccessful insanity pleas were imprisoned.

[5] While a request for psychiatric evaluation can occur at any time in the process, it usually occurs at arraignment.

Figure 3.1 STATISTICAL DISCRIMINATION

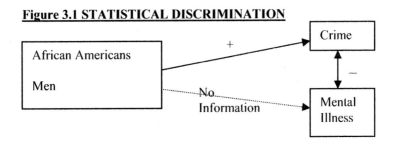

Figure 3.2 LABELING THEORY (Adapted from Pescosolido et al. 2000)

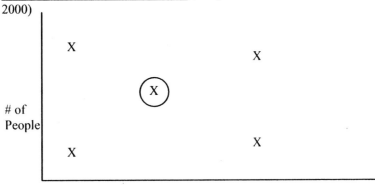

Figure 3.3 FEMINIST THEORY

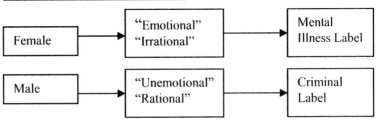

Figure 3.4 SOCIAL CONTROL THEORY

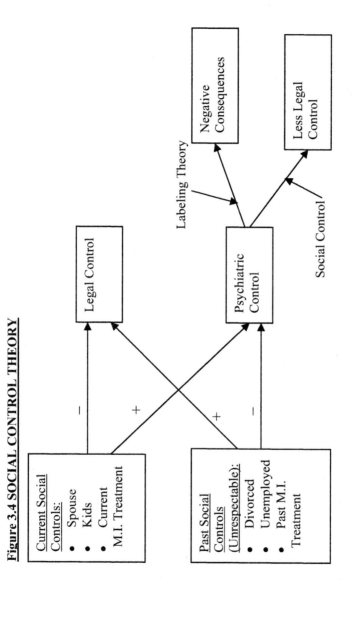

Figure 3.5 THEORETICAL MODEL

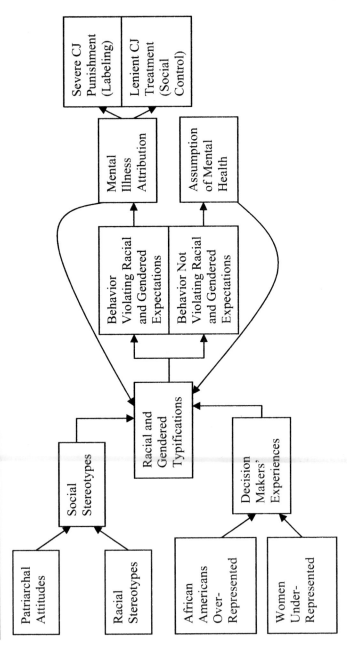

## CHAPTER 4

DATA, MEASURES, AND STATISTICAL PROCEDURES

To test the hypotheses, this project used data collected from two sources, both maintained by Hennepin County, Minnesota. To gather data on the use of psychiatric evaluations in criminal court processing, records maintained by Hennepin County's Psychological Services were used. These records include every felony criminal defendant who received a psychiatric evaluation to determine mental state at the time of an offense. These data are not publicly available and had never before been analyzed, therefore they provide an important new avenue for a sociological examination of ideas long debated in the sociology of gender and race.

For purposes of this project, these psychiatric evaluation files are better data sources than NGRI acquittals, since (1) these files provide information about cases prior to NGRI acquittal and offer information even on those who eventually dropped the plea; (2) these files also provide detailed information about mental states and the evaluator's recommendations; and, (3) the determination of who receives these evaluations is made by lawyers and/or judges, individuals who are not typically trained in determining mental states, and therefore most subject to social expectations regarding appropriate and typical behavior. The result is that this stage may be the most likely to include disparities and discretion based on incomplete information. Using these psychiatric evaluations, the researcher gathered data on psychological and criminal history, family and demographic detail, the evaluator's recommendation, and final disposition.

The comparison or control group consists of individuals who did not receive a psychiatric evaluation as part of their criminal court processing. Since requests for psychiatric evaluations are usually made early in criminal processing (typically at arraignment), this project randomly selected individuals arraigned for a felony in the same years as the psychiatric cases (see Figure 4.1 for a representation of case flow through the criminal justice system). From these individuals' pre-sentence investigation (PSI) reports, the same information as from the psychiatric evaluations was gathered (with the exception of the psychiatrist's evaluation of current mental status and recommendation for case outcome). These files are particularly useful since they provide detailed information about the crime, the offender's living arrangements, and the Probation Officer's perception of the offender's rehabilitative potential.

The procedure used for selection of the cases for comparison is commonly referred to as *case-control* methodology. While this process is rarely used in sociological and criminological research, and is not always called case-control (Lacy 1997), it has been instrumental in providing valuable information about rare events including violent crime (Heath, Kruttschnitt, and Ward 1986; Kruttschnitt, Ward, and Sheble 1987; Shepherd and Brickley 1996), homicide (Goodman et al. 1988; Kleck and Hogan 1999), and rape (Kruttschnitt 1989). Since mental health evaluations of criminal defendants are likewise rare, this methodology is useful in understanding the psychiatric evaluation process.

CASE-CONTROL METHODS FOR EFFICIENTLY STUDYING RARE EVENTS

Case-control studies are particularly useful for examining rare events. The simplest example of this is one in which the independent variables (e.g., African American race and gender) and event (psychiatric evaluation) are dichotomous, each being considered either present or absent; this sampling strategy is distinct from more traditional cohort sampling, which is more frequently used in sociological research.

Cohort sampling. The primary distinction between cohort and case-control designs is the method by which individuals are selected for study. If researchers used a cohort study to analyze gender and psychiatric evaluations, they would take random samples of men and women in the criminal justice system. Samples are "random" in the sense that, among men or women, a person who will be evaluated has the same chance of being studied as a person who will never be evaluated.

Rather than taking separate samples of men and women, a cohort study often begins by taking a sample of all individuals, irrespective of gender. Subjects are then followed over time to observe the occurrence of a psychiatric evaluation, and individuals are later stratified into gender groups. Since sampling would not depend on either the gender or evaluation status, the odds of female gender and the odds of evaluation in the sample would agree (apart from sampling variability) with their values in the target population (Schlesselman 1982). Because it is exceedingly difficult to sample a sufficiently large number of felony defendants to enable a cohort study, this research instead relies on data gathered using case-control sampling.

Case-control sampling. Case-control methods were developed for use in epidemiological and bio-statistical research. Since ethical or practical considerations often prevent the use of experimental methods in these settings, case-control methodology was developed with the tactic of working from the effect to the cause (Schlesselman 1982:5). In case-control studies, individuals with a particular condition or disease (the *cases*) are selected for comparison with a series of individuals in whom the condition or disease is absent (the *controls*). Cases and controls are then compared with respect to existing or past attributes or exposures thought to be relevant to the development of the condition or disease under study (Schlesselman 1982:14). Using this methodology, researchers can find the ratio of incidence rates in the cases as compared to the controls, or the *relative risk* associated with certain characteristics. In the simplest case, that of a binary independent variable and its effect on a binary dependent variable, effects can be summarized as either a "rate difference" or a "rate ratio" (Lacy 1997).

The defining feature of a case-control study is that the sample is stratified on a discrete *dependent* variable, not, as in conventional sociological practice, on one or more *independent* variables (Lacy 1997). Due to this methodology's selection of cases on the basis of outcome, case-control methods are especially economical for the study of rare events since a prospective longitudinal study of rare events requires large numbers of cases and significantly more funding (Schlesselman 1982:17; Loftin and McDowall 1988; King and Zeng 2001a; 2001b). Therefore, studies using this methodology have several advantages; in particular they are relatively quick to mount and conduct, are relatively inexpensive, and require comparatively few subjects. Also, existing records can be used, there are no risks to subjects, and they allow for the study of multiple causes (Schlesselman 1982:18). The disadvantages of this method are that they rely on records for information about the past, validation of this information is sometimes difficult, control of extraneous variables may be incomplete, selection of an appropriate comparison group may be difficult, rates of the disease/event in exposed and unexposed individuals cannot be determined, the method is relatively unfamiliar, and detailed study of the mechanism is rarely possible (Schlesselman 1982:18). Since the scarcity of psychiatric evaluations makes selection on this characteristic necessary, this chapter highlights this methodology's advantages while explaining how this research attempted to avoid its drawbacks.

Case and Control Selection and Matching

Whenever possible in the case-control selection process, *all* cases fulfilling selection criteria are chosen for analysis. The selection process for the cases is therefore relatively simple. The primary determinant of whether a case-control study is feasible is how easy it is to obtain some sort of listing of persons who experienced the rare event (Lacy 1997). This makes this methodology well-suited to the study of government documents and psychiatric evaluations in particular, since detailed case files are maintained for all cases. Thus, for this research, cases are all individuals fulfilling the selection criteria; all felony defendants referred for psychiatric evaluations between 1993 and 2001 were selected.

The important sample selection criterion, however, is deciding which controls to use. Researchers using this methodology will frequently match their cases and controls on one or more variables. In many case-control studies, however, matching can actually create confounding that otherwise would be absent and generally biases effect estimates toward the null, regardless of the direction of the true effect

(Lacy 1997; Rothman and Greenland 1998). For example, suppose a researcher matched on a variable (B, or SES in this analysis) that is intermediate in the causal pathway between gender and psychiatric evaluation ([A→ B→ C] or [female → SES → evaluation]). An analysis that ignored the pairing would result in an odds ratio biased toward zero (Schlesselman 1982:110; see also Lacy 1997; King and Zeng 2001a; 2001b). This would occur because matching on a consequence of being female (such as lower SES) would spuriously equate the proportion of individuals in the case and control series that are female. Even if researchers performed the analysis with appropriate controls for this matching, the female-evaluation odds ratio would tend to underestimate the correct value (Schelesselman 1982:110). According to Schlesselman, "if one has a procedure for ascertaining all incident cases occurring within a geographic area in a defined period of time, then the use of controls selected at random from the general population is undoubtedly the option of choice" (1982:82). Therefore, unless a researcher has a good theoretical or methodological rationale for matching cases, most case-control methodologists recommend randomly selecting controls (Lacy 1997; Rothman and Greenland 1998). Consequently, rather than match cases and controls, the control group was randomly selected from all felony cases arraigned in Hennepin County, Minnesota in the same nine years (1993-2001).

CASES, CONTROLS, AND SAMPLE SIZE

As in any sample-based study, increasing sample size will increase precision and reduce sampling error (Lacy 1997). Assuming all cases are sampled, only the sample size of the control group can be increased, so case-control studies usually involve at least as many controls as cases (Lacy 1997). The primary function of these controls is to provide information on the distribution of the independent variables within the case-generating population. The carefully executed case-control study is valid and efficient for exploring multiple independent variables (Rothman and Greenland 1998). If a researcher wanted to use a longitudinal study to explore the effect of several different independent variables on the hazard rate for a rare event, a panel large and diverse enough to exhibit a reasonable distribution of all the independent variables among both event and nonevent subjects would be needed. Follow-up costs for such a panel would be prohibitively expensive and would still suffer from a small number of cases with the rare event (see e.g., King and Zeng 2001a; 2001b). In contrast, a case-control study uses the much larger sample of persons who experienced the rare event, allowing for statistically precise estimates for a variety of independent variables (Schlesselman 1982; Carroll, Wang, and Wang 1995; Lacy 1997; King and Zeng 2001a; 2001b).

With such flexibility and apparent ease comes risk, however, as the validity of effect estimates depends on the controls having been sampled independently of each of the causal variables of interest. For example, using the research design, if controls were sampled on mental health history or SES, the use of mental illness as a causal variable would be subject to bias. A randomly sampled control series from a well-defined population at risk eliminates this concern; if a nonrandom control group is used, the chance of bias increases, since it may accurately represent the distribution for one independent variable, but not others (Schlesselman 1982; Carroll, Wang, and Wang 1995; Lacy 1997:143). Because the cases are limited to felony defendants, and all felony defendants are potential recipients of these psychiatric evaluations, the "well-defined population at risk" is all defendants arraigned for a felony in Hennepin County, Minnesota. If only certain felony defendants are at risk for a psychiatric evaluation (for example, if evaluations are given only to murderers or sex offenders), this sampling strategy would inaccurately represent the at-risk population. There are, however, no statutory limitations on the type of offenders who can be evaluated; also, as will be demonstrated in Chapter Five, those who are evaluated are charged with the entire range of felony offenses: from drug offenses to murder.

Based on information from Hennepin County, it was clear that data were available on approximately 400 felony defendants who received psychiatric evaluations. Since most researchers using case-control methods suggest an approximately equal (or slightly large) number of controls to compare to cases, it was decided to sample approximately 400-500 controls, with the knowledge that increasing sample size reduces sampling error (Lacy 1997; Rothman and Greenland 1998). Since there are approximately 40-50 of these evaluations in Hennepin County each year, obtaining a sample of this size required data collection covering a 9-year period (1993-2001). While Minnesota's insanity defense law has not changed in the past decade, year-to-year changes in procedural norms may alter the effects, so this analysis statistically controls for the year of the evaluation.

THE HENNEPIN COUNTY RESEARCH SETTING AND GENERALIZABILITY

This research is based in Hennepin County, Minnesota, and its largest city, Minneapolis. How does this research setting compare to other locations? To determine the generalizability of these data, it is important to compare characteristics of Hennepin County with other locations and explain how the research might be affected by the locality.

With its population of 1,116,200, Hennepin is the largest county in Minnesota; approximately 23 percent of Minnesota's population resides here and the 99,943 African Americans living here represent over 58 percent of the state's total African American population (U.S. Census Bureau 2003b). Socioeconomic indicators for Hennepin County, documented by the 2000 Census, indicate that Minnesotans and Hennepin County residents generally fare better than the national average. Per capita income (in 1999) was $28,789 in Hennepin County, $23,198 in Minnesota, and $21,587 in the nation (U.S. Census Bureau 2003c). In Hennepin County, 8.3 percent of persons fall below the poverty line, in comparison to 12.4 percent in the United States (the comparable number for Minnesota is 7.9 percent) (U.S. Census Bureau 2003c). Hennepin County residents also have a higher educational attainment than the national average; among those 25 or older, 39.1 percent are college graduates versus 24.4 percent of the U.S. population in this age group (U.S. Census Bureau 2003c). As in Minnesota generally, the labor market in Hennepin County presents good employment opportunities, with a relatively low unemployment rate (2.6 percent in 2000 versus 4.0 percent nationally) (U.S. Bureau of Labor Statistics 2003).

Thus, there are comparatively more economic opportunities in Hennepin County. To the extent that legal agents view low SES as a consequence and a possible indication of mental illness, Hennepin

County decision-makers may be less likely to perceive some defendants as mentally ill compared to other more economically stricken locations. If this is the case, the estimations of mental illness attributions will be conservative. Alternatively, Minnesota's comparatively strong socioeconomic position and its reputation for a treatment philosophy, stemming from professionalized criminal justice and mental health systems (Levin 1977), might affect legal agents in the opposite direction: decision-makers in Minnesota may be more inclined to perceive mental illness than in other jurisdictions.

Gender. Minnesota tends to be more progressive on gender issues than other states; for example, the earning power of women in Minnesota is seventh in the nation, with median weekly earnings of $598 in 2001 compared to the national average of $511 (U.S. Department of Labor 2002; see also Peterson 2003). Minnesota also ranks in the top 20 states in women's earnings as a percentage of men's earnings (77.8 percent) (U.S. Department of Labor 2002). Consequently, the notion of passive women who are economically dependent on their spouses may be less salient for Minnesotans. Legal agents in this setting might be less inclined to perceive criminal women as abnormal (and therefore in need of psychiatric treatment) because they violate gender expectations to a lesser extent than do criminal women in Mississippi—where women are 49th in median weekly earnings ($494) and 44th in earnings as a percentage of men's earnings. Thus, for purposes of this project, the result of the relative economic strength of Minnesota women should be more conservative estimates of the effect of gender on mental illness attributions.

Race. Despite Minnesota having the nation's second lowest incarceration rate with 139 inmates per 100,000 residents (U.S. Department of Justice 2003), Minnesota's African American imprisonment rate is 1,405, which ranks 33rd highest in the nation (U.S. Department of Justice 1998d; U.S. Census Bureau 2000). Almost 38 percent of Minnesota's prisoners are African American (U.S. Department of Justice 1998d), significantly more than are found in the state's population (3.5 percent of Minnesotans are African American) (U.S. Census Bureau 2003b). In this research, the hypothesized effect of disproportionate minority representation in the criminal justice system is the development of typifications of "normal" offenders who are perceived to be African American. Comparisons across jurisdictions, however, may depend on the degree of minority overrepresentation. For example, the results of this project may not generalize as well to states like North Dakota, which has a comparatively low African American imprisonment rate (753 per 100,000 in 1998)[1] (U.S. Department of Justice 1998d; U.S. Census Bureau 2000). In states with less racial disparity in criminal justice outcomes, this research may overestimate the effect of race on psychiatric attributions. Compared to states with a higher racial disparity, however (such as Delaware with its 4,413 African American imprisonment rate [U.S. Department of Justice 1998d; U.S. Census Bureau 2000]), data obtained in Minnesota should conservatively estimate the effect of racial typifications.

Due to important differences across various social indicators, generalizations beyond Hennepin County should be cautiously stated. Nevertheless, to the extent that racial and gendered typifications are pervasive throughout American society (see, e.g., Devine and Elliot 1995; Chiricos et al. 2001; Emerson et al. 2001; Chiricos, Welch, and Gertz 2004; Oliver 2004) this research provides evidence of this phenomenon. Because there is little local or national information available about racial and gendered effects on attributions of mental illness in the criminal justice system, this research addresses unanswered questions and provides a starting point for future research on typifications and institutions of social control.

INDEPENDENT AND DEPENDENT VARIABLES

Independent Variables

The independent variables that were collected for this project reflect individual demographic characteristics and familial, legal, and psychiatric status. These variables provide insight into how "type-scripts" or different social expectations of men and women affect case outcome for male and female defendants.

Demographic, Criminal History, and Offense Variables. The key independent variables in this analysis include the demographic characteristics of gender, age, and race. Although the statutory requirement for psychiatric evaluations does not require a certain criminal history or type of current offense, decision-makers in the criminal justice system are aware of this information and have been socialized to rely on this information to form other decisions about the offender. Legally relevant factors are also important controls when analyzing case outcomes. Therefore, this research gathered data for a control variable for the most serious current offense charge—whether it was a violent offense. It also obtained controls for the number of previous adult arrests for violence and the number of felony convictions as an adult.

    Mental Health, Socioeconomic Status, and Family. Mental health history is measured with dichotomous indicators of whether the defendant has ever received various mental illness diagnoses. A dichotomous indicator of whether the arresting police officer reported that the defendant acted in a "bizarre" manner was also obtained. Bizarre behavior on the part of the defendant would include talking to people who are not present, discussing why God told you to commit the offense, and rambling in an incoherent manner. Strange behavior that was attributable to intoxication or drug use was not considered as part of this bizarre behavior dichotomy. Mental health history was further measured with dichotomous indicators of previous mental hospitalization and previous outpatient psychiatric treatment.

    Some have argued that the criminal justice system is more lenient on mothers with children due to fears that punishment of mothers will harm their children (Daly 1994). Social control theory also indicates that those subject to informal social controls via marriage may be less subject to legal controls (Black 1976; Horwitz 1990; 2002a; 2002b). Consequently, indicators of whether the defendant is responsible for any children and whether the defendant is married or cohabiting with a significant other were also gathered. Finally, because mental illness is strongly associated with socioeconomic status, data were collected on the defendant's salary, unearned income—including SSI income, AFDC, and food stamps,—the defendant's educational attainment, and whether they had a private defense attorney.

Dependent Variables

The dependent variables measure mental health evaluations and the processing of these cases throughout the criminal justice system. The research primarily considers two stages of criminal justice processing. The first stage measures whether the defendant received a psychiatric evaluation (yes/no) to determine mental state at the time of the offense (referred to as a 20.02 evaluation under the *Minnesota Rules of Criminal Procedure*). The second stage looks to case outcome for those who received this evaluation in comparison to those who did not (see Figure 1 for a representation of the stages of interest).

The dependent variable used in the first stage of this analysis is a dichotomous variable indicating whether the felony defendant was given a psychiatric evaluation to determine mental state at the time of the offense (this analysis is presented in Chapter Five). The request for an evaluation typically comes from the defense side, but can be made by the prosecution or judge, if deemed necessary. Once the request is made, the defendant is referred to the county's psychiatric services division, which conducts the evaluation. This evaluation may ultimately be used in mounting an insanity defense, although this is not required. This dichotomous variable is used to indicate that actors in the criminal justice system are looking for a possible psychiatric explanation for the criminal behavior. If the defendant is found to have a mental impairment at the time of the offense, it might mitigate the defendant's responsibility for the criminal behavior. Thus, a psychiatric evaluation in the criminal justice system points to an understanding on the part of criminal justice officials that the defendant may be abnormal or ill such that he or she should not be held accountable.

The second stage of this analysis models case outcomes and is presented in Chapter Six. To obtain the dependent variable, the initial case outcome was coded based on five outcomes: a NGRI finding, the decision to dismiss all charges, whether the defendant is found guilty or pleads guilty, whether the defendant is sentenced to prison, and the length of the prison sentence. While some cases may initially receive a probationary sentence but ultimately result in a prison sentence once the offender recidivates or violates probation conditions, only the initial sentencing decision was coded. This decision was made to model the effect of the psychiatric control factors on sentencing outcome, regardless of the later behavior of the individual. Additionally, because the follow-up period is not the same for all offenders (e.g., cases from 1993 had 8 years in which to recidivate while cases from 2000 only had one year to recidivate), only the initial decision was coded and offenders were not followed beyond this point.[2]

CONCLUSION

The following chapters look for evidence of the role of racial and gendered expectations in determinations of insanity outcomes. While this research will not definitively answer the question of whether women and non-African Americans are more likely to be funneled into the psychiatric role in all jurisdictions, it will provide some evidence either to support this notion of race and gender typifications, or it will point to equality in mental illness attributions. The desirability of such racial and gendered differences, however, will not be answered in this research. If the criminal justice system is not arbitrarily lenient in its treatment of women and non-African American offenders, potential differences may not be a social problem;[3] racial and gendered differences in criminal justice and mental health treatment may instead be the result of "real" differences in rehabilitation potential, mental illness, or criminality. Conversely, if differences are arbitrary and the result of typifications about the appropriate behavior of women and African Americans, these typifications may negatively affect defendants who violate these expectations.

If there are different expectations based on race and gender, differential treatment on the basis of these factors can become institutionalized. As Baskin et al. (1989) demonstrated, the institutional response to violence and aggression is disciplinary confinement for men and mental health housing for females engaging in similar behavior. The institutionalization of differential treatment has several serious consequences for all who deal with the criminal justice system. "When the penal system adopts, in effect, a "madness" definition of role-incongruent behavior, it leaves female inmates open to such abuses as the improper use and the overuse of psychotropic drugs as well as to the effects of longer sentences in order to permit treatment" (Baskin et al. 1989:312). Similarly, when the legal system assumes that all African Americans are "normal" criminals, it fails to provide potentially important psychiatric treatment that may alter future criminal behavior and mental illness.

Conversely, if men and women are treated equally in determinations of insanity and psychiatric evaluations, this research will provide evidence to counter claims made by feminist and labeling theorists. Feminists contend that gender differences should be expected since the legal system reflects the masculine point of view and approaches women the way men approach women (see MacKinnon 1987; 1989). If this research fails to provide evidence to support this feminist perspective, it may be that recent changes in the legal system—reflecting the presence of more women—have altered the legal system's perception of women (see Spohn 1990); it may also be possible that societal expectations have changed to the point that the notion of violent women no longer seems contradictory or bizarre (see Worrall 2002). If this is the case, feminist assertions may need to be modified to reflect changes in social expectations and their influences in criminal justice processing. Race also determines who is "rational" for most feminist and labeling theorists. The standard for rationality in the criminal justice system may mirror typifications of "normal" or expected offenders—African Americans. If the research presented in this book does not indicate that African Americans are perceived to be normal offenders, this would imply that rather than assuming that the race of a defendant provides information about the normalcy or irrationality of a defendant committing a crime, legal agents instead rely on more objective psychiatric indicators to provide clues of a defendant's rationality when committing an offense.

NOTES

[1] North Dakota has a similarly low total incarceration rate of 167 in 2002 (U.S. Department of Justice 2003), however, so there is still evidence of significant racial differences in the rate of incarceration.

[2] An event history model of recidivism would be possible, however, with offenders coded as censored when they are no longer at risk. Because this analysis would require a significant amount of additional data collection and it is beyond the scope of this analysis, an event history analysis was not conducted at this point, but will be considered in future research.

[3] As discussed in Chapter Two, the question of whether it is better to have equality of treatment or for women to receive lenient treatment in the criminal justice system is hotly debated by feminists (see Carlen 2002a). On one hand are the arguments that promote equality of treatment for men and women in the criminal justice system. The critique of this perspective is that it ignores potentially important factors such as economic need, which may be more relevant for women than for men (Carlen 2002b; Hudson 2002:36). On the other hand are arguments that women should be treated more leniently than men. These arguments are also harshly critiqued because the assumption that women are somehow less culpable than men for the same offense implies that women need to be pampered and treated like children (who are less culpable than adults) (Hudson 2002:41).

Figure 4.1: Flow of Cases and Controls through the Criminal Justice System

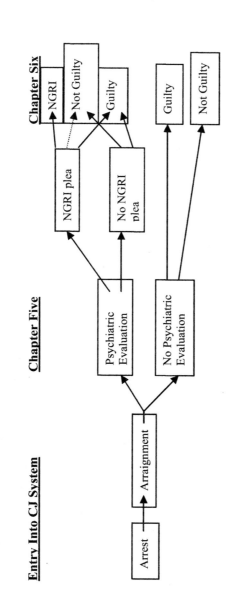

## CHAPTER 5

PREDICTORS OF PSYCHIATRIC EVALUATIONS

The theoretical perspective this chapter considers is that criminal responsibility in the justice system is influenced by social constructions of "normal" or expected behavior. Court actors face organizational constraints such as limited decision-making time and incomplete information about defendants (Kramer and Ulmer 1996). Consequently, these actors may view defendants in terms of stereotypes to reduce uncertainty in criminal processing decisions (Miethe 1987). Specifically, when court actors are faced with typical criminal defendants, such as African Americans and men, these actors may assume rationality. Conversely, when faced with "abnormal" criminal defendants, such as violent women, these legal actors may attribute criminal behavior to mental illness (see Holstein 1993:155).

The alternative to this social construction perspective is the "objectivist" account. This perspective asserts that the severity of the symptoms of mental illness is the sole criteria for determining who receives a psychiatric label. If mental illness is the only requirement for receiving a psychiatric evaluation, then psychiatric need should be the only significant predictor; thus only "objective" or "real" mental illness determines psychiatric labeling. This chapter compares the objectivist and social construction perspectives of legal decision-making affecting mental health evaluations for felony defendants.

Dependent Variable

The dependent variable for this analysis is a dichotomous indicator of whether the felony defendant was given a psychiatric evaluation to determine mental state at the time of the offense. The request for an evaluation typically comes from the defense, but can be made by the prosecution or judge if deemed necessary. Once the request is made, the defendant is referred to the county's psychiatric services division, which conducts the evaluation; every request for an evaluation is honored.

Both public defenders and private attorneys make use of this evaluation. In this sample, approximately 57 percent of the defendants with a private attorney received an evaluation; approximately 46 percent of the defendants with a public defender received an evaluation. This difference is statistically significant ($p < .05$, gamma $= .211$) (analysis not shown). While the rate of private attorneys among the evaluation population is greater than the rate of public defenders, the absolute number of evaluated defendants with public defenders ($N = 350$) is much larger than the number of evaluated defendants with private attorneys ($N = 60$). The analysis to follow includes a private attorney indicator to model this difference in defense attorneys and psychiatric evaluations.

The evaluation report, which is presented to the court, may ultimately be used in mounting an insanity defense, although this does not always occur. This dichotomous evaluation variable is used to indicate that actors in the criminal justice system are looking to a possible psychiatric explanation for the criminal behavior. If the defendant is found to have a mental impairment at the time of the offense, it might eliminate the defendant's responsibility for the criminal behavior. Thus, a psychiatric evaluation in the criminal justice system points to an understanding on the part of criminal justice officials that the defendant may be abnormal or ill such that he or she should not be held accountable.

Independent Variables

Demographic, Criminal History, and Offense Variables. The independent variables used for analysis in this chapter are described briefly in Chapter Four. The variables used are the demographic characteristics of gender, age, and race. These variables are used to determine whether typifications, based on social characteristics of defendants, alter the odds of being evaluated. This includes a dichotomous indicator of the most serious charged offense—whether it was a violent offense. This is done to control for the type of offense most commonly perceived as irrational and therefore requiring psychiatric investigation. Although all research only examines the last stages of the justice process, all available evidence implies that violent offenders are overrepresented in the insanity population.

Controls for the number of previous adult arrests for violence and the number of felony convictions as an adult are also included. These measures are added to indicate how entrenched defendants are in the criminal justice system. Legal agents may view chronic offenders as problematic and therefore seek out evaluations as a last-ditch effort to find any effective treatment; if this is the case, the effect of these factors will be to increase the odds of an evaluation. Alternatively, these factors, which are routinely used by legal agents, might be taken as evidence that criminal behavior is "normal" for this particular defendant; if this is true, these legally relevant factors will decrease the odds of an evaluation.

Mental Health, Socioeconomic Status, and Family. Because the most likely predictor of psychiatric evaluations is the presence of a real or perceived mental illness, measures of mental health history are included by including a dichotomous indicator of whether the defendant has ever received a major mental illness diagnosis. A major mental illness diagnosis refers to any diagnosis of schizophrenia/psychosis, major depression, or bipolar disorder. The dichotomous indicator of mental illness is limited to these three disorders because they tend to be most closely associated with bizarre behavior and also tend to be most closely associated with the successful use of the insanity defense (Callahan et al. 1991; Slovenko 1995).[1]

A dichotomous indicator is also added of whether the arresting police officer(s) indicated in the arrest report that the defendant acted in a "bizarre" manner. This indicator is important because with psychiatric evaluations the decision-makers are seeking to determine mental status at the time of the offense. Since the public defenders, county attorneys, and judges were not present at the time of the offense, this indicator is perhaps the best measure of the defendant's behavior while committing and immediately following the offense. It is asserted that this indicator is relatively objective because police officers report on the defendant's behavior at the time of the arrest for all defendants and make special note of any statements the defendant makes (e.g., mumbling, ranting, or conversations with God). Despite the contention that it is an objective indicator, this "bizarre" behavior variable is also subject to cultural stereotypes. For example, police officers may label the behavior of whites or women as "bizarre," but deem the same behavior to be "normal" for African Americans.

This research is also interested in testing whether the criminal justice system is more sympathetic to mothers with children and if those subject to the informal social controls of marriage may be less subject to legal controls (Black 1976; Horwitz 1990; Sampson and Laub 1993; Daly 1994). Thus, two other dichotomous indicators are also added: whether the defendant is primarily responsible for any children and whether the defendant is married or cohabiting with a significant other.

Finally, because mental illness is consistently found to be inversely associated with socioeconomic status, controls are included for the defendant's salary, unearned income—including SSI income, AFDC, and food stamps—and educational attainment. Controls are also included for the type of defense attorney: private or a public defender. This is done for two reasons: first, to provide an additional indicator of socioeconomic status; second, to control for any differences in the type and quality of representation provided by private defense attorneys.

Descriptive Statistics

Descriptive statistics are presented in Table 5.1. Due to the case-control sampling design, 44 percent of all defendants sampled received a psychiatric evaluation to determine mental status at the time of the offense. Less than 19 percent of the sample is female and over 51 percent is African American. At the time of the offense, the mean age for these offenders was more than 31 years and over one-third of the offenders in this sample are charged with a violent offense. The mean number of previous arrests for violence (.79) and the mean number of prior felony convictions (.90) are both less than one.[2]

Many of the defendants in this sample do not have family ties; only 20 percent were living with a significant other at the time of the offense and 17 percent were the primary caregiver for a child or children. Over 25 percent of all defendants in the sample received a diagnosis of a major mental illness prior to their arrest and almost 32 percent had been hospitalized for a mental illness. Arresting police officers reported bizarre behavior—unrelated to chemical abuse—from the defendant in less than 8 percent of all cases. The majority of defendants in this sample were represented by a public defender, with only 12 percent receiving private legal representation.[3] The mean monthly unearned income for defendants in this sample ($534) is higher than the mean earned income ($205) and the average level of education is slightly less than high school completion (11.97 years).

Bivariate Relationships

Table 5.2 presents the results of independent sample *t*-tests to determine characteristics that significantly differentiate between those who do and do not receive a psychiatric evaluation. This table demonstrates that female defendants are *less* likely to receive a psychiatric evaluation to determine mental state at the time of the offense, which is contrary to expectations based on a feminist perspective. African American defendants are significantly less likely than non-African Americans to be in the population of offenders who receive a psychiatric evaluation, consistent with stereotypes of African American criminals as "normal." Offenders who receive a psychiatric evaluation to determine mental status at the time of the offense are significantly older than those who do not receive an evaluation.

Consistent with previous research, violent offenders are significantly more likely to receive psychiatric evaluations than all other offense types (61 percent versus 21 percent). Defendants with a more significant criminal history are also more likely to be perceived as needing psychiatric evaluation: defendants with greater numbers of prior arrests for violence and felony convictions are more likely to be evaluated. Family status is important in differentiating between those with and without an evaluation; those who received an evaluation are less likely to cohabit with a significant other (15 percent versus 26 percent), and are less likely to be the primary caregiver for children (8 percent versus 26 percent).

As expected, mental health status is important in differentiating between those with and without an evaluation. Those with a past diagnosis of a major mental illness are significantly more likely to be referred for an evaluation, as are those who have a history of mental hospitalizations. If the arresting police officers report that the offender was acting in a bizarre manner at the time of the arrest, the defendant is significantly more likely to receive a mental health evaluation (14 percent versus 0.6 percent). This number of defendants who behaved in a bizarre manner yet failed to be referred for evaluation is very small; nevertheless, this variable is very important because it is the only "objective" indicator of bizarre behavior at the time of the offense that is available to decision-makers.[4] Again, because the dependent variable in this analysis is an evaluation to determine mental status *at the time of the offense*, this variable is perhaps the most valid indicator of which defendants truly should receive this evaluation.

Defendants' socioeconomic status at the time of the offense also significantly distinguishes between those who did and did not receive an evaluation. Those who receive an evaluation are more likely to have private representation than those who are not evaluated. On average, those evaluated psychiatrically have lower earnings ($392 versus $670) but greater levels of unearned income ($289 versus $127), although there is a large amount of variation around these means. Finally, there is no significant difference in education between those who are and are not evaluated.

Predicting Psychiatric Evaluations

Since the results of the case-control technique are appropriate for finding the ratio of incidence rates in the cases as compared to the controls, this project uses logistic regression models to analyze these data (see Lacy 1997).[5] The results of these logistic regression models are presented in Table 5.3, where the dependent variable is the dichotomous indicator of mental health evaluation, with defendants receiving an evaluation coded 1 and those without an evaluation coded 0. Thus, the coefficients in Table 5.3 represent effects on the log of the odds of receiving a psychiatric evaluation to determine mental status at the time of the offense.[6]

Models 1 and 2 of Table 5.3 again demonstrate the bivariate relationships between evaluations and gender and race, respectively. Model 1 shows the negative effect of being female on receipt of a psychiatric evaluation while Model 2 demonstrates that African Americans are significantly less likely to be evaluated. These two models, however, do not control for other factors that are also clearly important in determining which defendants will be psychiatrically evaluated.

While the gender coefficient is negative in Model 1, it becomes positive (but non-significant) in Model 3, which includes controls for current offense and criminal history and mental health status. Also in this model, African Americans are significantly less likely than non-African Americans[7] to receive a psychiatric evaluation. Again citing Model 3, violent offenders are significantly more likely to be evaluated. To interpret these effects, the coefficients are exponentiated, so that the violent offense effect in Model 3 indicates that, net of other factors, the odds of an evaluation among those charged with a violent offense are 4.8 times the odds for those not charged with violence ($e^{1.56} = 4.76$). Those with more prior adult arrests for violence are also significantly more likely to be psychiatrically evaluated. A history of major mental health diagnosis and mental hospitalizations also significantly increase the likelihood of a psychiatric evaluation, as do reports of bizarre behavior (from police) at the time of the offense.

Model 4 adds family status variables. In this model, being married or cohabiting and being the primary caregiver for children significantly decreases the likelihood of a psychiatric evaluation. Of particular

interest in this model is the now significantly positive effect of gender
on receipt of psychiatric evaluations (compared to Model 1 where this
effect is significantly negative). This sign reversal signals a possible
suppression effect (Jeffords and Dull 1982; Hagan 1991).[8] The
bivariate results in Model 1 showed that women were significantly less
likely than men to receive an evaluation and Model 3, which controls
for criminal history, shows that gender has little effect. The family
status of defendants, however, appears to suppress the relationship
between gender and psychiatric evaluations. Overall, being married and
caring for children significantly decrease the likelihood of a psychiatric
evaluation and women are significantly more likely to have these
family statuses than men.[9] Family, in this case, appears to work as a
suppressor variable, concealing the relationship between gender and
psychiatric evaluation. This is further demonstrated in Tables 5.4 and
5.5. Table 5.4 demonstrates that women who are *not* caregivers for
children are actually somewhat *more* likely to receive an evaluation
than men without children (64.5 percent vs. 54.1 percent). Women *with*
children are significantly *more* likely to get an evaluation than men
with children (35.1 percent vs. 15.2 percent).[10] Table 5.5 provides some
further support for this suppression explanation. In this table, there is
little difference between non-cohabiting men and women in receipt of a
psychiatric evaluation, but women who do live with a significant other
are more likely to be evaluated than men who live with a significant
other (45.5 percent vs. 32.8 percent).[11] Thus, women with children and
women with partners are more likely to be evaluated.

   Due to the strong and well-documented inverse relationship
between socioeconomic status and mental illness (Faris and Dunham
1939; Hollingshead and Redlich 1953; Mirowsky and Ross 1989a;
Ortega and Corzine 1990; Turner, Wheaton, and Lloyd 1995),
indicators of the defendant's socioeconomic status are added in Model
5 of Table 5.3. Due to concerns about the number of cases missing data
on the SES variables, this model is adjusted using mean imputation.
For each case that has missing values for the income and education
variables, the mean value is substituted and a dichotomous indicator of
the missing value is included. This procedure should provide unbiased
estimates of the SES effects, but may artificially deflate the standard
errors (see Little and Rubin 1987; 1990). Under every specification,
however, the SES variables are close to zero. The only indicator of SES

that is statistically significant is the private attorney dichotomy; defendants who have private representation are significantly more likely to be psychiatrically evaluated than defendants with public defenders or those who represent themselves. In this model, women are still more likely to be evaluated than men. As is true for each of these models, African Americans are significantly less likely to receive an evaluation than non-African Americans.[12]

To determine the odds of an evaluation, the coefficients in Model 5 are exponentiated. From this, it is clear that more "objective" and legally relevant factors—those that probably should be considered when predicting psychiatric evaluations—are clearly very important in determining who receives an evaluation. The odds of an evaluation for those with a prior diagnosis of a major mental illness are 4.9 times ($e^{1.58}$ = 4.85) higher than the odds for those without this mental illness history; those with previous mental hospitalizations have a rate of evaluation 7.7 times higher than those without previous hospitalizations. Perhaps the best available "objective" account of mental status at the time of the offense is police report of bizarre behavior; the rate of evaluations for those considered "bizarre" is over 9 times ($e^{2.23}$ = 9.3) higher than for those not considered "bizarre."

While these "objectivist" factors would be expected to affect receipt of psychiatric evaluations, other non-objective factors also significantly predict evaluations. For example, Model 5 of Table 5.3 indicates that being African American reduces the odds of receiving an evaluation by 44 percent ($e^{-.58}$ = .56 and 1.0 - .56 = .44); this can alternatively be explained by stating that the odds of evaluation for non-African Americans are estimated to be 1.8 times the odds of evaluation for African Americans, all else constant. Also, for each additional year of age, the odds of an evaluation increase by 1.03 times. Thus, a defendant who is 31 years old (the mean age of the sample) is 1.43 times more likely to receive an evaluation than a 19-year-old defendant ($e^{.03*12}$ = 1.43). Finally, being the primary caregiver for children decreases the likelihood of an evaluation by 68 percent, or alternatively, not being responsible for children increases the likelihood of an evaluation by approximately 3 times over those with children.[13]

In conclusion, the results of this section point to a mixed relationship between gender and attributions of mental illness. Gender appears to be related to psychiatric evaluations, but indirectly through family status and perhaps via previous attributions of mental illness. Race, however, is clearly related to attributions of mental illness by criminal justice decision-makers. African Americans are much less likely to be sent for a psychiatric evaluation than non-African Americans, perhaps reflecting decision-makers' expectations that crime is "normal" behavior for African Americans.

Interaction Effects

The results presented in the previous section demonstrate how race and gender might affect attributions of mental illness. Because several hypotheses cannot be tested without analyzing the *interaction* of factors, this research also modeled interaction effects. This section focuses on the relationships between gender, race, and psychiatric evaluation, and determines whether offense, family, and mental health variables mediate these relationships. The first issue to be explored is whether the race effect interacts with gender. The results of the logistic regression models demonstrate that while the gender effects are mixed, the race effects are consistently negative, indicating that African Americans are significantly less likely to be psychiatrically evaluated than non-African Americans. However, because images of stereotypical criminals tend to focus on African American *males* rather than all African Americans (Smith 1991; Sniderman and Piazza 1993; Quillian and Pager 2001), the relationship between race, gender, and evaluations is examined in Table 5.6. As this table demonstrates, race effects are strong for both men and women. Non-African American women are significantly more likely to receive evaluations than African American women (46.5 percent vs. 30.0 percent) and non-African American men are significantly more likely to receive evaluations than African American men (53.3 percent vs. 38.8 percent).

Using logistic regression, this interaction of gender and race is tested, along with eight other interaction effects, and present the results in Table 5.7.[14] In Model 1, the direct effects of race and gender remain the same, with African Americans significantly less likely than non-African Americans to receive an evaluation, women more likely than men to receive an evaluation, and no significant interaction between gender and race. Thus, it appears that black women are at the same disadvantage as black men in the likelihood of receiving an evaluation.

Because some have argued that women who engaged in "deviant deviance" (i.e., role-incongruent acts) are most likely to be treated psychiatrically (Rosenfield 1982), an interaction effect is also modeled to gauge the impact of violent female offenders on receipt of psychiatric evaluations. This interaction is presented in Model 2, where it is clear that violent offenses significantly increase the likelihood of a psychiatric evaluation for all defendants, and that this dichotomous variable does interact significantly with gender. This indicates that women who act in a role-incongruent manner—or violently—are more likely than other women and men to be evaluated to determine mental status.[15]

Kathleen Daly (1994) and others argue that family status in interaction with gender is more important than gender alone. Daly suggests that women with children are treated more leniently than women without children. Being married is also a fulfillment of a traditional gender role for women. Thus, Models 3 through 6 of Table 5.7 consider the interaction of gender and family statuses. Models 3 and 4 examine the victim-offender relationship to see whether women who commit crimes against their children and/or significant others might be considered more in need of psychiatric treatment than other offenders. These models demonstrate no significant effect of the relationship between the victim and the offender.

The relationship depicted in Model 4 is modeled more explicitly in Table 5.8. Results of this Crosstabulation indicate that women who committed an offense against their child or against their significant other do appear to be slightly more likely to be treated psychiatrically than other women. Over 63 percent of these women with children or significant others as victims received psychiatric evaluations compared to 47 percent of women without a child or significant other as a victim. This difference, however, is not statistically significant. One possibility is that if there were a greater number of women in the sample, particularly with violent offenses against their children and/or spouses, a more pronounced gender effect might appear.

Models 5 and 6 of Table 5.7 test whether women in a relationship with a significant other or women who are the primary caregivers for children might be considered in need of more or less psychiatric treatment than other offenders. Again, there are no statistically significant interaction effects. Next, this project tests whether mental illness is perceived differently in the criminal justice system based on the gender of the defendant. Models 7 through 9 of Table 5.7 test three interactions of mental health status with gender; again, there are no statistically significant interaction effects.

Finally, this research also considers interactions of race, family, and offense type. It explores whether family factors and violent offenses are of particular importance for African American defendants. The results (not shown) demonstrate that the interaction of African American race and marriage, and the interaction of African American race and children, do not significantly affect the likelihood of receiving a psychiatric evaluation. Also, the interaction of African American race and violent offense is not statistically significant in predicting which defendants will receive a psychiatric evaluation.

In sum, few of the hypothesized interactions are statistically significant. Race, family status, and mental health are significant predictors of psychiatric evaluation for both women *and* men. This research does indicate that violent women are significantly more likely to be psychiatrically evaluated than men and women charged with other offenses. Thus, it does appear that legal agents view violent women as abnormal criminals and therefore in need of psychiatric treatment. This finding must be interpreted with caution, however, because this result is sensitive to the particular specification. Consequently, there is some evidence of gendered typifications based on offense type, but further investigation with a larger sample of violent women would bolster this conclusion.

Charged Offense

The analysis to this point has used a dichotomous indicator of whether the current offense was violent. Because this variable encompasses a wide range of activity—from assault to first-degree murder—an investigation of the type of current offense was examined in greater detail. Models 3 through 5 of Table 5.3 were re-run, but rather than controlling only for a violent offense dummy, these models followed Spohn and Spears (1997) and controlled for five separate categories of most serious offense: first degree murder; second-degree murder/manslaughter; robbery; assault; and other felonies.[16] The results of this analysis (not shown) are quite similar to the results presented in Table 5.3, with African Americans significantly less likely to be evaluated under every specification, and women more likely to be evaluated in the models that include controls for family status. Again, all three mental health conditions significantly increase the likelihood of an evaluation while both family indicators significantly decrease the likelihood of receiving a psychiatric evaluation.

Relative to murder/manslaughter, robbery, assault, and other felonies significantly decrease the likelihood of a psychiatric evaluation; first-degree murder is not significantly different from murder/manslaughter in these models. These results are consistent with previous research and indicate that defendants charged with murder (any degree) are most likely to be psychiatrically evaluated. The non-offense coefficients—including demographic characteristics, mental health, and family status—are quite robust both in models with the dichotomous violent offense variable and in models with five offense categories. Due to the similarity of coefficients between these two models, this book only reports the more parsimonious model with the violent offense dichotomy.

Decomposition

Researchers assessing racial and/or gender discrimination often argue that using a simple regression equation with a dummy variable for race or gender can over- or underestimate the extent of discrimination (Myers 1985:214-215). Decomposing the differences between these groups is offered as an alternative method for determining race and gender disparity (see Jones and Kelley 1984; Myers 1985; Cancio et al. 1996; Kay and Hagan 1998). Consequently, the models previously presented were re-run after selecting on race and gender categories. Table 5.9 presents mean values for four separate categories: men, women, African Americans, and non-African Americans. This table again demonstrates that non-African Americans are significantly more likely to be psychiatrically evaluated than African Americans. The women in this sample are significantly more likely to be African

American than the men in the sample. Not surprisingly, men are more likely than women to be charged with a violent offense, have a history of violence arrests, and have a longer record of felony convictions. African Americans in the sample are more likely than non-African Americans to have prior arrests for violence and African Americans have more felony convictions on average.

There were few gender differences in mental health status, but significant racial differences in mental health. African Americans had, on average, lower levels of mental disorder according to the measures of illness. Women were more likely than men in the sample to have children, while African Americans were significantly more likely than non-African Americans to report children. Finally, there were significant racial and gender differences in socioeconomic status. Non-African Americans were significantly more likely than African Americans to have a private attorney. Women reported less earned income, more unearned income, and less education than men. African Americans reported less earned income and less education than non-African Americans.

To follow up on these descriptive statistics, a series of logistic regression models were run, sampling on six separate race and gender categories. These results are presented in Table 5.10. This table presents the full model only, although the trimmed models were analyzed as well. These trimmed models were essentially the same as the full model for each race/gender category, so in the interest of parsimony and ease of comparison across one single table, only the full models are presented. The first two columns of this table represent models selecting on African Americans and non-African Americans. Female gender is positive but non-significant in both of these models, but age is only statistically significant for non-African Americans. Both groups have significant positive coefficients for violent offense, but only African Americans have a greater likelihood of a psychiatric evaluation with each additional adult arrest for violence. Mental health indicators are significant and positive for both groups, although "bizarre" behavior at the time of the offense is only marginally significant for African Americans. While marriage and caregiving are negative for both groups, the primary caregiver dichotomy is only statistically significant for African Americans while the cohabitation dichotomy is marginally significant only for non-African Americans.

These results indicate that the mental health status of the defendant is the most significant predictor of psychiatric evaluation for both racial categories. Nevertheless, there are racial differences in the remaining significant predictors. Age, for example, is only statistically significant for non-African Americans, which could indicate that older non-African American (mostly white) defendants are portrayed as abnormal criminals. Older African Americans, however, may be portrayed as "normal" criminals who are not expected to age out of crime.

The next two columns of Table 5.10 compare males and females. Because every female defendant who behaved bizarrely at the time of the arrest (according to arresting police officers) was given a psychiatric evaluation, this variable was a constant for women and was therefore excluded from the model. African American race is significantly negative for both men and women, although it is only marginally significant for male defendants. Being charged with a violent offense significantly increases the likelihood of an evaluation for both men and women, but the magnitude is much greater for women than for men. The same is true for a history of mental hospitalizations, with coefficients significantly positive for both men and women, but much larger for women. A history of major mental illness is not statistically significant for these women, however, which together with the exclusion of the bizarre behavior indicator might help explain the size of the hospitalization coefficient. Family decreases the likelihood of receiving an evaluation for both men and women, with the exception of the cohabitation indicator for women. Having a private attorney significantly increases the likelihood of an evaluation for men, but not for women. Earned monthly income is statistically significant for women only, indicating that for women, each one hundred dollars earned reduces the odds of a psychiatric evaluation by approximately 26 percent ($e^{-.003*100} = .74$ and $1.0 - .74 = .26$). Whereas earned income is significant only for women, unearned income is statistically significant only for men: each additional one hundred dollars of unearned income increases the odds of an evaluation by approximately 1.1 times.

These results again indicate that mental health status is the most important factor determining which defendants receive psychiatric evaluations. Nevertheless, there are important differences between men and women in the significant predictors. The effect of having a private attorney significantly increases the odds of an evaluation for men, but not for women. One possibility is that there is simply an insufficient number of women with private attorneys in the sample to demonstrate a statistically significant effect. Another interpretation of this gender difference is that private attorneys, who are typically portrayed as having the time and resources to investigate all options, are less subject to gendered typifications. Rather than reserving psychiatric evaluations only for the defendants who are considered abnormal due to gendered typifications, private attorneys may be able to seek out all possible options for the defendant. Thus, while public defenders might rely on typifications to sort defendants into mentally ill or non-mentally ill categories, private attorneys may routinely send many of their clients (including men who are typified as "normal" offenders) to be evaluated. These models also display other gender differences in the effect of SES variables. For women, earned income decreases the odds of an evaluation, while for men, unearned income increases the odds of an evaluation. These gender differences in the effect of income might represent gendered expectations of the appropriate method of receiving money. Norms of masculinity include an expectation that men are breadwinners for their family; for women, this is less of a stereotyped expectation. Consequently, when women are able to earn money, this might be taken as a sign they are functioning normally. When men receive unearned income such as TANF or unemployment, however, this could be perceived as a violation of their breadwinner role because they are not *earning* this money.

The final two columns of Table 5.10 compare African American males with non-African American males.[17] Age is a statistically significant factor for both groups, but in opposite directions; for African American males, older defendants are less likely to be evaluated whereas older non-African Americans are more likely to be evaluated. Prior adult arrests for violence are positive and significant for African American males, but not for non-African American males. Mental health indicators again significantly increase the likelihood of an evaluation for both groups of men. The primary caregiver indicator is the only statistically significant family indicator for these men; African American men taking care of children are significantly less likely to be evaluated than those not taking care of children. Finally, unearned income significantly increases the odds of an evaluation for African American men, but not for non-African American men.

Once again, this comparison of African American and non-African American men indicates that mental health status is the most important factor determining which defendants receive psychiatric evaluations. Nevertheless, there are important differences between these men. Age, for example, appears to be interpreted very differently depending on the race of the man. It is possible that older non-African American men are considered to be abnormal defendants who require psychiatric investigation; older African American men, however, do not seem to be perceived as atypical defendants.

An interpretation of the significantly negative effect of age on psychiatric evaluations for African American men is less straightforward, however. It seems unlikely that younger African American men are perceived as "abnormal" offenders who need psychiatric treatment. Instead, outliers on the age variable might be affecting this age coefficient. Further research finds that there are five African American men who were older than 54 years old at the time of their offense who were not psychiatrically evaluated; no African American men over 54 years old were psychiatrically evaluated. One possibility is that these older men who did not receive an evaluation are causing the age coefficient to be significantly negative. This was tested this by running the "African American Males" model after rejecting these outliers. In this model, age is no longer statistically significant and the coefficient is close to zero. Thus, rather than indicating that young African American males are more likely to be evaluated than older African American males, the significantly negative age effect is perhaps the result of older African Americans not receiving an evaluation (especially since the first two columns of Table 5.10 indicate that age is significant only for non-African Americans).

In general, the coefficients for the full model in Table 5.3 are in the same direction as all decomposed categories in Table 5.10. While some of these coefficients are not statistically significant in the decomposed models, it does not appear that a single group, such as African American men, drives all results. While there are some interesting differences in which variables are statistically significant from model to model (e.g. African Americans vs. non-African Americans), in general there are no major differences that might cast doubt on the main findings of this chapter.

"High Mental Illness" Defendants

As one final test of these data and as a check on the validity of the conclusions, a crosstabulation was run to compare high and low mental illness groups. First, a new variable was created, "High Mental Illness." Every defendant with a history of major mental illness diagnosis *and* a history of mental hospitalization was coded 1 and all other defendants coded 0.[18] This variable, therefore, is a more objective indicator of the defendants who *should* be evaluated to determine current psychiatric status. A crosstabulation of high mental illness with race and receipt of psychiatric evaluation was run and the results indicated that, as expected, over 94 percent of those in the "high mental illness" category received an evaluation (see Table 5.11). This is the same for both African American and non-African American defendants. The significant finding, however, is that among the "low mental illness" group, non-African Americans are significantly more likely than African Americans to be psychiatrically evaluated (45.5 percent versus 30.8 percent). This seems to indicate that when there are clearly "objective" factors to consider—including previous psychiatric diagnoses and hospitalizations—then decision-makers rely on this information to determine which defendants should be evaluated. But when there is an absence of objective factors to consider, decision-makers may fall back on typifications or assumptions about the typical offender. Most notably, practitioners send non-African American offenders out for explanations for seemingly "abnormal" criminal behavior and seek no further intervention for African American defendants.

SUMMARY OF CHAPTER FIVE

This project began with two competing hypotheses:

> ***Hypothesis 1A:*** *Psychiatric status will be the only significant determinant of psychiatric evaluations in the criminal justice system (objectivist account).*

> **Hypothesis 1B**: *Social factors, in addition to psychiatric status will predict which defendants receive psychiatric evaluations (social construction).*

The analyses presented in this chapter indicate that psychiatric history is clearly very important in determining which felony defendants will receive psychiatric evaluations to determine mental status at the time of the offense. It does not appear, however, that psychiatric status is the only factor criminal justice decision-makers take into account when seeking explanations for criminal behavior. Instead, demographic, family, and criminal factors are similarly important in predicting which defendants will be the recipients of psychiatric evaluations.

> **Hypothesis 2**: *Female felony defendants will be more likely than male felony defendants to receive a psychiatric evaluation (social construction).*

This research provides some mixed evidence that women in the criminal justice system are viewed psychiatrically while men are not. On average, *men* are more likely to be treated as mentally ill. But once the effects of family roles are statistically controlled, *women* are more likely to be viewed as mad rather than bad. Being female in itself does not appear to increase the likelihood of a psychiatric evaluation. Instead, ties to family are strong indicators apparently used by decision-makers to indicate a stable living and social situation and, for women, fulfillment of gender-stereotyped roles. These results also provide strong support for social control theory; as predicted by Black's theory, family ties (informal social controls) are significantly and inversely related to other social controls, including psychiatric control.

Untangling the causal relationships between gender, family roles, and attributions of mental illness is complicated, since they are likely to be endogenously related. For example, gender affects selection into family roles and family roles may be disrupted by prior mental illness. Gender is clearly related to mental illness attributions, but it is unclear how these factors are linked. While it is possible that factors such as unmeasured variation in mental health status explain this link between gender and mental illness attributions, it is also possible that women in the justice system are typified as mad rather than bad. Using a wide range of controls, this research finds that gender does not independently affect the likelihood of a psychiatric evaluation. The best available evidence seems to point to a contextual use of gender on the part of legal agents. These legal agents probably do not assume that all female offenders or even all violent offenders are mentally ill; instead these decision-makers take cues from the defendant's family status. Overall these decisions support Black's theory of law with its predicted inverse relationship between competing systems of social control. Offenders subject to family (informal) control are less subject to legal control. Female offenders, however, do not appear adequately controlled by these informal controls, because women cohabiting and taking care of children are significantly more likely than similar men to be subject to psychiatric controls.

> **Hypothesis 6:** *Female defendants charged with a violent offense (role-incongruent act) will be more likely to receive a psychiatric evaluation than men who engage in violence (role-congruent).*

Baskin et al. (1989) note that the likelihood of mental health placement in prison is significantly increased if female inmates engaged in prison violence and/or aggressive behavior (role-incongruent acts). In contrast, male inmates who participated in similar acts (but ones that were role-congruent) were placed in disciplinary confinement (Baskin et al. 1989). If constructionist arguments about typification are indeed correct, we would expect that women who violate gendered behavior norms most severely would be most likely to get evaluations. Indeed, there is some evidence that this is the case: violent females appear to be more likely to be treated psychiatrically than non-violent offenders, indicating that the mad/bad distinction may be most salient for violent female offenders. A larger sample, with a greater number of cases, would have greater statistical power to detect the interactions suggested by this analysis.

> **Hypothesis 3:** *African Americans will be less likely than non-African Americans to receive a psychiatric evaluation (social construction).*

While the evidence for gender is mixed, the strong race differences provide more clear support for the social constructionist perspective. There is strong evidence that African Americans are less likely than non-African Americans to receive a psychiatric evaluation to determine mental status at the time of the offense. This would appear to support the contention that stereotypes of "normal" or typical offenders affect criminal justice decision-making. If criminal justice decision-makers expect African Americans to be criminals, these decision-makers will not seek alternative (including psychiatric) explanations that might mitigate responsibility.

> **Hypothesis 5:** *Black men will be less likely to be psychiatrically evaluated than white men and black women will be less likely to be psychiatrically evaluated than white women (intersectionality).*

This project examines the interaction of race and gender because many of the stereotypes of "normal" criminals refer primarily to African American men, although African American women also tend to be viewed as more criminal than white women (Quillian and Pager 2001; Hudson 2002). Findings indicate that both African American men and African American women are less likely than white defendants to be psychiatrically evaluated. The interaction of race and gender is not statistically significant in predicting evaluations. Thus, hypothesis five is supported, although there appears to be little difference between African American men and women in the receipt of psychiatric evaluations.

> **Hypothesis 7:** *Violent offenders will be more likely to receive a psychiatric evaluation than non-violent offenders.*

In models using a dichotomous violent offense indicator, violent offenders are consistently more likely to be psychiatrically evaluated than non-violent offenders. In models that specify more nuanced current charge indicators, it was clear that the most serious violent offenses, particularly murder and manslaughter, were the offenses most likely to result in a psychiatric evaluation. Regardless of the type of measure used, it appears that criminal justice decision-makers tend to reserve this evaluation for offenders facing the most significant prison sentence. Nevertheless, there are a significant number of non-violent offenders who were evaluated. Almost 29 percent of the evaluated offenders had a property offense as the most serious charge; an additional 4 percent were charged with a drug offense, and almost 10 percent of those evaluated were charged with an "other" felony, such as absconding or illegally possessing a weapon.

> **Hypothesis 4**: *Older defendants will be more likely to receive a psychiatric evaluation.*

It was expected that stereotypically "normal" offenders would be *less* likely than other defendants to be referred for a psychiatric evaluation to determine criminal responsibility. Since the typical criminal defendant is young, it was expected that age would be positively associated with evaluations.[19] Indeed, it does appear that young offenders are not viewed as abnormal criminal defendants. In this analysis, older defendants are consistently more likely to be viewed psychiatrically than younger defendants.

This project presented two sets of competing hypotheses regarding gender and family:

> **Hypothesis 8A**: *Women who fulfill their expected familial role by providing care for their children will be less likely to receive a psychiatric evaluation than women who are not parents.*

> **Hypothesis 8B**: *Women who fulfill their expected familial role by providing care for their children will be more likely to receive a psychiatric evaluation than women who are not parents.*

> **Hypothesis 9A**: *Women who fulfill their expected familial role by being married will be less likely to receive a psychiatric evaluation than women who are not married.*

> **Hypothesis 9B**: *Women who fulfill their expected familial role by being married will be more likely to receive a psychiatric evaluation than women who are not married.*

Differences in gender role expectations are very important for determining what types of behavior are considered deviant and how the criminal justice system responds. Family roles, including marital status and primary caretaker roles, are important in influencing criminal case outcomes (see Daly 1987; Steffensmeier, Kramer, and Streifel 1993; Daly 1994), and might also alter psychiatric decision-making in the criminal justice system. As was discussed in detail in Chapter Three, it is unclear whether insanity is perceived as a beneficial outcome for criminal defendants. Hypotheses 8B and 9B—that women fulfilling gender expectations by taking care of children and living with a spouse are *more* likely to receive an evaluation—point to insanity outcomes as positive or beneficial to the defendant. Thus, when women behave as expected, legal agents may seek more lenient case outcomes to protect these women and their families. Since decision-makers will not want to punish defendants' children, they may seek to funnel women with children or married women into a psychiatric route, one that is viewed as more beneficial (Blau and McGinley 1995).

Conversely, there may be an inverse relationship between systems of social control, with decision-makers resorting to increased intervention (psychiatric treatment) only in cases where there is no familial control as is hypothesized in 8A and 9A (see Horwitz 2002b). Overall, for the entire sample of defendants, the results presented in this chapter support this competing social controls perspective; higher levels of familial control result in lesser levels of psychiatric control. Defendants living with a significant other and defendants caring for children are significantly less likely to be psychiatrically evaluated. For women, however, the relationship is slightly different. Women with children and/or cohabiting women are more likely than men with children and/or cohabiting men to be evaluated. Thus, it does appear that for women, fulfilling this stereotyped role of a married mother might lead to a greater chance of being evaluated. Legal agents might expect such evaluations to be beneficial for these women and their families by imposing a psychiatric rather than legal label.

Hypothesis 10: *Women charged with crimes against their intimates (children and significant others) will be more likely to receive a psychiatric evaluation than other women and men charged with any crime.*

Beyond the traditional gender roles there are also norms that define appropriate *deviant* behaviors for men and women. Mothers who *violate* their expected care-taking role by engaging in violence against their loved ones may be viewed as *so* abnormal that a psychiatric explanation is expected. It may seem incomprehensible to decision-makers that any wife or mother would deliberately harm her own child or spouse (see Kirwin 1997). The results presented in this chapter do not provide any support for this hypothesis. Not only is the interaction between gender and child/significant other victim not statistically significant, the bivariate relationship between this child/significant other variable and psychiatric evaluation is non-significant. It may be the case that this and other interaction hypotheses cannot be tested without a significantly greater number of female offenders.

CONCLUSION

This analysis indicates that criminal justice officials may have different theories about the causes of crimes for African Americans as compared to white defendants. By deeming some offenders to be ill, or not culpable, criminal justice officials make decisions based on limited knowledge. Since these decision-makers are not typically trained in psychiatry, they are making judgments based on past experiences and stereotypes, which are socially constructed in the course of their work. These judgments about which defendants to hold criminally responsible for their behavior and which to treat medically are important avenues for research and yield significant information about the social control of female and African American offenders.

NOTES

[1] To determine whether this limitation is reasonable, a separate analysis including all types of mental illness was also conducted (not shown). Results were very similar to those presented below, but the magnitude of the mental illness indicator is smaller. Because of this and the very different social reactions to psychoses as compared to other types of mental illness (Phelen et al. 2000), the use of only schizophrenia/psychosis, major depression, and bipolar disorder are retained as indicators of major mental illness.

[2] The descriptive statistics for this sample are equivalent to a national sample of felony defendants in the 75 largest urban counties in 1998 (U.S. Department of Justice 2001a).

[3] Most of the defendants who were not privately represented had a public defense attorney. Only 1.2 percent of defendants without a private attorney represented themselves pro se; the remaining 98.8 percent had a public defender.

[4] Again, while this project contends that this indicator is relatively objective, this "bizarre" behavior variable is also subject to cultural expectations; police officers may typify criminal suspects based on gender and race.

[5] With appropriate sampling, odds ratios obtained from logistic regression will yield valid estimates of the rate ratio (relative hazard rate) (Lacy 1997). One caveat, however, is that in logistic regression models, the intercept coefficient will be biased so that probabilities or absolute rates or risks cannot be inferred directly, but exponentiating the coefficients will yield the odds ratios associated with the independent variables, which will give estimates of rate ratios (Lacy 1997).

[6] Several models were run with the year of evaluation in the equation to determine whether non-case factors occurring in the particular year might alter likelihood of an evaluation. For example, a significant lack of jail beds, but openings in psychiatric wards, may affect a decision-maker's calculation. Results indicated no relationship between year of arraignment and likelihood of psychiatric evaluation.

[7] The reference category is mostly white; approximately 92 percent of the non-African Americans are white.

[8] Due to concerns that the drop in number of cases between Model 1 (N = 929) and Model 4 (N = 697) is responsible for the switch in direction of the gender coefficient, these models were re-run using this sample of 697 cases for which

all data were available. The results are essentially the same as those presented in Table 5.3, indicating that these lost cases were not the cause of the sign switch.

[9] Overall, 26.2 percent of women were living with a significant other while 19.4 percent of men lived with a significant other; 47.9 percent of women but only 11.7 percent of men were the primary caregiver for a child.

[10] Adding a product term for the interaction between gender and children to the full model in Table 5.3 does not result in a statistically significant effect.

[11] Again, this interaction is not statistically significant in Table 5.3.

[12] One limitation of the analysis is the possibility that wealthier defendants can afford to have private psychiatric evaluations and will therefore only appear in the Hennepin County psychiatric evaluation population if they decide to proceed with an insanity defense. By holding "private attorney" constant, this research attempts to control for this possibility, but this dichotomous variable may be insufficient and it may be the case that wealthy defendants receive psychiatric evaluations at a greater rate than is presented in this research. This possibility, however, would bolster the race findings. Since African Americans tend to be found in the lowest economic classes, it seems unlikely that they would be the defendants who receive private evaluations. Instead, non-African Americans (especially white defendants) are the most likely to be evaluated outside of the County system. Therefore, the possibility that some wealthy defendants are being evaluated, but are not included in the sample, only makes the race findings more remarkable. If the sampling strategy included those privately evaluated, it may be that the result would be an even greater difference between African American and non-African American defendants, with African Americans perceived to be "normal" offenders and non-African Americans perceived to be abnormal offenders.

[13] Because having children and living with a significant other are likely to be correlated, a series of models were re-run with only one of the two family status indicators. Results indicated essentially the same findings, with family status significantly reducing the odds of an evaluation, and all other indicators in the same direction and the same level of significance. The only exception is that the gender indicator in Models 4 and 5 of Table 5.3 is statistically significant only in the models that include the primary caregiver variable. Gender is positive but non-significant in Models 4 and 5 of Table 5.3 when marital status is the only family variable included in the model. Thus, this caregiver dichotomy appears to be the primary suppressor variable, as is also suggested by Tables 5.4 and 5.5.

[14] The logistic regression models presented in Table 5.7 include each of the statistically significant predictors from Table 5.3. Table 5.7 only presents the interaction effect and the relevant direct effects. The other predictors, which are not shown, remain statistically significant and in the same direction as shown Table 5.3.

[15] This significant interaction of violent offense and gender is not a consistent finding, however. This result is highly sensitive to the other indicators included in the equation; the product term is only statistically significant in the full model (Model 5 from Table 5.3). When this interaction is included in Models 1 through 4, it is not statistically significant (although it remains positive).

[16] Approximately 2.4 percent of the sample had first degree murder as the most serious offense, 3.4 percent murder/manslaughter, 6.9 percent robbery, 18.4 percent assault, and 68.9 percent other felony.

[17] A similar comparison of African American and non-African American females was not possible due to the small number of cases remaining once selection was made on these two categories.

[18] The indicator for "bizarre" behavior at the time of the offense is not included in this created "high mental illness" dichotomy due to the small number of cases with this status. Had this variable been used, there would have been only 28 people with "high mental illness" (only 28 individuals have "yes" for all three mental health indicators). Instead, by using prior mental hospitalization and major mental illness diagnosis, 173 individuals are classified as having this status.

[19] Again, this sample is *adult* felony defendants only, so the youngest offenders are age 18 or older, with the exception of a few 16 and 17 year-olds who were waived to adult criminal court.

Table 5.1. Descriptive Statistics (N=929)

Variable	Description	Mean/ Percent
Received a psychiatric evaluation	0=No evaluation; 1=evaluation	44.3%
Demographic Variables		
Female	0=Male; 1=female	18.5%
African American	0=non-African American; 1=African American	51.1%
Age at offense	Age in years	31.39 (10.57)
Current Offense & Criminal History		
Most serious current offense		
Violence	0=non-violent offense; 1=violent offense	36.3%
Property	0=non-property offense; 1=property offense	36.3%
Drugs	0=non-drug offense; 1=drug offense	16.0%
Other offense	0=non-other offense; 1=other offense	11.4%
# Prior adult arrests for violence	Number of prior arrests	.79 (1.57)
# Prior adult felony convictions	Number of prior felony convictions	.90 (1.90)
Family Status		
Married/cohabiting	Was defendant living with a significant other at the time of the offense? 0=no; 1=yes	20.4%
Defendant primary caregiver for child/ren?	0=not responsible for kids; 1=responsible for kids	17.2%
Mental Health		
Prior major mental illness diagnosis	0=no previous diagnosis; 1=diagnosis prior to arrest	25.3%
Prior mental hospitalizations	0=no prior hospitalization; 1=prior hospitalization	31.9%
Police report bizarre behavior at arrest	0=no report of bizarre behavior; 1=reported bizarre behavior	7.4%
Socioeconomic Status		
Private attorney	0=public defender or pro se; 1=private attorney	12.1%
Monthly earned income	Mean monthly salary in dollars	$534.04 (993.41)
Monthly unearned income	Monthly unearned income (SSI, AFDC, etc.) in dollars	$204.54 (389.66)
Education	Years of education	11.97 (1.72)

Note: Standard deviations for continuous variables in parentheses.

118

Table 5.2. Comparison of Means for Defendants Receiving and Not Receiving a Psychiatric Evaluation, 1993-2001 (N=929)

Variable	No Evaluation	Evaluation
Demographic Variables		
Female*	21.0%	15.0%
African American**	58.0%	42.5%
Age at offense**	29.2	34.1
	(9.9)	(10.7)
Current Offense & Criminal History		
Violent offense**	20.7%	60.9%
# prior adult arrests for violence**	.54	1.11
	(1.10)	(1.97)
# prior adult felony convictions**	.74	1.09
	(1.76)	(2.05)
Family Status		
Married/cohabiting**	26.3%	14.5%
Primary caregiver for child/ren**	26.1%	8.1%
Mental Health		
Prior major mental illness diagnosis**	4.3%	46.0%
Prior mental hospitalization**	5.2%	58.7%
Police report bizarre behavior**	0.6%	14.0%
Socioeconomic Status		
Private Attorney*	9.9%	14.6%
Monthly earned income**	$670.15	$391.58
	(995.47)	(972.29)
Monthly unearned income**	$127.13	$289.32
	(318.34)	(440.21)
Education	11.93	12.01
	(1.60)	(1.81)

Note: Standard deviations in parentheses for continuous variables.
* $p < .05$ ** $p < .01$

Table 5.3. Logistic Regression Models Predicting Psychiatric Evaluation

Variable	Model 1	Model 2
Demographic Variables		
Female	-.39*	
	(.17)	
African American		-.62**
		(.13)
Constant	-.156	.088
Number of Cases	929	928
-2 Log Likelihood	1270.8*	1252.8**

Note: Standard errors in parentheses. * p < .05 ** p < .01

Table 5.3, continued

Variable	Model 3	Model 4	Model 5
Demographic Variables			
Female	.24	.83*	.78*
	(.29)	(.34)	(.38)
African American	-.64**	-.64**	-.58*
	(.22)	(.22)	(.24)
Age at offense	.02*	.03**	.03*
	(.01)	(.01)	(.01)
Current Offense & Criminal History			
Violent current offense	1.56**	1.51**	1.36**
	(.22)	(.22)	(.24)
# Prior adult arrests for violence	.17*	.17*	.16*
	(.07)	(.07)	(.07)
# Prior adult felony convictions	-.05	-.05	-.03
	(.06)	(.06)	(.06)
Mental Health			
Prior diagnosis of major mental illness	1.60**	1.58**	1.58**
	(.35)	(.36)	(.38)
Prior mental hospitalization	2.24**	2.13**	2.04**
	(.31)	(.32)	(.34)
Police report bizarre behavior	2.60**	2.44**	2.23**
	(.78)	(.78)	(.78)
Family Status			
Married/cohabiting		-.69*	-.65*
		(.29)	(.30)
Primary caregiver for children		-1.13**	-1.14**
		(.35)	(.39)
Socioeconomic Status			
Private attorney			.84*
			(.37)
Earned monthly income			.00
			(.00)
Unearned monthly income			.00
			(.00)
Education			.07
			(.11)
Missing Values for Mean Imputation			
Missing monthly income			-.01
			(1.52)
Missing monthly unearned income			1.79
			(1.18)
Missing education			-1.65
			(1.01)
Constant	-2.15	-2.02	-2.12
Number of Cases	713	697	676
-2 Log Likelihood	588.8**	561.2**	516.2**

Note: Standard errors in parentheses.   * p < .05 ** p < .01

Table 5.4. Receipt of Evaluation by Sex and Caregiver Status

		Male	Female	*Total*
Not a Primary Caregiver	**No Evaluation**	45.9% (273)	35.5% (22)	44.9% (295)
	Evaluation	54.1% (322)	64.5% (40)	55.1% (362)
	Total	100.0% (595)	100.0% (62)	100.0% (657)
Primary Caregiver	**No Evaluation**	84.8% (67)	64.9% (37)	76.5% (104)
	Evaluation	15.2% (12)	35.1% (20)	23.5% (32)
	Total	100.0% (79)	100.0% (57)	100.0% (136)

Note: Cell counts are in parentheses.
Chi-Square (*not* primary caregiver) = 2.454 (1 d.f.); Gamma = .213
Chi-Square (primary caregiver) = 7.286 (1 d.f.)**; Gamma = .502

Table 5.5. Receipt of Evaluation by Sex and Cohabitation Status

		Male	Female	*Total*
Not Cohabiting with Significant Other	**No Evaluation**	46.0% (256)	49.5% (46)	46.5% (302)
	Evaluation	54.0% (301)	50.5% (47)	53.5% (348)
	Total	100.0% (557)	100.0% (93)	100.0% (650)
Cohabiting with Significant Other	**No Evaluation**	67.2% (90)	54.5% (18)	64.7% (108)
	Evaluation	32.8% (44)	45.5% (15)	35.3% (59)
	Total	100.0% (134)	100.0% (33)	100.0% (167)

Note: Cell counts are in parentheses.
Chi-Square (*not* living together) = .393 (1 d.f.); Gamma = -.070
Chi-Square (living together) = 1.845 (1 d.f.); Gamma = .261

Table 5.6. Receipt of Evaluation by Sex and Race

		Non-African American	African American	*Total*
Male	**No Evaluation**	46.7% (179)	61.2% (229)	53.9% (408)
	Evaluation	53.3% (204)	38.8% (145)	46.1% (349)
	Total	100.0% (383)	100.0% (374)	100.0% (757)
Female	**No Evaluation**	53.5% (38)	70.0% (70)	63.2% (108)
	Evaluation	46.5% (33)	30.0% (30)	36.2% (63)
	Total	100.0% (71)	100.0% (100)	100.0% (171)

Note: Cell counts are in parentheses.
Chi-Square (male) = 15.997 (1 d.f.)**; Gamma = -.286
Chi-Square (female) = 4.846 (1 d.f.)*; Gamma = -.339

Table 5.7. Logistic Regression Models with Interactions Predicting Psychiatric Evaluation

Variable	Model 1	Model 2	Model 3
Demographic Variables			
Female	1.33*	.46	.87*
	(.52)	(.42)	(.37)
African American	-.57*		
	(.25)		
Current Offense			
Violent current offense dummy		1.30**	
		(.24)	
Family Status			
Child victim			-.81
			(1.04)
Child or significant other victim			
Primary caregiver for child/ren			
Married/cohabiting			
Mental Health			
Prior diagnosis of major mental illness			
Prior diagnosis of mood disorder			
Prior psychiatric hospitalization			
Interaction Effect	-.69	1.73*	.86
	(.64)	(.73)	(1.34)
Constant	-2.12	-2.03	-2.06
Number of Cases	677	677	670
-2 Log Likelihood	534.2**	529.3**	528.7**

Note: Standard errors in parentheses. $^{\#}$ p < .10 * p < .05 ** p < .01

Table 5.7, continued

Variable	Model 4	Model 5	Model 6
Demographic Variables			
Female	.81*	.86[#]	.69[#]
	(.37)	(.44)	(.40)
African American			
Current Offense			
Violent current offense dummy			
Family Status			
Child victim			
Child or significant other victim	-.64		
	(.49)		
Primary caregiver for child/ren		-1.17*	
		(.50)	
Married/cohabiting			-.91**
			(.33)
Mental Health			
Prior diagnosis of major mental illness			
Prior diagnosis of mood disorder			
Prior psychiatric hospitalization			
Interaction Effect	.90	.05	.88
	(.88)	(.76)	(.68)
Constant	-2.05	-2.06	-2.06
Number of Cases	670	676	677
-2 Log Likelihood	527.5**	534.0**	533.7**

Note: Standard errors in parentheses.   [#]p < .10   * p < .05   ** p < .01

Table 5.7, continued

Variable	Model 7	Model 8	Model 9
Demographic Variables			
Female	.94*	.90*	.86*
	(.37)	(.39)	(.38)
African American			
Current Offense			
Violent current offense dummy			
Family Status			
Child victim			
Child or significant other victim			
Primary caregiver for child/ren			
Married/cohabiting			
Mental Health			
Prior diagnosis of major mental illness	1.64**		
	(.40)		
Prior diagnosis of mood disorder		.01	
		(.33)	
Prior psychiatric hospitalization			2.07**
			(.36)
Interaction Effect	-.06	.12	.41
	(.90)	(.68)	(.79)
Constant	-2.08	-2.00	-2.07
Number of Cases	677	676	677
-2 Log Likelihood	535.4**	555.4**	535.1**

Note: Standard errors in parentheses. $^{\#}$p < .10 * p < .05 ** p < .01

Table 5.8. Receipt of Evaluation by Sex and Child/Significant Other Victim

		No Child or Significant Other Victim	Child or Significant Other Victim	*Total*
Male	**No Evaluation**	49.2% (308)	43.6% (17)	48.9% (325)
	Evaluation	50.8% (318)	56.4% (22)	51.1% (340)
	Total	100.0% (626)	100.0% (39)	100.0% (665)
Female	**No Evaluation**	52.8% (56)	36.8% (7)	50.4% (63)
	Evaluation	47.2% (50)	63.2% (12)	49.6% (62)
	Total	100.0% (106)	100.0% (19)	100.0% (125)

Note: Cell counts are in parentheses.
Chi-Square (male) = .463 (1 d.f.); Gamma: .112
Chi-Square (female) = 1.648 (1 d.f.); Gamma: .315

Table 5.9. Means and Standard Deviations for Variables Used in the Analysis

Variable	Men	Women	t-Value
Psychiatric evaluation	.46	.37	2.26*
	(.50)	(.48)	
Demographic Variables			
African American	.49	.58	-2.15*
	(.50)	(.49)	
Female			
Age at offense	31.61	30.42	1.49
	(10.87)	(9.06)	
Current Offense & Criminal History			
Violent current offense dummy	.42	.22	5.00**
	(.49)	(.42)	
# Prior adult arrests for violence	.90	.33	4.30**
	(1.68)	(.85)	
# Prior adult felony convictions	1.03	.28	4.73**
	(2.06)	(.71)	
Mental Health			
Prior diagnosis of major MI	.25	.28	-.57
	(.43)	(.45)	
Prior mental hospitalization	.31	.35	-.71
	(.46)	(.48)	
Police report bizarre behavior	.07	.08	-.05
	(.26)	(.27)	
Family Status			
Married/cohabiting	.19	.26	-1.62
	(.40)	(.44)	
Primary caregiver for children	.12	.48	-7.60**
	(.32)	(.50)	
Socioeconomic Status			
Private attorney	.12	.13	-.50
	(.32)	(.34)	
Earned monthly income	556.84	409.21	1.94#
	(1035.22)	(713.37)	
Unearned monthly income	190.70	280.37	-2.35*
	(389.93)	(380.97)	
Education	12.03	11.68	1.85#
	(1.70)	(1.81)	
Number of Cases	757	172	

Note: Standard deviations in parentheses. # p < .10 * p < .05 ** p < .01

Table 5.9, continued

Variable	Non-African American	African American	*t*-Value
Psychiatric evaluation	.52	.37	4.73**
	(.50)	(.48)	
Demographic Variables			
African American			
Female	.16	.21	-2.15*
	(.36)	(.41)	
Age at offense	32.21	30.58	2.34*
	(11.16)	(9.91)	
Current Offense & Criminal History			
Violent current offense dummy	.37	.40	-.87
	(.48)	(.49)	
# Prior adult arrests for violence	.50	1.07	-5.64**
	(1.08)	(1.89)	
# Prior adult felony convictions	.71	1.07	-2.89**
	(1.66)	(2.10)	
Mental Health			
Prior diagnosis of major MI	.32	.19	4.03**
	(.47)	(.40)	
Prior mental hospitalization	.40	.25	4.60**
	(.49)	(.43)	
Police report bizarre behavior	.10	.05	2.45*
	(.30)	(.22)	
Family Status			
Married/cohabiting	.20	.21	-.37
	(.40)	(.41)	
Primary caregiver for children	.12	.22	-3.89**
	(.32)	(.42)	
Socioeconomic Status			
Private attorney	.18	.07	5.13**
	(.38)	(.25)	
Earned monthly income	618.07	456.95	2.28*
	(1030.42)	(952.95)	
Unearned monthly income	227.35	184.04	1.51
	(467.17)	(302.71)	
Education	12.19	11.74	3.56**
	(1.78)	(1.63)	
Number of Cases	454	474	

Note: Standard deviations in parentheses.　# p < .10　* p < .05　** p < .01

Table 5.10. Decomposition: Logistic Regression of Psychiatric Evaluation by Sex and Race Categories

Variable	African Americans	Non-African Americans	Males	Females
Demographic Variables				
Female	.93	.80		
	(.57)	(.57)		
African American			-.44$^{\#}$	-4.73*
			(.25)	(2.14)
Age at offense	-.02	.09**	.02$^{\#}$	.27*
	(.02)	(.02)	(.01)	(.11)
Current Offense & History				
Violent current offense dummy	1.61**	1.22**	1.16**	8.29**
	(.34)	(.37)	(.25)	(2.65)
# Prior adult arrests for violence	.21*	-.09	.13$^{\#}$	1.28
	(.09)	(.17)	(.07)	(.78)
# Prior adult felony convictions	.05	-.13	-.02	-.57
	(.07)	(.11)	(.06)	(.86)
Mental Health				
Prior diagnosis of major MI	1.53**	1.81**	1.59**	2.61
	(.58)	(.53)	(.41)	(1.76)
Prior mental hospitalization	2.49**	1.77**	1.87**	6.54**
	(.53)	(.47)	(.36)	(2.41)
Police report bizarre behavior	2.10$^{\#}$	2.25*	2.17**	
	(1.19)	(1.08)	(.79)	
Family Status				
Married/cohabiting	-.59	-.73$^{\#}$	-.78*	.03
	(.45)	(.44)	(.34)	(1.31)
Primary caregiver for children	-1.74**	-.70	-1.04*	-2.39$^{\#}$
	(.62)	(.55)	(.51)	(1.31)
Socioeconomic Status				
Private attorney	.59	.78	.81*	1.89
	(.71)	(.48)	(.39)	(1.83)
Earned monthly income	.00	.01$^{\#}$	.00	-.003**
	(.00)	(.00)	(.00)	(.001)
Unearned monthly income	.001*	.00	.001*	-.00
	(.001)	(.00)	(.000)	(.00)
Education	.18	-.08	.07	.16
	(.16)	(.17)	(.11)	(.40)
Mean Imputation Values				
Missing monthly income	-1.67	1.36	-4.57	4.64
	(2.10)	(32.97)	(13.28)	(48.14)
Missing monthly unearned income	1.34	6.87	6.23	.65
	(1.37)	(23.59)	(13.25)	(1.64)
Missing education	-2.61$^{\#}$	-.78	-1.63	-2.93
	(1.51)	(1.56)	(1.09)	(3.53)
Constant	-1.95	-2.99	-1.96	-8.70
Number of Cases	336	340	571	110
-2 Log Likelihood	255.0**	230.9**	450.9**	36.3**

Note: Standard errors in parentheses. $^{\#}$ p < .10   * p < .05   ** p < .01

Table 5.10. Decomposition, continued

Variable	African American Males	Non-African American Males
Demographic Variables		
Female		
African American		
Age at offense	-.05*	.08**
	(.02)	(.02)
Current Offense & History		
Violent current offense dummy	1.36**	1.20**
	(.38)	(.38)
# Prior adult arrests for violence	.19*	-.15
	(.10)	(.17)
# Prior adult felony convictions	.10	-.13
	(.08)	(.11)
Mental Health		
Prior diagnosis of major MI	1.33*	2.00**
	(.64)	(.57)
Prior mental hospitalization	2.29**	1.62**
	(.58)	(.50)
Police report bizarre behavior	2.18#	2.15*
	(1.21)	(1.09)
Family Status		
Married/cohabiting	-.85	-.80
	(.53)	(.49)
Primary caregiver for children	-2.22*	-.63
	(.96)	(.67)
Socioeconomic Status		
Private attorney	.70	.60
	(.76)	(.51)
Earned monthly income	.00	.00
	(.00)	(.00)
Unearned monthly income	.003**	.00
	(.001)	(.00)
Education	.18	-.02
	(.18)	(.18)
Mean Imputation Values		
Missing monthly income	-6.14	2.20
	(16.63)	(35.67)
Missing monthly unearned income	6.02	6.01
	(16.54)	(25.75)
Missing education	-3.24#	-.84
	(1.80)	(1.65)
Constant	-1.22	-3.05
Number of Cases	272	299
-2 Log Likelihood	205.0**	208.1**

Note: Standard errors in parentheses. # $p < .10$ * $p < .05$ ** $p < .01$

Table 5.11. Receipt of Evaluation by Race and Prior Mental Illness Level

		Non-African American	African American	*Total*
High Prior Mental Illness	**No Evaluation**	5.7% (6)	5.9% (4)	5.8% (10)
	Evaluation	94.3% (99)	94.1% (64)	94.2% (163)
	Total	100.0% (105)	100.0% (68)	100.0% (173)
Low Prior Mental Illness	**No Evaluation**	54.5% (164)	69.2% (247)	62.5% (411)
	Evaluation	45.5% (137)	30.8% (110)	37.5% (247)
	Total	100.0% (301)	100.0% (357)	100.0% (658)

Note: Cell counts are in parentheses.
Chi-Square (High Mental Illness) = .002 (1 d.f.); Gamma: -.015
Chi-Square (Low Mental Illness) = 15.056 (1 d.f.)**; Gamma: -.305

## CHAPTER 6

THE EFFECT OF MENTAL HEALTH EVALUATIONS ON CASE OUTCOMES

This chapter examines the effect of these psychiatric evaluations on various case outcomes, asking how attributions of mental illness alter case outcomes in the criminal justice system. The specific theoretical perspective tested in this chapter is Black's (1976) social control perspective. One of the principles of Black's theory of law is that law varies inversely with other social control (1976:107). Specifically, Black contends that "the treatment of mental illness varies inversely with other social controls" (1976:119). Consequently, in the criminal justice system, this theory of law suggests that defendants who are treated psychiatrically will be subject to less law since the social control of psychiatry supersedes legal control. Previous social control, however, lowers an individual's respectability, leading to increased legal control. Thus, Black's theory predicts more severe legal control for defendants with prior criminal and psychiatric histories, but decreased control over those currently subject to psychiatric and family control.

A competing perspective to Black's theory of law comes from labeling theory, with its emphasis on the negative consequences of labels. Laberge and Morin (2001) contend that despite observing compelling evidence of a mental disorder, defense attorneys frequently avoid pursuing a mental illness defense because of censorious public opinion and negative case outcomes that are the result of this defense. While public perception of the insanity defense is that it is positive, that the defendant "gets away with murder," studies of length of confinement (prison or mental hospital) demonstrate a punishment philosophy where the punishment fits the crime, regardless of whether the defendant is considered responsible (Silver 1995; Callahan and Silver 1998; Lymburner and Roesch 1999). This type of research leads Menzies to conclude that mental health clinicians in the criminal justice system actually tailor their analysis to fit into a punishment framework, supporting dispositions that require punishment (1989:xvii). Even defendants who reject or fail with an NGRI plea might be punished more harshly; Perlin (2000) contends that defendants who plead insanity and are ultimately found guilty of their charges serve *longer* sentences than defendants who do not assert an insanity defense (see also Braff, Arvinites, and Steadman 1983).

Because these two perspectives make contradictory predictions about the relationship between psychiatric evaluations in the criminal justice system and eventual case outcomes, two competing hypotheses are tested in this chapter. Black's theory of law implies that receipt of this evaluation and increased psychiatric control will diminish legal control, or decrease sentence severity. In contrast, labeling theory emphasizes the negative effect of labels, including psychiatric labels; thus, using labeling theory, one would expect sentencing decisions and sentence length to be more severe for those with the added burden of a psychiatric label in contrast to those with only a criminal label.

Dependent Variables

In seeking the effect of an evaluation on outcomes, case outcomes were coded based on five factors: the decision to dismiss all charges, whether the defendant is found or pleads guilty, whether the defendant is found NGRI, whether the defendant is sentenced to prison, and the length of this prison sentence. The first four dependent variables are dichotomous outcomes and the last dependent variable is a continuous indicator of the sentenced imprisonment in months. While some cases may initially receive a probationary sentence but ultimately result in a prison sentence once the offender violates the conditions of probation, only the initial sentencing decision was coded. This decision was made to model the effect of the psychiatric control factors on sentencing outcome, regardless of the later behavior of the individual. Because the follow-up period is not the same for all offenders (e.g., cases from 1993 had eight years in which to recidivate while cases from 2000 only had one year to recidivate), only the initial decision was coded and offenders were not followed beyond this point.

Independent Variables

To test the effect of psychiatric controls on legal case outcomes, four psychiatric indicators are included. The first three indicators measure past psychiatric control, which lowers respectability and increases legal control according to Black (1976). Labeling theory similarly argues that these past labels negatively affect defendants, resulting in more severe case outcomes. These indicators of past psychiatric treatment include the following: First, an indicator for a prior diagnosis of a major mental illness is included. This dichotomous indicator refers to a diagnosis assigned by a mental health professional and includes major depression, bipolar disorder, and schizophrenia or any other psychosis. Second, this research indicates whether the individual has ever been hospitalized for psychiatric treatment. Third, a measure of whether the individual has ever been treated for a mental illness on an outpatient basis is included. Thus, these three measures of previous social control are expected to decrease respectability and therefore increase legal control of defendants.

The fourth psychiatric control variable represents current psychiatric control, which, according to Black (1976), results in lower legal control (because these are competing systems of social control), whereas labeling theory continues to imply heightened legal control, with its emphasis on the negative consequences of a label. This indicator of psychiatric control within the legal system is a dichotomous measure of whether the defendant received a psychiatric evaluation to determine his/her mental status at the time of the current offense. If there were indeed an inverse relationship between competing systems of social control, one would expect to find that this fourth psychiatric indicator significantly reduces the likelihood of conviction and prison sentences for defendants. Conversely, if labeling theory is correct and defendants are treated more harshly for an additional label, one would expect that defendants with mental health evaluations who fail to proceed with an insanity defense would actually receive more severe sentences than those without this psychiatric label.

Because criminal justice decisions about case dismissal and sentencing are most obviously affected by severity of offense, criminal history, and the strength of the case against the defendant, controls for these three important factors are included.

First, this project controls for offense severity. Originally, this research followed Spohn and Spears (1997) in controlling for five separate categories of most serious offense: first degree murder; second-degree murder/manslaughter; robbery; assault; and other felonies. Upon further investigation, however, it was noted that there is insufficient variation on the most severe offenses (particularly murder and manslaughter); it was also noted that all of the models were nearly identical when a dichotomous indicator of violent offense was substituted. As a result, for most of the analysis, only models that use this violent offense dichotomy are reported. The severity of the offense is also indicated by a dichotomous indicator of whether a weapon was used during the offense.

Second, because criminal history alters sentencing using the sentencing guidelines, this research includes a measure of the total number of adult felony convictions.

Third, because the odds of a successful prosecution increase with the strength of evidence in the case, this project follows Spohn and Spears (1996) and includes two quality of evidence indicators: (1) was there a witness to the offense? And (2) is there physical evidence of the crime?[1] Because the witness indicator is non-significant in all models, it is excluded from the analysis and only the physical evidence variable is reported.

To determine how social controls from employment and education affect criminal justice processing, indicators of socioeconomic status are also included. These indicators include monthly earned income, monthly unearned income (including AFDC, SSI, and welfare), and the highest year of education completed. Finally, indicators of family control are added to model the relationship between these competing systems of social control; two dichotomous indicators are used: whether the defendant was living with a significant other at the time of the offense, and whether the defendant was the primary caregiver for a child or for children. Black's theory predicts an inverse relationship between these family controls and legal control.

RESULTS
Descriptive Statistics

Descriptive statistics for these variables are presented in Table 6.1. Approximately 28 percent of the sample had all charges dismissed, 5 percent had an NGRI finding, 71 percent had a guilty finding (either as the result of a guilty plea, a jury, or a bench trial), 57 percent pled guilty, and approximately 24 percent of the sample received a prison sentence at the conclusion of their case. For the entire sample, the mean incarceration sentence was almost 19 months. Because not everyone in the sample was at risk for a prison sentence (i.e., some were not guilty or NGRI), the mean prison sentence for the 24 percent of the sample that actually received a prison sentence is presented, which is almost 77 months.

The various case outcomes are presented for the cases and controls in Figures 6.1A and 6.1B. Of the cases displayed in Figure 6.1A (offenders who received a psychiatric evaluation), approximately 11 percent are found NGRI, 19 percent are considered not guilty, and 69 percent are considered guilty. Not guilty encompasses a wide rage of final outcomes: 11 percent were deemed not guilty after a jury or bench trial, 58 percent had the charges against them dropped, and 30 percent still have their case pending, have died, or were found incompetent to stand trial (IST). Thus, this last group is yet to be found guilty, but might at some point be found guilty. For instance, a defendant found IST might be sent to a psychiatric hospital until competence is regained; once deemed competent, the offender might plead guilty or otherwise be found guilty. Of the 69 percent found guilty, most (84 percent) pled guilty whereas 16 percent were found guilty after a bench or jury trial. Consistent with previous research, individuals who plead guilty are less likely to be sentenced to prison than those found guilty

by trial (55 percent versus 69 percent), although this does not control
for other important legal factors such as offense seriousness or criminal
history.

The various outcomes for the controls (non-psychiatric
evaluations) are presented in Figure 6.1B. None of these controls had
an NGRI outcome because a psychiatric evaluation is necessary for this
outcome. This leaves the other two possible outcomes: guilty and not
guilty. Forty-three percent of the controls were not guilty. Of this
group, 4 percent were found not guilty by a trial, over 90 percent had
the charges against them dropped, and 6 percent either had pending
cases, died before final case outcome, or were found IST. This 43
percent of controls found not guilty is slightly higher than the
combined 30 percent found either not guilty or NGRI among the cases
(in Figure 6.1A). Whereas 69 percent of the cases are considered guilty,
approximately 57 percent of the controls are guilty. Of these guilty
outcomes, over 94 percent pled and less than 5 percent were found
guilty after a trial. In comparison to the guilty controls, the guilty cases
were slightly more likely to be found guilty by a trial (16 percent versus
5 percent). Again consistent with previous research and the trend noted
for cases, control defendants who pled guilty were less likely to be
sentenced to prison than those who went through a trial (30 percent
versus 50 percent). One important distinction between cases and
controls is the percent sent to prison. Of the defendants in the control
group who pled guilty, roughly 70 percent are not incarcerated; among
the cases who pled guilty, only 45 percent are not incarcerated. While
these figures might provide some evidence supportive of labeling
theory—that the psychiatric label has additional negative consequences
for defendants—these frequencies do not provide any statistical
controls for important legal variables such as offense seriousness and
criminal history. These and other important controls are added in the
multivariate models that follow.

To determine whether there are any race differences in final
outcomes for cases and controls, outcomes for African Americans and
non-African Americans are presented in Figures 6.2 and 6.3. As was
found in Chapter Five, non-African Americans have a larger percentage
of cases than African Americans (52.2 percent versus 36.9 percent).
Comparing controls (see Figures 6.2B and 6.3B) there is very little
difference in case outcomes between African Americans and non-

African Americans. Not guilty and guilty outcomes occur at roughly the same percentage for both racial categories (approximately 42 percent not guilty and approximately 57 percent guilty). A slightly higher percentage of African American controls were found guilty by trial (7.0 percent versus 1.6 percent for non-African Americans); once these offenders are considered guilty, however, there are no obvious racial differences in the likelihood of a prison sentence.[2]

While Figures 2 and 3 present few racial differences for controls, there are many differences among the cases (see Figures 6.2A and 6.3A). Among non-African American defendants who received a psychiatric evaluation there is a greater percentage of NGRI outcomes (13.1 percent) than for African American cases (8.6 percent). A larger percentage of African American cases were ultimately considered guilty (74.9 percent versus 65.7 percent for non-African Americans). Of these cases who are guilty, African Americans appear more likely to receive a prison sentence; this race difference is apparent both for those who plead guilty (57.9 percent of African Americans receive prison versus 39.8 percent of non-African Americans) and for those who are found guilty (75.0 percent versus 57.1 percent). While these figures provide some evidence that African American defendants, and especially African American cases, receive harsher punishment in the criminal justice system, these frequencies do not provide any statistical controls for important legal variables such as offense seriousness and criminal history. These and other important controls are added in the multivariate models that follow.

Continuing with descriptive statistics in Table 6.1, approximately 44 percent of the sample received a psychiatric evaluation to determine mental status at the time of the offense and over 30 percent had a history of psychiatric outpatient treatment for a mental illness. The most serious offense was first-degree murder for 2.4 percent of the sample; while over 68 percent of the sample had a non-violent felony offense as the most serious charge. Almost 20 percent of the defendants sampled used a weapon in committing their offense, and in approximately 13 percent of the sample, prosecutors had physical evidence to implicate the defendant in the offense.

The remaining independent variables used in the analyses discussed in this chapter are presented in Chapter Five. Rather than repeat the variables here in great detail, these descriptive statistics are summarized (not shown in this chapter, but displayed in Table 5.1). Roughly 19 percent of the defendants are female and the sample population is approximately 51 percent African American. Over one-third of the offenders in this sample are charged with a violent offense, and the mean number of previous adult felony convictions is less than one. Many of the defendants in this sample do not have family ties, for approximately 20 percent were living with a significant other at the time of the offense and 17 percent were the primary caregiver for a child or children. Over 25 percent of all defendants in the sample received a diagnosis of a major mental illness prior to their arrest.

The mean monthly unearned income for defendants in this sample ($534) is higher than the mean earned income ($204), while the average level of education is slightly less than high school completion (11.97). These independent variables are used to determine how psychiatric and family controls and the demographic characteristics of race and gender affect various case outcomes.

Not Guilty by Reason of Insanity Outcome

Chapter Five modeled the predictors of psychiatric evaluations in the criminal justice system. Because the apparent purpose of a psychiatric evaluation is to determine whether the defendant was legally insane at the time of the offense, the ultimate case outcome for some of these offenders is NGRI.

As reported in Chapter Two, the outcome of an insanity case is highly dependent on the ultimate decision-maker; successful insanity pleas are much more likely when judges, rather than juries, make the decision of whether to accept an insanity outcome (Boehnert 1989; Callahan et al. 1991). Expert mental health testimony also significantly alters the likelihood of an NGRI outcome, with judges relying on the expertise of psychiatrists to determine legal sanity or insanity (Ewing 1983; Dahl 1985; LaFond 1994). This implies that this research should include measures of the decision-maker (judge or jury) and the opinion of the psychiatric evaluator. Because these variables are very closely correlated with the NGRI outcome, however, there is insufficient variation in these independent variables to allow a multivariate analysis. A bench trial, for example, almost perfectly predicts NGRI outcome; only 0.4 percent of the defendants who chose a jury trial were found NGRI. When the psychiatric evaluator offers the opinion that the defendant was sane at the time of the offense, the defendant is found NGRI in only 2.7 percent of the cases. Consequently, because these variables lack sufficient variation, they are excluded from the NGRI analysis.

Because both psychiatric evaluation and NGRI outcome are dichotomous variables, this research uses a univariate probit procedure to estimate initial models of psychiatric evaluation and NGRI outcome. As Figure 6.1B demonstrates, a psychiatric evaluation is necessary for an NGRI outcome, so the most direct way to measure the effect of psychiatric controls on NGRI outcome might be to simply eliminate all defendants who were not evaluated. This, however, might obscure important unmeasured factors affecting both NGRI and selection into the psychiatric evaluation pool. This project therefore estimates two-equation probit models that allow for interdependence in the factors leading to psychiatric evaluation and NGRI outcome. The first equation predicts the likelihood of NGRI and the second equation models the selection process predicting psychiatric evaluation, or the sub-group of potential NGRI outcomes.

The probit estimates of NGRI are presented in Table 6.2. The first three models display the uncorrected univariate probit models, which were run using only defendants who received the psychiatric evaluation. Probit coefficients are interpreted as the result of a unit change in the independent variable on the cumulative normal probability of the dependent variable, or effects on z-scores (see e.g., Hardy 1989; Uggen 1999). Model A fits only a constant, indicating that the probability of NGRI relative to other outcomes is .11, which is associated with a z-score of -1.22.

Model B adds psychiatric and demographic characteristics. Rather than using the constructed major mental illness dichotomy (which includes major depression, bipolar disorder, and schizophrenia/psychosis) as a control for previous mental status, instead, this research focuses on the most severe mental illness type, schizophrenia/psychosis, in modeling NGRI outcome. Because this NGRI outcome is most often decided by psychiatric rather than legal agents (Steadman et al. 1983; Steadman et al. 1993), an indicator of the mental disorder most commonly associated with violence among mental health experts is used (Link, Andrews, and Cullen 1992; Link et al. 1999a; Silver and Teasdale 2005).[3] Also, because insanity is highly dependent on the psychiatrist's report (Mechanic 1969; Ewing 1983; Dahl 1986; LaFond 1994), rather than using previous mental illness diagnosis, the psychiatrist's report of whether the current diagnosis is schizophrenia or another psychosis is used. This dichotomous indicator significantly increases the likelihood of an NGRI finding; African Americans are marginally less likely to be found NGRI in this model. Model C adds criminal offense and history and SES variables. Here, prior adult felony convictions significantly reduce the likelihood of NGRI; high education levels, however, increase likelihood of NGRI.

Because the bivariate probit selection model considers selection into evaluation, Models D, E, and F are run using the entire sample, rather than deleting all defendants who did not receive a psychiatric evaluation, as is done in Models A, B, and C. This bivariate probit selection model tests whether unmeasured characteristics that increase the probability of evaluation alter the likelihood of NGRI outcome. For example, if those evaluated had higher levels of unmeasured NGRI propensity, this would appear in a positive correlation between the error terms of the evaluation and NGRI equations. Alternatively, if unmeasured NGRI propensity was lower among those evaluated than those who were not evaluated, then this correlation would be negative.

Model D displays the effect of unmeasured traits that increase the likelihood of psychiatric evaluation on the probability of NGRI. Here the correlation of the error terms (ρ) is significantly negative. Therefore, it appears that unmeasured factors associated with a psychiatric evaluation actually *decrease* the probability of NGRI.[4] The constant term in the corrected equation (D) is smaller in absolute magnitude than in the uncorrected model (A); the probability of NGRI net of unmeasured factors related to evaluation is approximately .19, the probability associated with a z-value of -.87.

In the corrected equation presented in Model F and the uncorrected equation in Model C, the number of previous adult felony convictions is statistically significant. While criminal history is significant in determining which defendants will be evaluated, it is also an important consideration for mental health clinicians. Demographic characteristics such as gender and race are also significant in predicting evaluations; these variables do not provide much explanation for NGRI outcome.

Whereas previous research had emphasized a greater likelihood of women being successful with an NGRI defense, the available evidence does not replicate this finding once psychiatric factors are taken into account. Although the coefficients for women are positive, they are not statistically significant. It may be that prior research demonstrating a consistent gender difference failed to adequately control for important psychiatric factors; conversely, it may be that there was an insufficient number of women remaining in the models to accurately demonstrate this gender difference.

The results in Models D, E, and F in Table 6.2 provide little evidence that the single equation estimates are biased by selectivity. Thus, it does not appear that unmeasured characteristics are causing individuals who are unlikely to be found NGRI to be sent for a psychiatric evaluation. Instead, it is clear that the most important factor in NGRI determinations is current mental illness diagnosis. Mental illness alone, however, is not the only significant predictor of NGRI. Number of previous felony convictions is apparently used by psychiatrists to determine who the "real" (and thus responsible) criminals are. In addition, education increases the likelihood of NGRI; these decision-makers apparently view defendants with higher levels of education as more appropriate recipients of this outcome. Thus, while mental illness is the most significant predictor of NGRI, it appears that psychiatric agents also have expectations of the appropriate insanity acquittees, and these individuals are better educated with a shorter criminal history. The robustness of these coefficients across both specifications—with and without correction for sample selection—indicates that the results of the uncorrected models do not appear to be an artifact of analyzing just the sub-group of evaluation defendants.

Charges Dismissed Outcome

Table 6.3 presents the results of probit analysis of the charges dismissed outcome. This research determines what factors significantly predict which defendants will have changes against them dismissed. The dependent variable in this analysis is a dichotomous indicator of all charges dismissed, with defendants receiving a dismissal coded 1 and those without a dismissal coded 0.

The results presented in Model 1 of Table 6.3 indicate that defendants who received a psychiatric evaluation to determine their mental status at the time of the offense were significantly less likely to have their charges dismissed relative to those without a psychiatric evaluation. This is also true in Model 2, although the magnitude of the evaluation effect is diminished by the inclusion of current offense and criminal history factors. As might be expected, violent offenders and those with a greater number of adult felony convictions are significantly less likely to have their charges dismissed. Use of a weapon and physical evidence, however, are non-significant and have little effect on the likelihood of dismissal.

Model 3 of Table 6.3 adds SES and family status indicators. In this model, defendants who were psychiatrically evaluated are still significantly less likely to have their criminal charges dismissed relative to those who were not psychiatrically evaluated. Similarly, those charged with a violent offense are also significantly less likely to have charges dismissed. SES and family status indicators have little effect on this case outcome. Thus, while current offense is the strongest predictor, psychiatric evaluations also significantly reduce the likelihood of dismissal. This result provides support for the labeling perspective that psychiatric labels result in a negative outcome for the labeled defendant.

Guilty Outcome

Table 6.4 models the predictors of a guilty outcome. In this table, those who were found guilty of their offense were coded as 1 and those with all other outcomes (including NGRI) were coded as 0. Model 1 of Table 6.4 demonstrates that defendants who received a psychiatric evaluation were significantly more likely to be found guilty of their offense than those without an evaluation. This remains true in Model 2, although the magnitude of this coefficient is reduced when criminal offense and history are included. Violent offenders, defendants with a greater number of adult felony convictions, and those who used a weapon during the commission of their offense are more likely to be found guilty than other offenders. These results are essentially the same in Model 3, which adds SES and family status, although the marginally significant number of prior convictions and use of weapon are no longer statistically significant in this model. Despite these significant offense and criminal history variables, it is clear that receipt of psychiatric evaluations significantly increases the likelihood of a guilty outcome. The violent offense dichotomy is the only indicator larger in magnitude than this psychiatric evaluation coefficient; clearly, receipt of this evaluation results in a more negative outcome when looking at the guilty/not guilty dichotomy. Again, these results provide support for labeling theory's emphasis on negative case outcomes for labeled defendants.

Prison Sentence Outcome

For offenders who are deemed guilty of their offense, Table 6.5 presents the likelihood of a prison sentence for this offense. In Model 1 of Table 6.5, defendants with a history of outpatient psychiatric treatment are marginally more likely to be sent to prison relative to those without outpatient treatment. Defendants receiving a psychiatric evaluation, however, are much more likely to be sentenced to prison than those who are not evaluated. Gender is statistically significant for the first time in the analysis of case outcomes. Relative to men, women are significantly less likely to receive a prison sentence, which is consistent with previous research indicating that the most significant gender differences in criminal justice processing appear in the in/out decision. Also in Model 1, African Americans are significantly more likely to be sent to prison than non-African Americans.

Model 2 of Table 6.5 adds current offense and criminal history factors. In this model, the psychiatric evaluation coefficient is reduced to marginal significance, although it remains positive. Women are still less likely and African Americans remain marginally more likely to be sent to prison. As might be expected, criminal history and current offense indicators are significant predictors of which offenders receive a prison sentence. Relative to second degree murder/manslaughter, defendants charged with assault or other non-violent felonies are significantly less likely to be sent to prison (using offense coding consistent with Spohn and Spears [1997]). A greater number of adult felony convictions, use of a weapon, and physical evidence of the offense all significantly increase the likelihood of a prison sentence.

Finally, Model 3 adds SES and family status indicators. In this model, both psychiatric evaluation and African American race are positive, but are no longer statistically significant. Women remain marginally less likely to be sent to prison, and criminal offense and history indicators still significantly alter the likelihood of a prison sentence. The major legal factors considered in the sentencing guidelines (offense severity and criminal history) best predict which defendants receive prison sentences; nevertheless, extralegal factors also contribute: women and defendants with higher levels of education are significantly less likely to be sent to prison. This education effect is particularly strong considering the metric is *years* of education rather than a simple dichotomy. Psychiatric control variables, however, appear to be less important in the decision to incarcerate. Nevertheless, psychiatric evaluations are positive and statistically significant in the first two models, although not in the full model. The number of cases, however, drops precipitously between Models 2 and 3 and the non-significant evaluation coefficient might be the result of this drop in cases. Thus, it does appear that psychiatric evaluations slightly increase the likelihood of imprisonment, even controlling for the greater levels of violence found among the evaluation cases; this again provides some support for labeling theory.

Incarceration Length

The previous section modeled the predictors of prison sentence. Because the in/out variable was a dichotomous indicator, use of probit analysis was appropriate; but since sentence length is a continuous variable, it requires a different analytic technique. As Table 6.1 indicates, approximately 76 percent of all sampled defendants did not receive a prison sentence. Consequently, the distribution of the dependent variables is skewed and OLS regression would produce biased and inconsistent estimates (see e.g., Edelman, Uggen, and Erlanger 1999). Tobit analysis is appropriate when studying dependent variables for which a large proportion of cases have zero as the lowest possible value (Roncek 1992; Winship and Mare 1992). Thus, this research estimated maximum likelihood Tobit models of length of incarceration. In these Tobit models, among defendants with no prison sentence, varying values of the independent variables imply different probabilities of experiencing prison. For defendants with at least one month of incarceration ordered, varying values on the independent variables imply variation in the severity (length) of a prison sentence (Roncek 1992).

Because only guilty defendants are even subject to imprisonment, this research estimated uncorrected Tobit equations after eliminating all non-guilty defendants. Corrected Tobit equations were also estimated, which consider unmeasured variation in selection into a guilty finding. Model 6.6 presents these uncorrected Tobit estimates and models corrected for sample selection.

Models A and B of Table 6.6 present Tobit estimates of sentence length in months, deleting all offenders without a guilty outcome. Thus, these coefficients represent sentenced incarceration among those found guilty, adjusting for the in/out decision. The results presented in Model A indicate that those with a psychosis or schizophrenia diagnosis receive prison sentences slightly shorter than those without this diagnosis. In contrast, a psychiatric evaluation significantly increases sentence length. Consistent with previous research, women receive shorter prison sentences while African Americans receive significantly longer sentences than non-African Americans. Model B adds offense and criminal history and family status indicators. As is usual in the criminal justice system, violent offenders with a history of felony convictions receive longer prison sentences than other defendants. Family status variables, however, do not significantly impact sentence length in these models.

Models C and D present the same analysis as above, but with a correction for guilty outcome. Because all offenders are not equally likely to be found guilty (as discussed earlier, referring to Table 6.4), this analysis uses all defendants but alters the model to incorporate information from the selection into a guilty outcome. The uncorrected tobits in Models A and B are modeled using only guilty defendants. Thus, the resulting coefficients represent sentence severity for guilty defendants after adjusting for the propensity to receive a prison sentence. The corrected models (C and D) take one step back and model the propensity to be found guilty, as well. Thus, Models C and D represent the sentence length for all defendants, adjusting for the propensity to receive a prison sentence and the selection into a guilty outcome. Thus, the coefficients displayed in Models C and D represent the propensity for imprisonment (in months) for all defendants, with selection corrections for guilty outcome and the in/out decision.

As demonstrated in Model C, the selection correction does not alter many of the significant coefficients. A diagnosis of schizophrenia or other psychosis decreases sentence length, as does female gender. A psychiatric evaluation and African American race both significantly increase the length of a prison sentence. Compared to Model A, the race coefficient is much smaller in Model C, which indicates that at least some of the race effect on sentence length is due the greater propensity to be selected into a guilty outcome. The coefficients in Model D are also similar to Model B, which does not correct for sample selection. The only differences are African American race and the number of prior adult felony convictions, both of which significantly increase sentence length in the uncorrected model (Model B), but are non-significant in the corrected model (Model D). This comparison of Tobit models with and without selectivity appears to indicate that the uncorrected Tobit models are not significantly altered by unmeasured characteristics that both cause individuals to be found guilty and make them likely to be sent to prison. The magnitudes of several coefficients in the corrected models are reduced, however, suggesting that the determinants of sentence are to some extent affected by which defendants are being sentenced.

This Tobit analysis, however, appears to provide a better analysis of length of imprisonment than an OLS model (see Appendix 6A). After sampling only on offenders found guilty *and* sentenced to prison, OLS regression is used to model length of sentenced incarceration. In this analysis, results are similar to the Tobit analysis above. A psychosis diagnosis decreases sentence length by approximately 64 months, whereas a psychiatric evaluation increases length of imprisonment by 82 months. Also similar to the Tobit analysis, the coefficients in Model 2 indicate that those who committed a violent offense received longer sentences than those who did not. A few differences between Tobit and OLS models are apparent, however. While bizarre behavior is not statistically significant in the Tobit analysis, it significantly increases length of imprisonment in the OLS models. The OLS models do not demonstrate any significant race or gender effects on sentence length, whereas the Tobit analysis indicates that women receive less severe and African Americans more severe prison sentences. In addition, the Tobit coefficients for family status were non-significant. The OLS coefficient for living with a significant other is marginally significant and positive, indicating that those with a spouse may receive slightly longer sentences than those without. While there are a few differences between the Tobit and OLS estimates, both estimation techniques provide strong evidence that defendants who receive psychiatric evaluations are sentenced to longer prison terms than those not evaluated. This project emphasizes the tobit estimates over the OLS, however, because in addition to providing important information about sentence lengths for offenders sent to prison, tobit also provides key information about the propensity for a prison sentence for those who ultimately are not incarcerated—information that is unavailable in the OLS model. Thus, this analysis indicates that receipt of psychiatric evaluations clearly increases sentence severity for defendants, even after controlling for current criminal offense, criminal history, and these selection processes.[5] Again, these results provide support for labeling theory: receipt of a psychiatric label significantly increases negative outcomes, which in this case, means lengthier imprisonment.

SUMMARY OF CHAPTER SIX

Consistent with previous research, it was expected that the largest racial and gender differences in case processing to appear in the earliest stage, the decision of whether to evaluate the defendant for a psychiatric disorder. This was because lawyers and judges, who are not trained in evaluating mental states, play a pivotal role in determining who will be evaluated (see Bonnie et al. 1996). As a result, it was expected that these legal actors will be the most free to incorporate prejudice or typifications of "normal" offenders.

> **Hypothesis 11:** *The greatest gender disparity will be found in the earliest stage, the decision to request a psychiatric evaluation.*

The analysis presented here provides mixed evidence for this hypothesis. Gender is occasionally significant in predicting psychiatric evaluations (as discussed in Chapter Five), and gender is not an important factor is explaining case dismissal, guilty finding, and NGRI. Gender is important, however, in explaining whether guilty defendants receive a prison sentence and the length of this sentence. Overall, at this late stage of the justice process, women are less likely than men to be sentenced to prison, and the prison sentences that women receive are significantly shorter than men's sentences. Thus, while there is some evidence that legal agents base decisions on typifications of "normal" women in deciding which defendants require an evaluation, there is even more evidence of lenient treatment of women in the later stages of the criminal justice system.

> **Hypothesis 12:** *The greatest racial disparity will be found in the earliest stage, the decision to request a psychiatric evaluation.*

There is evidence to support this hypothesis. African Americans are significantly less likely to be psychiatrically evaluated than non-African Americans. This finding is robust under a variety of specifications. In the later stages, however, the effect of race is less conspicuous. The only case outcomes significantly altered by race are the imprisonment (in/out) decision and the sentence length, with African Americans more likely to be imprisoned and to receive a lengthier sentence. These effects are non-significant, however, in the full models which control for SES and family status. Thus, it appears that the typifications of African Americans play an important role in the earliest stages of the criminal justice system, but that typifications are less important in the later stages. Perhaps the sentencing guidelines and other efforts to prevent extralegal factors from affecting case outcomes have succeeded in reducing the effect of typifications at the latest stages of the criminal justice system.

The third relevant hypothesis for this chapter was based on Black's theory of law. From a social control perspective, defendants subject to psychiatric controls are less subject to legal controls. Consequently, the evaluation results in less severe legal sanctions. On the level of individual decision-making, defense attorneys may advocate for a mental illness defense in an attempt to obtain immediate mental health treatment for their clients (Perlin 2000). From this perspective, as part of their legal strategy defense attorneys will advocate for a psychiatric defense in an attempt to force prosecutors to negotiate a plea disposition that includes limited criminal justice penalties in favor of mental health treatment (Blau and McGinley 1995; Laberge and Morin 2001).

> ***Hypothesis 13:*** *Defendants in the criminal justice system who receive psychiatric evaluations will receive less severe sanctions than those who do not receive evaluations.*

Black's theory of law indicates that as psychiatric controls increase, legal controls will decrease. There is no support for this perspective using psychiatric evaluations and their effect on severity of case outcome. In all of the analyses, the effect of a psychiatric evaluation is either non-significant or significantly increases the likelihood of a harsher outcome. Thus, Black's theory is not supported by the current analysis. In contrast, labeling theory suggests that the psychiatric evaluation label negatively alters case outcome; this suggests the following hypothesis, which is a competing hypothesis to number 13.

> ***Hypothesis 14:*** *Defendants in the criminal justice system who receive mental health evaluations will receive more severe sanctions than those who do not receive evaluations.*

There is quite a bit of support for this hypothesis. As suggested by Figures 6.1A and B, and confirmed in the multivariate analysis, receipt of a psychiatric evaluation typically results in a harsher outcome for defendants who are not found NGRI. Those who receive this evaluation are significantly less likely to have charges against them dismissed. This evaluation also significantly increases the likelihood of a guilty finding, a prison sentence, and the length of this prison sentence. These outcomes appear to provide stronger support for labeling theory's assumption that mental illness labeling actually harms criminal defendants, in particular those defendants who do not successfully plead NGRI.

CONCLUSION

Some have argued that the institutions of mental health and justice are not, as is usually depicted in sociological analysis, two opposing systems that meet and compete in an adversarial process (Spohn 1990; Dallaire et al. 2000; Laberge and Morin 2001). Rather, these two systems may actually work together and in effect become one actor in a treatment-control system that has as its function and aim to "take care of" residual cases viewed as problematic for society (Dallaire et al. 2000). In fact, rather than seeking medical and non-punitive dispositions for mentally ill offenders, psychiatrists in the criminal justice system may instead focus their recommendations on issues such as perceived dangerousness and community risk (Menzies 1989; Steadman et al. 1999; Arrigo 2002), which may require incarceration for safety and treatment issues. As a result, Menzies argues that psychiatrists' reports to the court "reflect the collusion between clinical and judicial agents" (1989:160; see also Scheff 1974). This "collusion" is the result of the increasing use of psychiatrists to determine criminal sanctions. Because clinicians have the weight of medical authority behind their opinion, this chapter indicates that rather than Donald Black's notion of two competing systems of social control, the introduction of psychiatry actually undermines the adversarial nature of justice decisions, leading to increases in legal controls for these defendants.

Consequently, decision-makers in the criminal justice system may inadvertently be causing differential treatment on the basis of a perceived mental illness. In an attempt to determine whether the mental health or criminal justice system should have control over offenders who might be mentally ill, decision-makers may seek psychiatric evaluations and unknowingly cause disparity in case outcome.

NOTES

---

[1] This physical evidence variable includes DNA and fingerprints.

[2] There is a large racial difference in the percent of defendants found guilty by trial who receive a prison sentence: only 50 percent of African Americans found guilty received a prison sentence while 100 percent of non-African Americans found guilty received a prison sentence. Since the number of cases is so small (seven African Americans and two non-African Americans), this difference is likely the result of the number of cases rather than "real" racial differences.

[3] Although other mental illness indicators are also strongly related to NGRI outcomes—including prior mental hospitalizations and bizarre behavior at the time of the offense—this research is unable to include these variables in the analysis of the NGRI outcome. All mental illness indicators cannot be included in the same model because they are highly correlated; including each of these indicators causes problems with multicollinearity. This research therefore uses the variable (whether the current mental illness is schizophrenia/other psychosis) that is the strongest predictor of an NGRI outcome.

[4] This significantly negative ρ perhaps suggests that the factors legal agents use to make psychiatric attributions are quite different than the factors used by psychiatric agents. For example, Chapter Five demonstrated that African Americans in this sample are much less likely than non-African Americans to receive an evaluation. Perhaps this negative correlation of the error terms reflects the inaccurate assessment of mental disorder on the part of legal agents. It may be that by relying on typifications of offenders to determine who *could* be mentally disordered, these legal decision-makers are failing to observe "real" mental illness. But once psychiatric agents—who are better trained in evaluating mental disorder—are asked to make decisions, they focus more on mental illness rather than typifications.

Conversely, the significant negative ρ may be the result of the sampling strategy. Using the case-control methodology, psychiatric evaluations were over-sampled and as a result, the sample does not reflect average felony defendants. Because selection was made on the dependent variable in the selection equation, this analysis may diverge from typical sample selection models that do not follow a case-control methodology. Regardless of the interpretation of ρ, the estimates in Models E and F are similar to those in Models B and C. Thus, the uncorrected univariate probit model appears to be a reasonably accurate portrayal of the factors affecting NGRI outcome.

[5] To determine whether the effect of mental health evaluations is different for women and African Americans, the four primary case outcomes (dismissal, guilty, prison, and prison sentence) were modeled using interaction effects. Interactions of gender and evaluation and race and evaluation were examined; none of these interactions were statistically significant, indicating that the effect of psychiatric evaluations does not differ because of the defendant's race or gender.

Table 6.1. Descriptive Statistics (N=929)

Variable	Description	Percent/Mean
Dependent Variables		
All charged dismissed	0=charges not dismissed; 1=all charged dismissed	27.5%
Found Not Guilty by Reason of Insanity	0=no; 1=yes	5.0%
Guilty	0=defendant not guilty; 1=guilty	70.7%
Guilty plea	0=no guilty plea; 1=guilty plea	56.9%
Received a prison sentence	0=no prison; 1=prison	24.2%
Mean prison sentence (entire sample)	Length of sentence in months	18.6 (67.8)
Mean prison sentence (prison only)	Length of sentence in months	76.8 (120.6)
Psychiatric Controls		
Received a psychiatric evaluation	0=No evaluation; 1=evaluation	44.3%
Previous outpatient psychiatric treatment	0=no outpatient treatment; 1=previous outpatient treatment	30.6%
Schizophrenia/psychosis current diagnosis (entire sample)	0=no schizo/psych diagnosis; 1=schizo/psych diagnosis	17.9%
Schizophrenia/psychosis current diagnosis (evaluations only)	0=no schizo/psych diagnosis; 1=schizo/psych diagnosis	35.3%
Current Offense & Criminal History Most serious conviction offense		
First degree murder	0=no; 1=yes	2.4%
Second degree murder, manslaughter	0=no; 1=yes	3.4%
Robbery	0=no; 1=yes	6.9%
Assault	0=no; 1=yes	18.4%
Other felony	0=no; 1=yes	68.9%
Use of weapon	0=no; 1=yes	19.9%
Physical evidence	0=no; 1=yes	13.4%

Note: Standard deviations in parentheses.

155

Table 6.2. Probit Estimation of NGRI with and without Selectivity Correction

Variable	Uncorrected Univariate Probit			Bivariate Probit with Selectivity		
	A	B	C	D	E	F
Intercept	-1.22**	-1.47**	-2.93**	-.87**	-1.20**	-2.71**
	(.08)	(.18)	(.68)	(.11)	(.19)	(.83)
Psychiatric Controls						
New schizophrenia or		.79**	.82**		.64**	.69**
psychosis diagnosis		(.18)	(.19)		(.21)	(.22)
Demographic Variables						
Female		.11	.01		.14	.03
		(.24)	(.27)		(.24)	(.28)
African American		-.32$^{\#}$	-.25		-.19	-.12
		(.18)	(.20)		(.20)	(.24)
Current Offense &						
Criminal History						
Violent offense			.13			.002
			(.20)			(.24)
# Prior adult felony			-.16*			-.15*
convictions			(.07)			(.06)
Socioeconomic Status						
Years of education			.12*			.13*
			(.05)			(.07)
P Covariance ($\varepsilon_1,\varepsilon_2$)				-.67**	-.55**	-.54**
				(.12)	(.17)	(.20)
Number of Cases	411	397	380	697,	688,	619,
				411	397	380
Log-Likelihood	-144.06	-128.44	-115.17	-408.53	-398.03	-368.66

Note: Standard errors in parentheses. $^{\#}$ p < .10 * p < .05 ** p < .01

Table 6.3. Univariate Probit Estimation of Charges Dismissed

Variable	Model 1	Model 2	Model 3
Intercept	-.66**	-.70**	-.35
	(.17)	(.19)	(.52)
Psychiatric Controls			
Major mental illness diagnosis	.06	-.04	.04
	(.18)	(.19)	(.21)
Previous mental hospitalization	.15	.29	.22
	(.18)	(.19)	(.21)
Previous outpatient psychiatric treatment	-.10	-.09	-.07
	(.13)	(.14)	(.16)
Psychiatric evaluation	-.72**	-.47**	-.47**
	(.14)	(.16)	(.18)
Demographic Variables			
Female	.06	-.08	-.18
	(.14)	(.16)	(.21)
African American	.00	.10	.08
	(.11)	(.12)	(.14)
Age at offense	.00	.00#	.01
	(.00)	(.00)	(.01)
Current Offense & Criminal History			
Violent offense		-.60**	-.60**
		(.14)	(.16)
# Prior adult felony convictions		-.07*	-.05
		(.03)	(.03)
Use of weapon		-.30	-.33
		(.19)	(.23)
Physical evidence		.09	.07
		(.17)	(.20)
Socioeconomic Status			
Earned monthly income			-.00
			(.00)
Unearned monthly income			.00
			(.00)
Education			-.03
			(.04)
Family Status			
Primary caregiver for child/ren			-.09
			(.21)
Living with significant other			-.15
			(.18)
Number of Cases	786	717	599
Log Likelihood	-395.55	-324.91	-245.30
Chi-Squared	39.92	66.65	49.71
	(7 df)**	(11 df)**	(16 df)**

Note: Standard errors in parentheses.   #p < .10 * p < .05 ** p < .01

Table 6.4. Univariate Probit Estimation of Guilty Outcome

Variable	Model 1	Model 2	Model 3
Intercept	.64**	.67**	.60
	(.17)	(.19)	(.50)
Psychiatric Controls			
Major mental illness diagnosis	-.02	.07	.08
	(.17)	(.19)	(.20)
Previous mental hospitalization	-.19	-.33[#]	-.30
	(.17)	(.19)	(.20)
Previous outpatient psychiatric treatment	.11	.10	.10
	(.12)	(.13)	(.15)
Psychiatric evaluation	.67**	.44**	.39*
	(.13)	(.15)	(.17)
Demographic Variables			
Female	-.09	.02	.09
	(.14)	(.15)	(.20)
African American	.02	-.07	-.08
	(.10)	(.12)	(.13)
Age at offense	-.01	-.01[#]	-.01
	(.00)	(.01)	(.01)
Current Offense & Criminal History			
Violent offense		.54**	.57**
		(.14)	(.16)
# Prior adult felony convictions		.05[#]	.03
		(.03)	(.03)
Use of weapon		.31[#]	.34
		(.18)	(.22)
Physical evidence		-.15	-.04
		(.16)	(.20)
Socioeconomic Status			
Earned monthly income			.00
			(.00)
Unearned monthly income			-.00
			(.00)
Education			.00
			(.04)
Family Status			
Primary caregiver for child/ren			.02
			(.20)
Living with significant other			.10
			(.17)
Number of Cases	786	717	599
Log Likelihood	-412.39	-344.21	-260.73
Chi-Squared	35.37	60.16	46.83
	(7 df)**	(11 df)**	(16 df)**

Note: Standard errors in parentheses. [#]p < .10 * p < .05 ** p < .01

158

Table 6.5. Univariate Probit Estimation of Prison Sentence (Selecting on Guilty)

Variable	Model 1	Model 2	Model 3
Intercept	-.67**	-.12	1.51*
	(.20)	(.37)	(.67)
Psychiatric Controls			
Major mental illness diagnosis	-.12	-.02	.13
	(.16)	(.17)	(.19)
Previous mental hospitalization	-.12	-.10	-.09
	(.16)	(.17)	(.19)
Previous outpatient psychiatric treatment	.21[#]	.05	.08
	(.12)	(.14)	(.15)
Psychiatric evaluation	.58**	.28[#]	.20
	(.13)	(.15)	(.17)
Demographic Variables			
Female	-.50**	-.37*	-.38[#]
	(.16)	(.17)	(.21)
African American	.35**	.22[#]	.20
	(.11)	(.12)	(.14)
Age at offense	-.00	-.01	-.00
	(.01)	(.01)	(.01)
Current Offense & Criminal History			
First degree murder[1]		.44	-.01
		(.46)	(.57)
Robbery[1]		-.64	-.49
		(.34)	(.44)
Assault[1]		-.69*	-1.28**
		(.30)	(.40)
Other felony[1]		-.65*	-1.08**
		(.30)	(.41)
# Prior adult felony convictions		.16**	.14**
		(.03)	(.03)
Use of weapon		.53**	.70**
		(.17)	(.19)
Physical evidence		.57**	.67**
		(.17)	(.19)
Socioeconomic and Family Status			
Earned monthly income			-.00
			(.00)
Unearned monthly income			-.00
			(.00)
Education			-.11**
			(.04)
Primary caregiver for child/ren			-.04
			(.22)
Living with significant other			.02
			(.17)
Number of Cases	601	563	490
Log Likelihood	-370.44	-306.90	-255.66
Chi-Squared	40.57	120.99	138.27
	(7 df)**	(14 df)**	(19 df)**

Note: Standard errors in parentheses.   [#] p <.10   * p < .05   ** p < .01
[1] Second degree murder/manslaughter is the reference category.

Table 6.6 Maximum Likelihood Tobit Regression of Sentence Length with & without Selectivity Correction

Variable	Uncorrected Tobit		Tobit with Selectivity	
	A	B	C	D
Intercept	-133.70**	-180.73**	6.20	-10.23
	(18.00)	(21.10)	(6.43)	(7.37)
Psychiatric Controls				
Schizophrenia or psychosis diagnosis	-45.09[#]	-40.56[#]	-20.62*	-19.53[#]
	(23.88)	(23.69)	(10.31)	(10.39)
Previous mental hospitalization	-24.69	-38.08[#]	-17.18[#]	-18.73*
	(20.78)	(20.63)	(9.19)	(9.20)
Bizarre behavior at time of offense	-34.36	-21.28	5.95	7.70
	(31.00)	(30.46)	(12.42)	(12.49)
Psychiatric evaluation	113.28**	90.63**	46.51**	38.84**
	(19.23)	(19.50)	(8.04)	(8.40)
Demographic Variables				
Female	-64.54**	-52.54*	-16.60[#]	-17.23[#]
	(24.18)	(26.21)	(9.31)	(10.37)
African American	44.54**	27.14[#]	12.51[#]	7.53
	(16.02)	(15.97)	(6.70)	(6.83)
Current Offense & Criminal History				
Violent offense		95.70**		34.08**
		(16.94)		(7.05)
# Prior adult felony convictions		12.05**		2.52
		(3.67)		(1.70)
Family Status				
Living with significant other		10.10		6.57
		(20.39)		(8.56)
Primary caregiver for child/ren		33.34		17.30
		(25.57)		(10.59)
Sigma	151.92**	145.69**		
	(8.23)	(7.91)		
Lambda			.010	.001
			(1.05)	(.109)
Log-Likelihood	-1467.06	-1419.50	-3251.92	-3172.35
Number of Cases	564	552	722, 564	704, 552

Note: Standard errors in parentheses.   [#] p <.10 * p < .05 ** p < .01

Figure 6.1A Outcomes for Cases (Offenders Who Received a Psychiatric Evaluation)

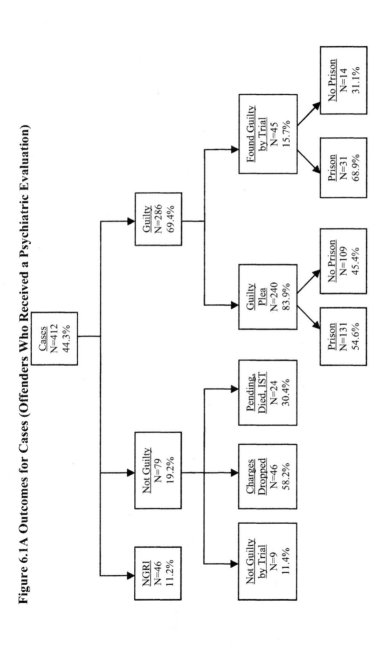

Figure 6.1B Outcomes for Controls (Offenders Who Did Not Receive a Psychiatric Evaluation)

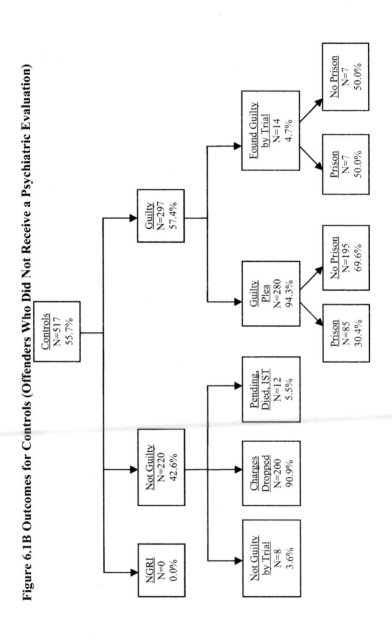

Figure 6.2A Outcomes for African American Cases (Offenders Who Received a Psychiatric Evaluation)

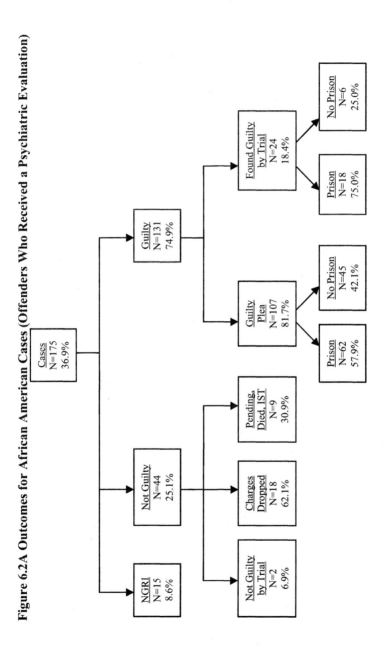

Figure 6.2B Outcomes for African American Controls (Offenders Who Did Not Receive a Psychiatric Evaluation)

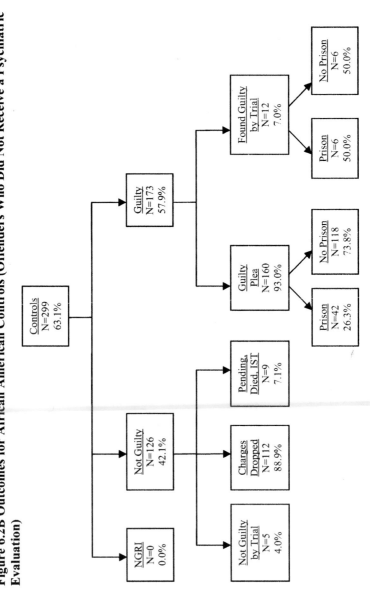

Figure 6.3A Outcomes for non-African American Cases (Offenders Who Received a Psychiatric Evaluation)

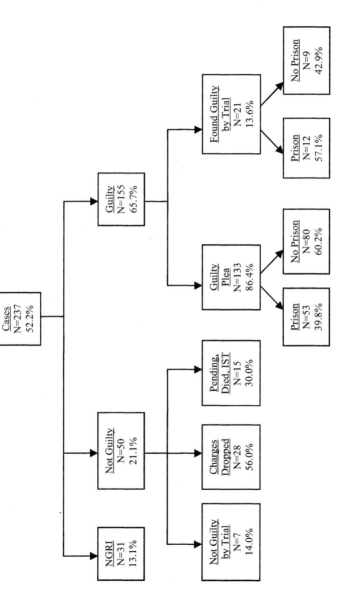

Figure 6.3B Outcomes for non–African American Controls (Offenders Who Did Not Receive a Psychiatric Evaluation)

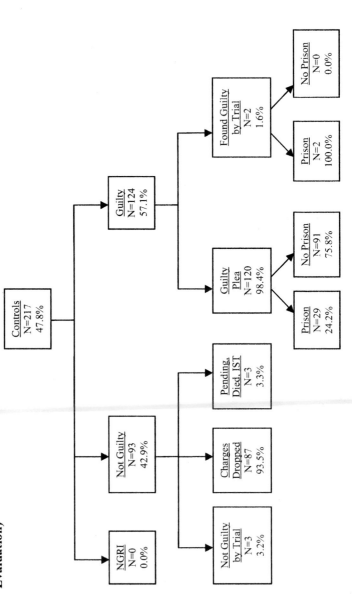

Appendix 6A. OLS Regression of Prison Sentence Length

Variable	Model 1	Model 2
Intercept	49.23*	-.63
	(22.47)	(27.22)
Psychiatric Controls		
Schizophrenia/Psychosis diagnosis	-63.94*	-48.29[#]
	(28.52)	(27.57)
Previous mental hospitalization	-19.20	-45.52[#]
	(24.92)	(25.19)
Bizarre behavior at time of offense	117.80**	107.65*
	(43.89)	(42.61)
Psychiatric evaluation	81.94**	82.23**
	(24.22)	(24.33)
Demographic Variables		
Female	-31.47	-49.56
	(33.96)	(34.79)
African American	-2.02	-14.39
	(20.40)	(20.15)
Current Offense & Criminal History		
Violent offense		81.66**
		(23.14)
# Prior adult felony convictions		-3.03
		(3.84)
Family Status		
Living with significant other		48.06[#]
		(26.75)
Primary caregiver for child/ren		44.43
		(32.54)
R^2	.132	.238
Number of Cases	160	158

Note: Standard errors in parentheses. * $p < .05$ ** $p < .01$

## CHAPTER 7

IMPLICATIONS FOR THEORY AND RESEARCH ON CRIME AND MENTAL ILLNESS

What effects do racial and gendered expectations have on the criminal justice system? Are women labeled "mad" while men are labeled "bad?" Are African American defendants "criminal" while non-African Americans are "ill?" How do psychiatric and criminal labels affect criminal justice outcomes? This chapter returns to these research questions asked in Chapter One and discusses the weight of the empirical evidence presented in Chapters Five and Six.

OVERVIEW OF THE RESEARCH
Case-Control Methods for Studying Rare Events

To obtain estimates of the effects of race and gender typifications on psychiatric evaluations, this project uses case-control methods. While case-control methodology was originally developed for use in epidemiology and is rarely used in sociological research, this procedure can provide important information on rare events that otherwise might be ignored by sociologists (see Lacy 1997; King and Zeng 2001a; 2001b). Consequently, this method is particularly useful for this analysis of the use of psychiatric evaluations in the criminal justice system due to the relative paucity of defendants who are psychiatrically evaluated. Because this methodology is used, this project takes advantage of the defining characteristic of case-control methods: selection on the case outcome. As a result, inferences are drawn from a large number of cases based on previously existing records, which ensures no risks to the research subjects.

Of course, these data are not without their drawbacks. These data are forced to rely on records gathered and maintained by others, with little opportunity for independent validation. Further, the research was limited to the information that legal agents chose to collect and report, meaning that it was impossible to gather complete data on some relevant and potentially significant variables. Although these are important caveats to this project, they are perhaps less significant concerns than might be evident in other case-control studies. The psychiatric evaluation reports and the PSIs reflect the level and amount of information that legal agents *know* and *choose* to report to the court. The decision to include this information is an indication of what the decision-maker believed was most relevant, and therefore at least part of the information on which evaluation and case-outcome decisions were based.[1] Therefore, as James A. Holstein explains in his analysis of civil commitment, it is unnecessary to attempt a "sociology of error" to determine whether the family status, criminal history, and psychiatric history reported in these documents is "real" (1993:15). Instead, what is important is what the decision-makers *believe* to be real—what is reported in court documents (Holstein 1993). Thus, this project follows Holstein in paraphrasing W.I. Thomas (1931): if labels are thought to be accurate—thus "real"—they are real in their consequences (Holstein 1993:175). Of course, as discussed in Chapter Two, there are numerous criticisms of the psychiatric labeling process. These criticisms focus on the validity and reliability of psychiatric labeling and how race and gender might affect the labeling process. While the question of whether previous mental illness diagnoses are "real" or accurate is a concern in this project, the Thomas Theorem is again important to note: for the research questions posed, what is most vital is what legal agents know (e.g., that the defendant had previously been diagnosed as schizophrenic) rather than what is "really" true.

A final disadvantage to case-control methods is that they do not enable researchers to report precise rates of the event under study. This is not available in the current analysis because the selection on outcome (evaluation/no evaluation) overestimates the rate of psychiatric evaluations for felony defendants; if these data were used to estimate the rate of evaluations, we would expect that 44 percent of all felony defendants are evaluated (because 44 percent of the sample are cases), which is obviously incorrect. While this is a limitation in precise understanding of the rate of psychiatric evaluations for felony defendants, it does not interfere with answering the research questions posed in this project. Thus, for women and African Americans, we can determine the relative risk of receiving a psychiatric evaluation as compared to not receiving an evaluation. Further, a rough approximation of this rate of evaluations can be made using the 413 evaluations conducted between 1993 and 2001 and making a comparison to the total number of felony defendants in Hennepin County in the same years. This approximate rate for other states is also reported elsewhere (Callahan et al. 1991; Steadman et al. 1993; Hiday 1999). Despite these caveats, the benefits of using case-control methodology in this research setting are considerable, providing rare and valuable information about attributions of mental illness in the criminal justice system.

Research Questions

In the first chapter of this book, three primary research questions were posed related to the use of psychiatric evaluations in the criminal justice system. This project sought to answer the first two questions in Chapter Five and the third question was addressed in Chapter Six.

1. *What are the characteristics of defendants who are evaluated to determine their mental state at the time of a criminal offense?*

2. *What is the role of race and gender expectations in predicting*
    psychiatric evaluations for felony defendants?

Chapter Five considered the factors that best predict which
defendants receive a psychiatric evaluation. The goal of this chapter
was to determine whether criminal justice responses are socially
constructed so that expectations of the "typical" defendant alter
perceptions of the mental status of women and non-African Americans.
It does not appear that psychiatric history or need is the only factor
criminal justice decision-makers take into account when seeking
alternative explanations for criminal behavior. Instead, demographic,
family, economic, and criminal factors are all important in predicting
which defendants will be the recipients of psychiatric evaluations.

Gender. The results of the analysis do not consistently indicate that
women are significantly more likely than men to receive psychiatric
evaluations. In fact, the bivariate relationship shows that men are
actually more likely than women to receive these evaluations. In the
full models, females are significantly more likely to be evaluated, but
this effect is quite sensitive to the other causal variables in the model;
consequently, these results should be interpreted with caution.
Nevertheless, gender does appear to be related to receipt of psychiatric
evaluations, but indirectly through offense type, mental health, and
family status.

This research also indicates that in general, violent women are
viewed psychiatrically, but only after controlling for family status and
previous mental illness. There is also evidence that women without
children are treated psychiatrically more often than other women and
men. These results may indicate that women who violate two gender
roles by committing acts of violence *and* by failing to have traditional
nurturing relationships (i.e., have children) are considered to be
especially in need of psychiatric treatment.

One explanation for the lack of a consistent gender effect is that
the major independent variables used to measure mental health history
are dichotomies of whether the defendant had ever received a major
psychiatric diagnosis, or been hospitalized, or if the defendant acted
bizarrely at the time of the offense. These measures may be capturing
gender differences that occur earlier in this process. Women are more
likely than men to seek psychiatric help, even when holding psychiatric

need constant (Greeley and Mullen 1990; Hankin 1990). Thus, despite having a diagnosed psychiatric condition, women with a history of mental illness may be less severely affected than men with the same history, because men often wait to seek treatment until forced to do so (Horwitz 1977; Thoits 1985; Greeley and Mullen 1990; Hankin 1990). If this is the case, by including a control for prior psychiatric diagnosis this research may also be controlling for gendered differences in the likelihood of previous psychiatric diagnosis. Further, there may be gender differences in the labeling of "bizarre" behavior by police officers. While this research uses this variable as a more "objective" indicator of the defendant's behavior at the time of the offense, it is possible that police officers view certain behaviors by certain offenders as so disturbing that they highlight this strangeness in their report; conversely, if police consider an offender's behavior to be routine, they might deemphasize the oddity of this offense. Thus, if police officers consider violent women to be very bizarre, whereas violent men are expected, the inclusion of this "bizarre behavior" indictor could mask typifications made earlier in the justice system. If so, the lack of consistent significant gender effects may be a product of "overcontrolling" for these endogenous factors.

This research does, however, offer evidence to counter claims made by some feminists that women in the criminal justice system are viewed as "mad" while men are "bad." These theorists have asserted that gender differences should be expected since the legal system reflects the masculine point of view and approaches women the way men approach women (see MacKinnon 1987; 1989). There is some indication that certain types of women may receive psychiatrically-based treatment more often than other women or men, but the current research provides little support for the idea that female defendants—simply on the basis of being female—are more likely to be viewed as "mad" than male defendants. One possible explanation for the lack of a consistent gender effect is that recent changes in the criminal justice system, reflecting the presence of more women, has altered the legal system's perception of women (see Spohn 1990; Stepnick and Orcutt 1996).

It may also be the case that societal expectations have changed to the point that the notion of criminal women no longer seems contradictory or bizarre (see Spohn 1990; Goodkind 2005). In fact, recent feminist thought points to a "contemporary search for equivalence" in offending; this search for equivalence involves a social construction of women as "real criminals" whose crimes should be taken seriously and not medicalized or sexualized away (Worrall 2002:48). This search for equivalence is predicated on a symmetrical world, where men suffer from the same things as women and, conversely, women engage in the same deviant behavior as men (see MacKinnon 1987:170). Thus, men are battered just as women are battered; and men are victims of female sexual abusers just as women are victims of male sexual abusers (although in vastly different numbers). These social constructions that women can be just as criminal and violent as men began after the advent of the women's movement (see e.g., Adler 1975; Simon 1975); they are also to some extent the product of media constructions of "twisted sisters" (Worrall 2002:61). Portrayals of the few women who commit violent acts and are then generalized through inaccurate statements like the following, reported in *Psychology Today* by journalist Barry Yeoman:

> Violence by women has skyrocketed in the latter part of this century. Have they taken 'women's liberation' one step too far, or are they just showing their natural killer instinct? (1999:54, cited by Worrall [2002]).

As a result of this search for equivalence, female offenders and even violent female offenders may no longer be viewed as abnormal and thus in need of psychiatric treatment. While historically female offenders could have been typified as mentally ill, social constructions of women might have changed to the point that women are now considered normal offenders.

Age and Race. In addition to gender, legal actors develop other expectations of typical criminal defendants. Since African Americans and younger defendants are over-represented in the criminal justice population, it was hypothesized that these groups would be less likely to be evaluated since they would not be viewed as abnormal criminal defendants. This was supported for both age and race; older defendants are significantly more likely to be treated psychiatrically and to be viewed as less responsible for their offenses than younger defendants. This research finds strong and consistent evidence that African

American defendants are less likely than all others to receive psychiatric evaluations to determine mental status at the time of the offense, despite controls for mental health and criminal history. These results imply that criminal justice decision-makers have expectations about the "normal" or typical offender—based on race—and that the typical offender (African American) is held fully responsible for criminal offenses, while the atypical offender (non-African American) is thought to be less responsible for criminal offenses.

Bridges and Steen explain that "officials may have different theories about the causes of crimes for blacks and whites and perceive minority youths as more threatening than white youths." They state that this "indicates that a perceptual logic of explanation and assessment directs the disposition of offenders" (1998:568). This research contends that this assessment of offenders also occurs in the context of appraising mental health and defining criminal responsibility. By deeming some white offenders to be ill, or not culpable, criminal justice officials make decisions based on limited knowledge. Since judges and attorneys aren't typically trained in psychiatry, these decision-makers are making judgments based on past experiences and stereotypes, which are socially constructed in the course of their work. These judgments about which defendants to hold criminally responsible for their behavior and which ones to treat medically yield important information about how agents of social control respond to African American offenders; the implication of this project is that criminal justice officials may perceive African Americans as more culpable and "normal" criminals than non-African American (particularly white) offenders.

One potential consequence of expectations and attributions of criminal responsibility based on race is that differential treatment on the basis of race becomes institutionalized. As Baskin et al. (1989) demonstrated for prisoners, the institutional response to violence and aggression is disciplinary confinement for men and mental health institutionalization for females engaging in similar behavior. If the criminal justice system is similarly responding to criminal defendants on the basis of race and assigns different levels of responsibility to defendants based on expectations of the "normal" defendant, there are serious consequences for the criminal justice system. For example, if the justice system assumes rationality for African Americans, it will fail to treat mental illness among these offenders. As discussed in Chapter Two, the idea that some offenders should be excused from criminal culpability because of their mental state has long been recognized in criminal law. These offenders are considered morally blameless for their wrongful conduct (Smith 1985; Palermo and Knudten 1994; Finkel and Slobogin 1995). This research indicates that African Americans do not have access to this opportunity to be found blameless. Instead, African Americans appear to be considered "typical" criminals who are held fully accountable for their crimes.

Policy. The results of this project indicate that legal agents use typifications of some defendants as "normal" offenders and some defendants as "abnormal" or mentally ill. This is especially true for African American defendants who are significantly less likely to be psychiatrically evaluated than non-African Americans. Because this attribution reflects an assumption on the part of legal agents about the level of responsibility African American defendants assume, it might result in more punitive treatment for African Americans, who are considered fully responsible for their conduct. Further, these racial differences in attributions may reinforce social constructions of "normal" or typical defendants, resulting in negative outcomes for African Americans across a wide range of social indicators such as housing, employment, and income (see Emerson et al. 2001; Quillian and Pager 2001; Kerley et al. 2004; Pager 2004). Thus, to lessen some of this differential treatment within the criminal justice system, one policy option would be to increase awareness of racial differences in attribution of mental illness among legal agents. This could result in a more systematic psychiatric labeling process in the criminal justice system. For example, if every felony defendant, or those charged with offenses such as homicide, in the criminal justice system received a brief screen for mental illness, this would help the justice system gauge possible illness, regardless of gender and racial typifications that might color interpretation of events and behaviors. Defendants with indications of mental illness could then be looked at more closely to determine whether a full mental illness evaluation is necessary. Of course, this would also be subject to typifications of "normalcy," but a more objective screening process would at least allow some defendants—especially African Americans—to have their criminal responsibility questioned before sentences are imposed.

3. *How does receipt of a psychiatric evaluation alter case outcomes?*

Chapter Six examines Black's theory of law and its contention that as psychiatric controls increase, legal controls will decrease. This perspective is not supported by the current research. The effect of a psychiatric evaluation to determine mental status at the time of the offense significantly predicts all modeled case outcomes. Receipt of a psychiatric evaluation reduces the likelihood of defendants having the charges against them dismissed. This evaluation also increases the likelihood of a guilty outcome, a prison sentence, and a lengthier sentence. These outcomes appear to provide stronger support for the notion that raising this issue of mental illness actually harms criminal defendants, in particular those defendants who do not successfully plead NGRI. Thus, this project provides some support for labeling theory with its emphasis on labels and how they can have negative effects other than the creation or maintenance of deviance (Link 1982:202; Walsh 1990; Rosenfield 1997).

Thus, this research does not support Donald Black's notion that the law and psychiatry are two opposing systems that meet and compete in an adversarial process (1976). Instead, these two systems may actually work together in a treatment-control system to "take care of" problem cases (Dallaire et al. 2000). Thus, psychiatric evaluation reports may focus on the need for psychiatric treatment for these "problem" defendants. This psychiatric treatment may best be met—according to psychiatrists—through incarceration (Menzies 1989; Steadman et al. 1999; Arrigo 2002).

Defense attorneys may also be reluctant to waste their hard-earned capital on mentally ill defendants. These attorneys may view themselves as intermediaries between the court and the accused, and their job is to assist the system in dealing with these offenders (Laberge and Morin 2001). Because people with mental health problems are perceived by legal actors as difficult, the defense may consider it important to spare their "partners"—the judge and prosecution—by pushing for an expeditious conclusion to the case (Laberge and Morin 2001; see Spohn 1990). This may result in the defense attorney advocating for a guilty plea from the defendant, in order to ensure immediate psychiatric treatment (Laberge and Morin 2001). Defense attorneys may consider it beneficial to their clients to receive a sentence where treatment is possible; prison sentences may serve a function of providing access to psychiatric treatment that would not be provided on the outside. This response is guided by a medical ideology, which contends that it is safer to treat someone who may be mentally ill than it is to fail to treat someone who is mentally ill (Holstein 1993). Thus, the criminal justice system and eventual incarceration are often seen as the best option for mentally ill individuals with diminishing access to hospital care (Laberge and Morin 2001).

The results of this research indicate that psychiatric evaluations do increase the severity of punishment.[2] This is of particular concern because the decision to request this evaluation is often forced on the defendant. Bonnie et al. (1996) found that when approached with the idea of a defense of insanity, 10 percent of defendants resisted the plea. Another 15 percent were unreceptive to the attribution of mental illness. These researchers found that when the decision was made to pursue the defense, the attorneys pre-empted their clients' participation in the decision-making process in 36 percent of the cases, acting in the absence of consultation (Bonnie et al. 1996). Even when the client was consulted, the degree of participation was relatively low; they attribute this behavior to "a distinct tendency toward paternalistic decision-making in cases involving defendants with documented histories of serious mental illness" (Bonnie et al. 1996). With 35 percent of U.S. jurisdictions permitting the insanity defense to be imposed on an unwilling defendant, even defendants who are competent to make an informed decision regarding whether they wish to utilize the insanity defense are not always free to choose (Miller et al. 1996). These results imply that attorneys, and especially defense attorneys, have enormous power in determining who receives a psychiatric evaluations and who proceeds with a mental illness defense in a criminal trial. Consequently, decision-makers in the criminal justice system may inadvertently be causing differential treatment on the basis of a perceived mental illness. In an attempt to determine whether the mental health or criminal justice system should have control over offenders who might be mentally ill, decision-makers may force psychiatric evaluations and unknowingly cause disparity in case outcome.

Policy. Because the current research points to the negative consequences of a psychiatric evaluation on criminal justice treatment—with more severe treatment imposed on those with an evaluation—legal agents may be choosing to seek imprisonment as an additional level of social control. In an era of decreased community psychiatric care (Tausig et al. 1999; Cockerham 2000), prison may be the best method of ensuring that mentally ill defendants receive some form of institutionalization and possibly some psychiatric treatment (Cockerham 2000).[3] Consequently, the best policy for reducing institutionalization of these offenders who were psychiatrically evaluated but not found NGRI might be to ensure sufficient treatment opportunities within the community. If legal agents have the option of community treatment rather than simply institutionalization for "problem" defendants, the negative effect of psychiatric evaluations on criminal sentences might be eliminated and these defendants might receive necessary psychiatric treatment.

Reconciling Chapters Five and Six

Chapter Five explained that psychiatric evaluations are important to study because they represent the assumptions of legal agents and typifications of female and African American defendants as either "normal" or "abnormal" offenders. This project particularly finds that African Americans are less likely to be psychiatrically evaluated than non-African Americans. Chapter Six examines the effect psychiatric evaluations have on case outcome and find that these evaluations result in negative case outcomes in terms of prospects for freedom. Does this mean that African Americans actually benefit from the psychiatric evaluation process? This researcher argues that the answer is "no" because these results indicate that the legal agents do indeed rely on typifications of defendants to alter case outcome. Thus, regardless of the apparent negative final outcome for the evaluated defendants, the fact that African Americans are less likely to be evaluated signals an assumption on the part of legal agents that African Americans are "normal" criminals and therefore fully responsible for their criminal actions. As a result, even if some individual African Americans "benefit" from more lenient sentences[4] (in comparison to those non-African Americans who are evaluated and sentenced to longer imprisonment), overall, the assumption that they are expected criminals has significant implications for *all* African Americans—even those not in the criminal justice system.

Recommendations for Future Research

An issue of critical importance in the sociology of law and social control is the role of institutions such as the courts in reflecting and reproducing the patterns of inequality present in the larger society (Bridges and Steen 1998). If legal decision-making by court officials is altered by perceptions of the offender, we must question the legitimacy of these perceptions and the system in which they are situated. It is conceivable that these typifications speed up the criminal justice process and thereby provide some benefit to society. When these perceptions result in detrimental criminal penalties for certain groups, however, the desirability of these attributions is questionable. Therefore, we clearly need additional research on legal decision-making, detailing how court officials define and treat criminal offenders.

To advance sociological understanding of attributions of mental illness among agents of social control and address questions unanswered in this project, future research should respond to at least four general questions.

First: How do lawyers and judges reach the decision to seek an evaluation? This might be answered using the vignette approach that Loring and Powell (1988) use to examine race and gender differences in mental illness attributions by psychiatrists. Using this approach, descriptions of clients would be sent to lawyers and judges; each vignette would be exactly the same, with the exception of the gender and race of the case. This type of research would provide some verification and clarification that race and possibly gender influence the likelihood of psychiatric evaluation.

Second: Is the lack of consistent gender effects in this project due to an insufficient number of female (especially violent female) cases? A similar analysis with a larger sampling of violent female defendants would provide evidence to answer this question.

Third: Which label (criminal justice or mental illness) results in the worst stigma? As discussed in Chapter Three, labeling theory implies that those with the least amount of power to resist a label are the most likely to receive a negative label. It is unclear, however, if an evaluation (and the corresponding mental illness label) are worse for a defendant than the criminal label. Link's work suggests that widely held perceptions of dangerousness may play a role in the public's unwillingness to interact with people with mental illness (Link et al. 1999b). It is uncertain, however, whether this unwillingness to interact with mentally ill individuals is greater than the unwillingness to interact with criminals (Emerson et al. 2001; Quillian and Pager 2001). This question could be addressed through survey questions designed to measure the public's willingness to interact with people with either a mental illness or criminal history. Martin, Pescosolido, and Tuch (2000), for example, ask respondents about mentally ill individuals and if they are willing to: live next door to them, make friends with them, spend an evening with them, work closely with them, have a group home in their neighborhoods, and have this person marry into the family. Similar questions could be asked about various types of ex-offenders (e.g., sex offenders, burglars, and drug offenders) and compared for the degree of desired social distance.

Lastly, future research should ask: What are the long-term consequences of criminal labels as compared to NGRI outcomes? Eric Silver compares length of hospital confinement for NGRI acquittees to length of imprisonment for similar convicted offenders and reports that some jurisdictions hold insanity acquittees longer than convicts, while other jurisdictions hold convicted offenders for lengthier periods; Silver also reports that in some jurisdictions there are no differences in length of confinement between these populations (1995). Because these findings remain contradictory, future research should focus on this question in greater detail, drawing on what has been learned the current research. Thus, future investigations might question whether African Americans found NGRI are involuntarily hospitalized longer than similar African American offenders who are convicted of their offense and sentenced to prison. Further, this research might question how differences in case outcome (NGRI and hospitalization versus conviction and imprisonment) affect behavior and prospects post-release. For example, are ex-patients or ex-prisoners more likely to be hired for the same job? How do these different treatments affect criminal recidivism and future mental status?

SUMMARY OF MAJOR FINDINGS

Link et al. (1987) group labeling theory's important debates into two broad questions: (1) who gets labeled? and (2) what are the consequences of this label? This research responds to both of these questions by considering two institutions of social control: the mental health system and the criminal justice system; three major findings are highlighted. First, although related to psychiatric evaluations, gender alone does not significantly affect psychiatric evaluations for felony defendants. Despite this, it remains possible that legal agents view female offenders as irrational. Some evidence indicates that gender works through family status: women without families are more likely to be evaluated than men without families; as Schur (1984) explains, women without families are considered to be especially deviant. The failure to find a consistent gender effect may be a limitation of the data, with an insufficient number of violent women and women with and without families. Another possibility is that the status of women in the criminal justice system has changed to reflect more general social changes in the status of women. As a result, legal agents might no longer view criminal females—even violent ones—as so aberrant that they require investigation into the cause of the offense. Also, as discussed in Chapter Four, Minnesota tends to be more progressive on gender issues than other states. As a result, the notion of passive women who are economically dependent on their spouses may be less salient for Minnesotans. Legal agents in Minnesota might be less inclined to perceive criminal women as abnormal compared to legal agents in a state with more with more "traditional" gender expectations. Nevertheless, there is some evidence of a gender effect on receipt of a psychiatric evaluation; the strength of this finding, however, varies under different specifications and should therefore be interpreted with caution.

A second major finding in this research project is that African Americans are significantly less likely than non-African Americans to be psychiatrically evaluated. Under several specifications African Americans, regardless of gender, are less likely to be evaluated. This is true despite controls for criminal history and mental illness. Thus, it would appear that legal agents have developed typifications of "normal" or "expected" defendants, which include African Americans.

Consequently, when faced with these defendants decision-makers assume they are responsible for the offense and do not seek alternative explanations. This race difference is a strong and robust finding and provides compelling evidence of racial attributions of criminal culpability.

Finally, this research finds that offenders who receive psychiatric evaluations but are not deemed NGRI tend to receive harsher punishment than similar non-evaluated offenders. There appears to be a punitive response to defendants who utilize this psychiatric option and either fail with the attempt or decide against continuing down this path. One possible explanation can be drawn from defendants who refuse to plead guilty and consequently receive harsher treatment for taking up the court's resources (see e.g., Engen et al. 2003); the defendants analyzed in this project also appear to "waste the court's time" in seeking extra attention that is not afforded to all offenders. Whereas defendants who are "truthfully" mentally ill and unable to control their behavior (at least in the eyes of the court) might be accorded pity or lenient treatment, these defendants who are now apparently responsible for causing their condition are therefore viewed as wasting time and resources, resulting in negative consequences (see Corrigan et al. 2003).

While these defendants are deemed responsible for their offenses, most are still considered to be mentally ill. While only 46 (11.2 percent) of those evaluated were found NGRI, the vast majority of defendants who were evaluated *did* receive a diagnosis from the evaluator.[5] Of the 350 evaluated offenders who were *not* found NGRI, only 36 (10.3 percent) received no diagnosis from the psychologist or psychiatrist conducting the evaluation. Consequently, it is possible that legal agents, desiring some type of treatment for these problematic mentally ill (but legally sane) offenders, seek outcomes that require institutionalization, where some sort of treatment program might be implemented.

CONCLUSION

This research provides evidence that legal agents—facing organizational constraints such as limited information about defendants and brief periods in which to make decisions—may view defendants in terms of socially constructed typifications to reduce uncertainty in their decision-making process (Kramer and Ulmer 1996:98; see also Miethe 1987). These results also point to some differences in the criteria used to judge the behavior of felony defendants. African Americans are significantly less likely to be psychiatrically evaluated than non-African Americans, indicating that decision-makers in the criminal justice system expect African Americans to be criminals: that is, they are thought to be "normal" criminals. In addition, the use of psychiatry in the legal system seems to provide support for increased social control of felony defendants. Rather than reducing punitive sanctions, psychiatric evaluations within the criminal justice system increase sentence severity for felony defendants.

Feeley and Simon (1992) argue that the penal system has moved from an individualistic system of punishment to a managerial type of incapacitive justice; rather than a concern for punishing individuals, the criminal justice system has developed into a system for the management of aggregates of dangerous groups. Similarly, this research indicates that the legal system relies on typifications of "normal" offenders and on psychiatry to manage those deemed to be mentally ill. To the extent that female criminality deviates from that of males, and African Americans differ from non-African Americans, this would warrant a differential response from the legal system. Basing such decisions on assumptions associated with the defendant's race or gender raises legal and ethical problems reflective of enduring social inequalities.

NOTES

[1] This research was unable to collect any information on which actor in the justice system made the decision to seek a psychiatric evaluation. Some research on the courtroom workgroup suggests that this may not be a significant factor. For example, Spohn provides some evidence of the "powerful influence of socialization on the legal profession and on the judicial role" (Spohn 1990:98), in that discretion is limited by informal agreements among members of the courtroom workgroup. Thus, which defendants to send for mental health evaluations may be commonly agreed upon by the courtroom workgroup.

[2] On the basis of this research, the possible beneficial aspects that receipt of psychiatric treatment has on NGRI acquittees cannot be addressed, although most would argue that psychiatric treatment is more beneficial for mentally ill individuals than prison or jail time (Torrey et al. 1992; Hodgins 1993; U.S. Department of Justice 1997a).

[3] This assumption that inmates will receive some mental health treatment in prison is supported by the available evidence. According to the U.S. Department of Justice (2001), 95 percent of state adult confinement facilities screen inmates for mental health problems. Due to these screens, 1 in 10 state inmates receive psychotropic medications and 1 in 8 receive mental health therapy or counseling (U.S. Department of Justice 2001:1).

[4] It should also be noted here that even in the analysis that controls for the lower likelihood of African Americans to be in the evaluation population, the direct effect of race *still* results in stricter sentences for African Americans relative to non-African Americans.

[5] There is considerable variation in the type of mental illness, however, for those who received a diagnosis. Overall, 33 percent received a mood disorder, 35 percent schizophrenia or psychosis, 39 percent personality disorder, and 45 percent substance abuse (these numbers sum to more than 100 percent because multiple diagnoses are possible for each defendant).

BIBLIOGRAPHY

Adler, Freda. 1975. *Sisters in Crime*. New York: McGraw-Hill.

Albonetti, Celesta A. 1997. "Sentencing Under the Federal Sentencing Guidelines: Effects of Defendant Characteristics, Guilty Pleas, and Departures on Sentence Outcomes for Drug Offenses, 1991-1992." *Law & Society Review* 31:789-824.

Albonetti, Celesta A. and John R. Hepburn. 1996. "Prosecutorial Discretion to Defer Criminalization: The Effects of Defendant's Ascribed and Achieved Status Characteristics." *Journal of Quantitative Criminology* 12:63-81.

Alcoff, Linda. 1988. "Cultural Feminism versus Post-Structuralism. The Identity Crisis in Feminist Theory." *Signs* 13:405-436.

American Psychiatric Association. 1994. *Diagnostic and Statistical Manual of Mental Disorders: DSM-IV.* Washington, DC: American Psychiatric Press.

Aneshensel, Carol S., Carolyn M. Rutter, and Peter A. Lachenbruch. 1991. "Social Structure, Stress, and Mental Health: Competing Conceptual and Analytical Models." *American Sociological Review* 56:166-78.

Arrigo, Bruce. 2002. *Punishing the Mentally Ill: A Critical Analysis of Law and Psychiatry.* Albany, NY: State University of New York Press.

Baskin, Deborah R., Ira Sommers, Richard Tessler, and Henry J. Steadman. 1989. "Role Incongruence and Gender Variation in the Provision of Prison Mental Health Services." *Journal of Health and Social Behavior* 30: 305-314.

Becker, Howard S. 1963. *Outsiders: Studies in the Sociology of Deviance.* New York: The Free Press.

Becker, Gary. 1971. *The Economics of Discrimination.* 2d ed. Chicago: University of Chicago Press.

_____. 1985. "Human Capital, Effort and the Sexual Division of Labor." *Journal of Labor Economics* 3:S33-S58.

Berberoglu, Linda, Mary Alice Conroy, and Michael Schaefer. 1998. "Treating Incompetence to Stand Trial: Development and Use of Psycholegal Games." Presented at the American Psychology-Law Society Biennial Conference, Redondo Beach, FL.

Bickle, Gayle and Ruth D. Peterson. 1991. "The Impact of Gender Based Family Roles on Criminal Sentencing." *Social Problems* 38:372-394.

Black, Donald. 1976. *The Behavior of Law.* New York: Academic Press.

Blakey, Katherine P. 1996. "The Indefinite Civil Commitment of Dangerous Sex Offenders is an Appropriate Legal Compromise Between "Mad" and "Bad"—A Study of Minnesota's Sexual Psychopathic Personality Statute." *Notre Dame Journal of Law, Ethics and Public Policy* 10:227.

Blau, George L. and Hugh McGinley. 1995. "Use of the Insanity Defense: A Survey of Attorneys in Wyoming." *Behavioral Sciences and the Law* 13:517-528.

Bloom, Joseph D. and Mary H. Williams. 1994. *Management and Treatment of Insanity Acquittees: A Model for the 1990s.* Washington, DC: American Psychiatric Press.

Blumstein, Alfred. 1982. "On the Racial Disproportionality of U.S. Prisons' Populations." *Journal of Criminal Law and Criminology* 73:1259-1281.

Boehnert, Caryl E. 1989. "Characteristics of Successful and Unsuccessful Insanity Pleas." *Law & Human Behavior* 13:31-39.

Bonnie, Richard J., Norman G. Poythress, Steven K. Hoge, John Monahan, and Marlene M. Eisenberg. 1996. "Decision-Making in Criminal Defense: An Empirical Study of Insanity Pleas and the Impact of Doubted Client Competence." *Journal of Criminal Law & Criminology* 87:48-62.

Boritch, Helen. 1992. "Gender and Criminal Court Outcomes An Historical Analysis." *Criminology* 30:293-326.

Boritch, Helen and John Hagan. 1990. "A Century of Crime in Toronto: Gender, Class, and Patterns of Social Control, 1859-1955." *Criminology* 28: 567-599.

Borum, Randy and Solomon M. Fulero. 1999. "Empirical Research on the Insanity Defense and Attempted Reforms: Evidence toward Informed Policy." *Law & Human Behavior* 23:117-135.

Bourdon, K. H., D. S. Rae, B. Z. Locke, W.E. Narrow, and Darrel A. Reiger (1992). "Estimating the Prevalence of Mental Disorders in U.S. Adults from the Epidemiologic Catchment Area Study." *Public Health Report* 107:663-8.

Braff, Jeraldine, Thomas Arvanites, and Henry J. Steadman. 1983. "Detention Patterns of Successful and Unsuccessful Insanity Defendants." *Criminology* 21:439-448.

Bridges, George S. and Gina Beretta. 1994. "Gender, Race, and Social Control: Toward an Understanding of Sex Disparities in Imprisonment." Pp. 158-175 in *Inequality, Crime and Social Control* (Crime and Society Series), edited by George S. Bridges and Martha A. Meyers. Boulder, CO: Westview Press.

Bridges, George S. and Sara Steen. 1998. "Racial Disparities in Official Assessments of Juvenile Offenders: Attributional Stereotypes as Mediating Mechanisms." *American Sociological Review* 63:554-570.

Brown, George W. and Tirril Harris. 1978. *Social Origins of Depression: A Study of Psychiatric Disorder in Women.* New York: The Free Press.

Burns, Jan. 1992. "Mad or Just Plain Bad: Gender and the Work of Forensic Clinical Psychologists." in *Gender Issues in Clinical Psychology,* edited by J.M. Ussher and P. Nicolson. London: Routledge.

Burton, Velmer S. 1990. "The Consequences of Official Labels: A Research Note on Rights Lost by the Mentally Ill, Mentally Incompetent, and Convicted Felons." *Community Mental Health Journal* 26:267-276.

Busfield, Joan. 1988. "Mental Illness as Social Product of Social Construct: A Contradiction in Feminists' Arguments?" *Sociology of Health and Illness* 10:521-542.

Bushway, Shawn D. and Anne Morrison Piehl. 2001. "Judging Judicial Discretion: Legal Factors and Racial Discrimination in Sentencing." *Law & Society Review* 35:733-764.

Caesar, B. 1982. "The Insanity Defense: The New Loophole." *The Prosecutor* 16:19-26.

Callahan, Lisa A. and Eric Silver. 1998. "Factors Associated with the Conditional Release of Persons Acquitted by Reason of Insanity: A Decision-Tree Approach." *Law & Human Behavior* 22:147-163.

Callahan, Lisa A., Henry J. Steadman, Margaret A. McGreevy, and Pamela Clark Robbins. 1991. "The Volume and Characteristics of Insanity Defense Pleas: An Eight-State Study." *Bulletin of the American Academy of Psychiatry and Law* 19:331-338.

Campbell, M.J., S.A. Julious, and D.G. Altman. 1995. "Estimating Sample Sizes for Binary, Ordered Categorical, and Continuous Outcomes in Two Group Comparisons." *British Medical Journal* 311:1145-1148.

Carlen, Pat, ed. 2002a. *Women and Punishment: The Struggle for Justice.* Portland, OR: Willan Publishing.

Carlen, Pat. 2002b. "Introduction: Women and Punishment." Pp. 3-20 in *Women and Punishment: The Struggle for Justice,* edited by Pat Carlen. Portland, OR: Willan Publishing.

Carroll, R.J., Suojin Wang, and C.Y. Wang. 1995. "Prospective Analysis of Logistic Case-Control Studies." *Journal of the American Statistical Association* 90:157-169.

Chan, Wendy. 1994. "A Feminist Critique of Self-Defense and Provocation in Battered Women's Cases in England and Wales." *Women & Criminal Justice* 6:39-65.

Chan, Wendy. 1999. "Gender, Murder and Madness." Presented at the annual meeting of the American Society of Criminology, Toronto, Canada.

Chesney-Lind, Meda and Randall G. Shelden. 1998. *Girls, Delinquency, and Juvenile Justice.* Belmont, CA: Wadsworth Publishing Company.

Chiricos, Ted and Sarah Eschholz. 2002. "The Racial and Ethnic Typification of Crime and the Criminal Typification of Race and Ethnicity in Local Television News." *Journal of Research in Crime and Delinquency* 39:400-420.

Chiricos, Ted, Ranee McEntire, and Marc Gertz. 2001. "Perceived Racial and Ethnic Composition of Neighborhood and Perceived Risk of Crime." *Social Problems* 48:322-340.

Chiricos, Ted, Kelly Welch, and Marc Gertz. 2004. "Racial Typification of Crime and Support for Punitive Measures." *Criminology* 42:359-390.

Cirincione, Carmen. 1996. "Revisiting the Insanity Defense: Contested or Consensus?" *Bulletin of the American Academy of Psychiatry and Law* 24:165-176.

Cirincione, Carmen, Henry J. Steadman, and Margaret A. McGreevy. 1995. "Rates of Insanity Acquittals and the Factors Associated with Successful Insanity Pleas." *Bulletin of the American Academy of Psychiatry and Law* 23:399-409.

Cirincione, Carmen, Henry J. Steadman, and John Monahan. 1994. "Mental Illness as a Factor in Criminality: A Study of Prisoners and Mental Patients." *Criminal Behaviour and Mental Health* 4:33-47.

Cirincione, Carmen, Henry J. Steadman, Pamela Clark Robbins, and John Monahan. 1992. "Schizophrenia as a Contingent Risk Factor for Criminal Violence." *International Journal of Law and Psychiatry* 15:347-358.

Clark, Charles R., Carol E. Holden, Judith S. Thompson, Patricia L. Watson, and Lois H. Wightman. 1993. "Forensic Treatment in the United States: A

Survey of Selected Forensic Hospitals." *International Journal of Law and Psychiatry* 16:71-81.

Clegg, Stewart and David Dunkerley. 1980. *Organization, Class and Control.* Boston, MA: Routledge and Kegan Paul.

Cloward, Richard A. and Frances F. Piven. 1979. "Hidden Protest: The Channeling of Female Innovation and Resistance." *Signs* 4:651-669.

Cockerham, William C. 1990. "A Test of the Relationship Between Race, Socioeconomic Status, and Psychological Distress." *Social Science and Medicine* 31:1321-26.

_____. 2000. *Sociology of Mental Disorder.* 5th ed. Upper Saddle River, NJ: Prentice Hall.

Collins, Patricia Hill. 1997. "Defining Black Feminist Thought." Pp. 241-259 in *The Second Wave,* edited by Linda Nicholson. New York: Routledge.

_____. 1998. *Fighting Words: Black Women and the Search for Justice.* Minneapolis, MN: University of Minnesota Press.

_____. 2000. *Black Feminist Thought: Knowledge, Consciousness, and the Politics of Empowerment.* 2nd ed. New York: Routledge.

Conrad, Peter. 1975. "The Discovery of Hyperkinesis: Notes on the Medicalization of Deviant Behavior." *Social Problems* 23:12-21.

Corley, Charles J., Stephen Cernkovich, and Peggy Giordano. 1989. "Sex and the Likelihood of Sanction." *Journal of Criminal Law & Criminology* 80:540-556.

Corrigan, Patrick, Fred E. Markowitz, Amy Watson, David Rowan, and Mary Ann Kubiak. 2003. "An Attribution Model of Public Discrimination." *Journal of Health and Social Behavior* 44:162-179.

Crew, B. Keith. 1991. "Sex Differences in Criminal Sentencing: Chivalry or Patriarchy?" *Justice Quarterly* 8:59-83.

Dahl, Peter R. 1985. "Legal and Psychiatric Concepts and the Use of Psychiatric Evidence in Criminal Trials." *California Law Review* 73:411-442.

Dallaire, Bernadette, Michael McCubbin, Paul Morin, and David Cohen. 2000. "Civil Commitment Due to Mental Illness and Dangerousness: The Union of Law and Psychiatry within a Treatment-Control System." *Sociology of Health and Illness* 22:679-699.

Daly, Kathleen. 1987. "Structure and Practice of Familial-Based Justice in a Criminal Court." *Law & Society Review* 21:267-290.

_____. 1989. "Neither Conflict Nor Labeling Nor Paternalism Will Suffice: Intersections of Race, Ethnicity, Gender, and Family in Criminal Court Decisions." *Crime & Delinquency* 35:136-168.

_____. 1994. *Gender, Crime, and Punishment*.: New Haven, CT: Yale University Press.

Daly, Kathleen and Rebecca L. Bordt. 1995. "Sex Effects and Sentencing: An Analysis of the Statistical Literature." *Justice Quarterly* 12:141-175.

Daly, Kathleen and Michael Tonry. 1997. "Gender, Race and Sentencing." Pp. 201-252 in *Crime and Justice*, vol. 22, edited by Michael Tonry. Chicago, IL: University of Chicago Press.

Daly, Martin and Margo Wilson. 1988. *Homicide*. New York: Aldine De Gruyter.

Dixon, T.L., C.L. Azocar, and M. Casas. 2003. "The Portrayal of Race and Crime on Television Network News." *Journal of Broadcasting & Electronic Media* 47:498-523.

Dohrenwend, Bruce P. and Barbara Snell Dohrenwend. 1969. *Social Status of Psychological Disorder*. New York: Wiley.

_____. eds. 1974. *Stressful Life Events: Their Nature and Effects*. New York: Wiley.

_____. 1976. "Sex Differences and Psychiatric Disorders." *American Journal of Sociology* 81:1447-58.

Eaton, William W., Christian Ritter, and Diane Brown. 1990. "Psychiatric Epidemiology and Psychiatric Sociology: Influences on the Recognition of Bizarre Behaviors as Social Problems." *Research in Community and Mental Health* 6:41-68.

Edelman, Lauren B., Christopher Uggen, and Howard S. Erlanger. 1999. "The Endogeneity of Legal Regulation: Grievance Procedures as Rational Myth." *American Journal of Sociology* 105:405-54.

Edwards, Susan. 1986. "Neither Bad Nor Mad: The Female Violent Offender Reassessed." *Women's Studies International Forum* 9:79-87.

Eigen, Joel Peter. 1999. "Lesion of the Will: Medical Resolve and Criminal Responsibility in Victorian Insanity Trials." *Law & Society Review* 33:425-459.

Elliott, Carl. 1996. *The Rules of Insanity: Moral Responsibility and the Mentally Ill Offender*. Albany, NY: State University of New York Press.

Engen, Rodney L. and Randy R. Gainey. 2000. "Modeling the Effects of Legally Relevant and Extralegal Factors under Sentencing Guidelines: The Rules Have Changed." *Criminology* 38:1207-29.

Engen, Rodney L., Randy R. Gainey, Robert D. Crutchfield, and Joseph G. Weis. 2003. "Discretion and Disparity Under Sentencing Guidelines: The Role of Departures and Structured Sentencing Alternatives." *Criminology* 41:99-130.

Erez, Edna. 1989. "Gender, Rehabilitation and Probation Decisions." *Criminology* 27:307-327.

_____. 1992. "Dangerous Men, Evil Women: Gender and Parole Decision-Making." *Justice Quarterly* 9:105-126.

Ewing. 1983. "'Dr. Death' and the Case for an Ethical Ban on Psychiatric and Psychological Predictions of Dangerousness in Capital Sentencing Proceedings." *American Journal of Law and Medicine* 8:407-508.

Faris, Robert E.L. and H. Warren Dunham. 1939. *Mental Disorders in Urban Areas: An Ecological Study of Schizophrenia and Other Psychoses.* Chicago, IL: University of Chicago Press.

Farnworth, Margaret and Raymond H.C. Teske, Jr. 1995. "Gender Differences in Felony Court Processing: Three Hypotheses of Disparity." *Women and Criminal Justice* 6:23-44.

Farrell, Ronald A. and Victoria L. Swigert. 1977. "Normal Homicides and the Law." *American Sociological Review* 42:16-32.

_____. 1978. "Prior Offense as a Self-Fulfilling Prophecy." *Law & Society Review* 12:437-53.

_____. 1986. "Adjudication in Homicide: An Interpretive Analysis of the Effects of Defendant and Victim Social Characteristics." *Journal of Research in Crime and Delinquency* 23:349-369.

Feeley, Malcolm M. and Deborah L. Little. 1991. "The Vanishing Female: The Decline of Women in the Criminal Process, 1687-1912." *Law & Society Review* 25:719-757.

Feeley, Malcolm M. and Jonathan Simon. 1992. "The New Penology: Notes on the Emerging Strategy of Corrections and its Implications." *Criminology* 30: 449-474.

Finkel, Norman J. 1991. "The Insanity Defense: A Comparison of Verdict Schemas." *Law & Human Behavior* 15:533-555.

Finkel, Norman J. and Christopher Slobogin. 1995. "Insanity, Justification, and Culpability: Toward a Unifying Schema." *Law & Human Behavior* 19:447-464.

Frazier, P.A. and J.S. Hunt. 1998. "Research on Gender and the Law: Where Are We Going, Where Have We Been?" *Law & Human Behavior* 22:1-16.

Freeman, Richard J. and Ronald Roesch. 1989. "Mental Disorder and the Criminal Justice System: A Review." *International Journal of Law and Psychiatry* 12:105-115.

Frerichs, Robert, Carol Aneshensel, and Virginia A. Clark. 1981. "Prevalence of Depression in Los Angeles County." *American Journal of Epidemiology* 113:691-99.

Freud, Sigmund. 1963. *Dora: An Analysis of a Case of Hysteria*. New York: Macmillan.

Gallagher, Bernard. 2002. *The Sociology of Mental Illness*. 4th ed. Upper Saddle River, NJ: Prentice Hall.

Gallo, C. 1982. "The Insanity of the Insanity Defense." *The Prosecutor* 16:6-13.

Gilligan, Carol. 1982. *In a Different Voice*. Cambridge, MA: Harvard University Press.

Goffman, Erving. 1963. *Stigma*. New York: Simon & Schuster, Inc.

Goodkind, Sara. 2005. "Gender-Specific Services in the Juvenile Justice System: A Critical Examination." *Affilia* 20:52-70.

Goodman, Richard A., James A. Mercy, Peter M. Layde, and Stephen B. Thacker. 1988. "Case-Control Studies: Design Issues for Criminological Applications." *Journal of Quantitative Criminology* 4:71-84.

Gottfredson, Michael R. and Travis Hirschi. 1990. *A General Theory of Crime*. Stanford, CA: Stanford University Press.

Gove, Walter. 1970. "Societal Reaction as an Explanation of Mental Illness: An Evaulation." *American Sociological Review* 35:873-84.

_____. 1980. "Labeling Mental Illness: A Critique." Pp. 53-109 in *Labeling Deviant Behavior*, edited by Walter R. Gove. Beverly Hills, CA: Sage.

_____. 1982. "The Current Status of the Labelling Theory of Mental Illness." Pp. 273-300 in *Deviance and Mental Illness*, edited by Walter R. Gove. Beverly Hills, CA: Sage.

Gove, Walter R. and Jeannette F. Tudor. 1973. "Adult Sex Roles and Mental Illness." *American Journal of Sociology* 78:812-35.

Greeley, James R. and Julia A. Mullen. 1990. "Help-Seeking and the Use of Mental Health Services." *Research in Community and Mental Health* 6:325-50.

Hagan, John. 1991. "Destiny and Drift: Subcultural Preferences, Status Attainments, and the Risks and Rewards of Youth." *American Sociological Review* 56:567-582.

Hagan, John, A.R. Gillis, and John Simpson. 1985. "The Class Structure of Gender and Delinquency: Toward a Power-Control Theory of Common Delinquent Behavior." *American Journal of Sociology* 90:1151-1178.

Hanke, Penelope J. 1995. "Sentencing Disparities by Race of Offender and Victim: Women Homicide Offenders in Alabama, 1929-1985." *Sociological Spectrum* 15:277-297.

Hankin, Janet R. 1990. "Gender and Mental Illness." *Research in Community and Mental Health* 6:183-201.

Hans, Valerie P. 1986. "An Analysis of Public Attitudes Toward the Insanity Defense." *Criminology* 24:393-414.

Hardy, Melissa A. 1989. "Estimating Selection Effects in Occupational Mobility in a 19th Century City." *American Sociological Review* 54:834-843.

Harris, Anthony R. 1977. "Sex and Theories of Deviance: Toward a Functional Theory of Deviant Type-Scripts." *American Sociological Review* 42:3-16.

Harris, Angela P. 1990. "Race and Essentialism in Feminist Legal Theory." *Stanford Law Review* 42:11-18.

Hartmann, Heidi. 1981. *Women and Revolution.* Boston, MA: South End Press.

Hawkins, Richard and Gary Tiedeman. 1975. *The Creation of Deviance.* Columbus, OH: Charles E. Merrill.

Heath, Linda, Candace Kruttschnitt, and David Ward. 1986. "Television and Violent Criminal Behavior: Beyond the Bobo Doll." *Violence and Victims* 1:177-190.

Hiday, Virginia Aldigé. 1999. "Mental Illness and the Criminal Justice System." Pp. 508-525 in *A Handbook for the Study of Mental Health: Social Contexts, Theories and Symptoms,* edited by Allan V. Horwitz and Teresa L. Sheid. New York: Cambridge University Press.

Hill, Gary D., Anthony R. Harris and JoAnn L. Miller. 1985. "The Etiology of Bias: Social Heuristics and Rational Decision Making in Deviance Processing." *Journal of Research in Crime and Delinquency* 22:135-162.

Hochstedler, Ellen. 1986. "Criminal Prosecution of the Mentally Disordered." *Law & Society Review* 20:279-292.

Hodgins, Sheilagh. 1993. "Mental Health Treatment Services in Quebec for Persons Accused or Convicted of Criminal Offenses." *International Journal of Law and Psychiatry* 16:179-194.

Hollingshead, August B. and Frederick C. Redlich. 1953. "Social Stratification and Psychiatric Disorders." *American Sociological Review:* 18:163-169.

Holstein, James A. 1987. "Producing Gender Effects on Involuntary Mental Hospitalization." *Social Problems* 34:141-155.

_____. 1993. *Court-Ordered Insanity. Interpretive Practice and Involuntary Commitment.* New York: Aldine de Gruyer.

Horowitz, Ruth and Anne E. Pottieger. 1991. "Gender Bias in Juvenile Justice Handling of Seriously Crime-Involved Youths." *Journal of Research in Crime and Delinquency* 28:75-100.

Horwitz, Allan V. 1977. "The Pathways into Psychiatric Treatment: Some Differences between Men and Women." *Journal of Health and Social Behavior* 18:169-78.

_____. 1990. *The Logic of Social Control.* New York: Plenum Press.

_____. 2002a. *Creating Mental Illness.* Chicago, IL: University of Chicago Press.

_____. 2002b. *The Social Control of Mental Illness.* Clinton Corners, NY: Percheron Press.

Horwitz, Allan V., Julie McLaughlin, and Helene Raskin White. 1998. "How the Negative and Positive Aspects of Partner Relationships Affect the Mental Health of Young Married People." *Journal of Health and Social Behavior* 39:124-136.

Hudson, Barbara. 2002. "Gender Issues in Penal Policy and Penal Theory." Pp. 21-46 in *Women and Punishment: The Struggle for Justice,* edited by Pat Carlen. Portland, OR: Willan Publishing.

Huffine, Carol and John A. Clausen. 1979. "Madness and Work: Short- and Long-Term Effects of Mental Illness on Occupational Careers." *Social Forces* 57:1049-62.

Janofsky, Jeffrey S., Mitchell H. Dunn, Erik J. Roskes, Jonathan K. Briskin, and Maj-Stina Lunstrum Rudolph. 1996. "Insanity Defense Pleas in Baltimore City: An Analysis of Outcome." *American Journal of Psychiatry* 153:1464-1468.

Jeffords, Charles R. and R.Thomas Dull. 1982. "Demographic Variations in Attitudes Towards Marital Rape Immunity." *Journal of Marriage and Family* 44:755-762.

Jeffrey, Richard W. and Richard A. Pasewark. 1983. "Altering Opinions about the Insanity Plea." *Journal of Psychiatry and Law* 29-40.

Johnson, Kirsten K. and Mary-Anne Kandrack. 1995. "On the Medico-Legal Appropriation of Menstrual Discourse: The Syndromization of Women's Experiences." *Resources for Feminist Research* 24:23-27.

Jones, F.L. and Jonathan Kelley. 1984. "Decomposing Differences Between Groups." *Sociological Methods & Research* 3:323-343.

Kahn, Marvin W. and Lawrence Raifman. 1981. "Hospitalization Versus Imprisonment and the Insanity Plea." *Criminal Justice and Behavior* 8:483-490.

Katz, Charles M. and Cassia C. Spohn. 1995. "The Effect of Race and Gender on Bail Outcomes: A Test of an Interactive Model." *American Journal of Criminal Justice* 19:161-184.

Kay, Fiona M. and John Hagan. 1998. "Raising the Bar: The Gender Stratification of Law-Firm Capital." *American Sociological Review* 63:728-743.

Kendall, Kathleen. 1991. "The Politics of Premenstrual Syndrome: Implications for Feminist Justice." *The Journal of Human Justice* 2:77-98.
_____. 1999a. "Beyond Grace: Criminal Lunatic Women." *Canadian Woman Studies* 19:110-115.
_____. 1999b. "Criminal Lunatic Women in 19th Century Canada." *Forum on Corrections Research* 11:46-50.

Kennedy, Randall. 1997. *Race, Crime, and the Law.* New York: Random House.

Kerley, Kent R., Michael L. Benson, Matthew R. Lee, and Francis T. Cullen. 2004. "Race, Criminal Justice Contact, and Adult Position in the Social Stratification System." *Social Problems* 51:549-568.

Kessler, Ronald C. 1979. "Stress, Social Status, and Psychological Distress." *Journal of Health and Social Behavior:* 20:259-72.

Kessler, Ronald C., K.A. McGonagle, M. Swartz, D.G. Blazer, and C.B. Nelson. 1993. "Sex and Depression in the National Comorbidity Survey I: Lifetime Prevalence, Chronicity, and Recurrence." *Journal of Affective Disorders* 29:85-96.

Kessler, Ronald C., K.A. McGonagle, S. Zhao, C.B. Nelson, M. Hughes, S. Eshleman, H.U. Wittchen, and K.S. Kendler. 1994. "Lifetime and 12-Month Prevalence of DSM-III-R Psychiatric Disorders in the United States: Results from the National Comorbidity Survey." *Archives of General Psychiatry* 51:8-19.

Kessler, Ronald C. and Jane D. McLeod. 1984. "Sex Differences in Vulnerability to Undesirable Life Events." *American Sociological Review* 49:620-31.

Kessler, Ronald C. and Harold W. Neighbors. 1986. "A New Perspective on the Relationships Between Race, Social Class, and Psychological Distress." *Journal of Health and Social Behavior:* 27:107-15.

Kessler, Ronald C. and Shanyang Zhao. 1999. "The Prevalence of Mental Illness." Pp. 58-78 in *A Handbook for the Study of Mental Health: Social Contexts, Theories and Symptoms*, edited by Allan V. Horwitz and Teresa L. Sheid. New York: Cambridge University Press.

King, Gary and Langche Zeng. 2001a. "Explaining Rare Events in International Relations." *International Organization* 55:693-715.

_____. 2001b. "Logistic Regression in Rare Events Data." *Political Analysis* 9:137-163.

Kirk, Stuart A. 1974. "The Impact of Labeling on the Rejection of the Mentally Ill: An Experimental Study." *Journal of Health and Social Behavior* 15:108-17.

Kirwin, Barbara R. 1997. *The Mad, the Bad, and the Innocent*. Boston, MA: Little, Brown and Company.

Kleck, Gary and Michael Hogan. 1999. "National Case-Control Study of Homicide Offending and Gun Ownership." *Social Problems* 46:275-293.

Klein, Stephen, Joan Petersilia, and Susan Turner. 1988. *Racial Equity in Sentencing*. Santa Monica, CA: Rand Corporation.

Konrad, Alison M. and Kathy Cannings. 1997. "The Effects of Gender Role Congruence and Statistical Discrimination on Managerial Advancement." *Human Relations* 50:1305-1328,

Kramer, John H. and Jeffery T. Ulmer. 1996. "Sentencing Disparity and Departures from Guidelines." *Justice Quarterly* 13:81-106.

Kruttschnitt, Candace. 1980-81. "Social Status and Sentences of Female Offenders." *Law & Society Review* 15:247-265.

_____. 1982. "Respectable Women and the Law." *Sociological Quarterly* 23:221-234.

_____. 1989. "A Sociological, Offender-Based, Study of Rape." *Sociological Quarterly* 30:305-329.

_____. 1996. "Contributions of Quantitative Methods to the Study of Gender and Crime, or Bootstrapping Our Way into the Theoretical Ticket." *Journal of Quantitative Criminology* 12:135-161.

Kruttschnitt, Candace and Daniel McCarthy. 1985. "Gender, Criminal Sentences and Sex Role Stereotypes." *Windsor Yearbook of Access to Justice* 5:306-323.

Kruttschnitt, Candace, David Ward, and Mary Ann Sheble. 1987. "Abuse-Resistant Youth: Some Factors That May Inhibit Violent Criminal Behavior." *Social Forces* 66:501-519.

Kupers, Terry A. 1999. *Prison Madness. The Mental Health Crisis Behind Bars and What We Must Do About It.* San Francisco, CA: Jossey-Bass Publishers.

Kutchins, Herb and Stuwart A. Kirk. 1997. *Making us Crazy. DSM: The Psychiatric Bible and the Creation of Mental Disorders.* New York: The Free Press.

LaFond, John Q. 1994. "Law and the Delivery of Involuntary Mental Services." *American Journal of Orthopsychiatry* 64:209-222.

LaFree, Gary D. 1989. *Rape and Criminal Justice: The Social Construction of Sexual Assault.* Belmont, CA: Wadsworth.

Laberge, Danielle and Daphné Morin. 2001. "Mental Illness and Criminal Justice Processing: The Strategies and Dilemmas of Defence Lawyers." *International Journal of the Sociology of Law* 29:149-171.

Lacy, Michael G. 1997. "Efficiently Studying Rare Events: Case-Control Methods for Sociologists." *Sociological Perspectives* 40:129-154.

Lee, C. 1998. "Race and the Victim: An Examination of Capital Sentencing and Guilt Attribution Studies." *Chicago-Kent Law Review* 73:533.

Lehman, Anthony F., Susan Possidente, and Fiona Hawker. 1986. "The Quality of Life of Chronic Patients in a State Hospital and in Community Residences." *Hospital and Community Psychiatry* 37:901-907.

Lemert, Edwin M. 1951. *Social Pathology.* New York: McGraw-Hill.

_____. 1972. *Human Deviance, Social Problems, and Social Control.* Englewood Cliffs, NJ: Prentice-Hall.

Levin, Martin A. 1977. *Urban Politics and the Criminal Courts.* Chicago, IL: University of Chicago Press.

Light, Donald W. 1982. "Learning to Label: The Social Construction of Psychiatrists." Pp. 33-47 in *Deviance and Mental Illness,* edited by W.R. Gove. Beverly Hills, CA: Sage.

Little, Roderick and Donald Rubin. 1987. *Statistical Analysis with Missing Data.* New York: Wiley.

_____. 1990. "The Analysis of Social Science Data with Missing Values." *Sociological Methods and Research* 18:292-326.

Link, Bruce G. 1982. "Mental Patient Status, Work, and Income: An Examination of the Effects of a Psychiatric Label." *American Sociological Review* 47:202-15.

_____. 1987. "Understanding Labeling Effects in the Area of Mental Disorders: An Assessment of the Effects of Expectations of Rejection." *American Sociological Review* 52:96-112.

Link, Bruce G., Howard Andrews, and Francis T. Cullen. 1992. "The Violent and Illegal Behavior of Mental Patients Reconsidered." *American Sociological Review* 57:275-292.

Link, Bruce G. and Francis T. Cullen. 1990. "The Labeling Theory of Mental Disorder: A Review of the Evidence." *Research in Community and Mental Health* 6:75-105.

Link, Bruce G., Francis T. Cullen, James Frank, and John F. Wozniak. 1987. "The Social Rejection of Former Mental Patients: Understanding Why Labels Matter." *American Journal of Sociology* 92:1461-1500.

Link, Bruce G., Francis T. Cullen, Elmer Struening, Patrick E. Shrout, and Bruce P. Dohrenwend. 1989. "A Modified Labeling Theory Approach to Mental Disorders: An Empirical Assessment." *American Sociological Review* 54:400-23.

Link, Bruce G., Bruce P. Dohrenwend, and Andrew D. Skodol. 1986. "Socio-Economic Status and Schizophrenia: Noisome Occupational Characteristics as a Risk Factor." *American Sociological Review* 51:242-58.

Link, Bruce G. and Jo C. Phelan. 1999. "The Labeling Theory of Mental Disorder: The Consequences of Labeling." Pp. 361-376 in *A Handbook for the Study of Mental Health: Social Contexts, Theories and Symptoms*, edited by Allan V. Horwitz and Teresa L. Sheid. New York: Cambridge University Press.

Link, Bruce G., John Monahan, Ann Stueve, and Francis T. Cullen. 1999a. "Real in Their Consequences: A Sociological Approach to Understanding the Association between Psychotic Symptoms and Violence." *American Sociological Review* 64:316-332.

Link, Bruce G., Jo Phelan, Michaline Bresnahan, Ann Stueve, and Bernice A. Pescosolido. 1999b. "Public Conceptions of Mental Illness: Labels, Causes, Dangerousness and Social Distance." *American Journal of Public Health* 89:1328-33.

Liska, Allen E., Fred E. Morkowitz, Rachel Bridges Whaley, and Paul Bellair. 1999. "Modeling the Relationship between the Criminal Justice and Mental Health Systems." *American Journal of Sociology* 104:1744-75.

Loftin, Colin and David McDowall. 1988. "The Analysis of Case-Control Studies in Criminology." *Journal of Quantitative Criminology* 4:85-98.

Loring, Marti and Brian Powell. 1988. "Gender, Race, and DSM-III: A Study of the Objectivity of Psychiatric Behavior." *Journal of Health and Social Behavior* 29:1-22.

Lymburner, Jocelyn A. and Ronald Roesch. 1999. "The Insanity Defense: Five Years of Research (1993-1997)." *International Journal of Law and Psychiatry* 22:213-240.

MacKinnon, Catherine A. 1987. *Feminism Unmodified.* Cambridge, MA: Harvard University Press.

_____. 1989. *Towards a Feminist Theory of the State.* Cambridge, MA: Harvard University Press.

Maitzen, Stephen. 1991. "The Ethics of Statistical Discrimination." *Social Theory and Practice* 17:23-45.

Mann, Coramae Richey. 1996. *When Women Kill.* Albany, NY: State University of New York Press.

March, James G. and Herbert A. Simon. 1963. *Organizations.* New York: Wiley.

Martin, Jack K., Bernice A. Pescosolido, and Steven A. Tuch. 2000. "Of Fear and Loathing: The Role of 'Disturbing Behavior,' Labels, and Causal Attributions in Shaping Public Attitudes Toward People with Mental Illness." *Journal of Health and Social Behavior* 41:208-223.

Mechanic, David. 1969. *Mental Health and Social Policy* Englewood Cliffs, NJ: Prentice-Hall.

Menkel-Meadow, Carrie and Shari Seidman Diamond. 1991. "The content, method, and epistemology of gender in sociolegal studies." *Law & Society Review* 25(2) Special Issue on Gender and Sociolegal Studies: 221-235.

Menzies, Robert J. 1989. *Survival of the Sanest. Order and Disorder in a Pretrial Psychiatric Clinic.* Toronto: University of Toronto Press.

Meyers, M. 2004. "African American Women and Violence: Gender, Race, and Class in the News." *Critical Studies in Media Communication* 21:95-118.

Miethe, Terance D. 1987. "Stereotypical Conceptions and Criminal Processing: The Case of the Victim-Offender Relationship." *Justice Quarterly* 4:571-593.

Miethe, Terance D. and Charles A. Moore. 1986. "Racial Differences in Criminal Processing: The Consequences of Model Selection on Conclusions about Differential Treatment." *Sociological Quarterly* 27:217-37.

Miles, Steven H. and Allison August. 1990. "Courts, Gender and 'The Right to Die.'" *Law, Medicine & Health Care* 18:85-95.

Miller, Robert D. 1993. "The Criminalization of the Mentally Ill: Does Dangerousness Take Precedence over the Need for Treatment?" *Criminal Behaviour and Mental Health* 3:241-250.

Miller, Robert D., J. Olin, D. Johnson, J. Dodge, D. Iverson, and E. Fantone. 1996. "Forcing the Insanity Defense on Unwilling Defendants: Best Interests and the Dignity of the Law." *Journal of Psychiatry and Law* 24:487-509.

Mirowsky, John and Catherine E. Ross. 1989a. *Social Causes of Psychological Distress.* New York: Aldine de Gruyter.

_____. 1989b. "Psychiatric Diagnosis as Reified Measurement." *Journal of Health and Social Behavior* 30:11-25.

Moran, Richard. 1981. *Knowing Right from Wrong.* New York: Free Press.

Morris, Amy V. 1992. *Insanity Defense: Gender Differences.* Unpublished Ph.D. dissertation. University of Wyoming, Laramie, WY.

Morse, Stephen J. 1985. "Excusing the Crazy: The Insanity Defense Reconsidered." *Southern California Law Review* 58:777-836.

Mowbray, Carol T. and Philip Chamberlain. 1986. "Sex Differences Among the Long-Term Mentally Disabled." *Psychology of Women Quarterly* 10:383-392.

Myers, Martha and Suzette Talarico. 1987. *The Social Contexts of Criminal Sentencing.* New York: Springer-Verlag.

Myers, Samuel L., Jr. 1985. "Statistical Tests of Discrimination in Punishment." *Journal of Quantitative Criminology* 1:191-218.

Nagel, Irene H. and Barry L. Johnson. 1994. "The Role of Gender in a Structured Sentencing System: Equal Treatment, Policy Choices, and the Sentencing of Female Offenders Under the United States Sentencing Guidelines." *The Journal of Criminal Law & Criminology.* 85:181-221.

Narayan, Uma. 1997. "Contesting Cultures. 'Westernization,' Respect for Cultures, and Third-World Feminists." Pp. 396-414 in *The Second Wave: A Reader in Feminist Theory,* edited by Linda Nicholson. New York: Routledge.

Neumann, C.S., E.F. Walker, J. Weinstein, and C. Cutshaw. 1996. "Psychotic Patients' Awareness of Mental Illness: Implications for Legal Defense Proceedings." *Journal of Psychiatry and Law* 24:421-442.

Nicholson, Linda. 1997. (Ed.) *The Second Wave: A Reader in Feminist Theory.* New York: Routledge.

Nicolson, Donald. 1995. "Telling Tales: Gender Discrimination, Gender Construction and Battered Women Who Kill." *Feminist Legal Studies* 3:185-206.

Offen, Liz. 1986. "The Female Offender and Psychiatric Referral: The Medicalization of Female Deviance?" *Medicine and Law* 5:339-348.

Ogloff, James R.P. 1991. "A Comparison of Insanity Defense Standards on Juror Decision Making." *Law & Human Behavior* 15:509-531.

Oliver, M.B. 2004. "The Face of Crime: Viewers' Memory of Race-Related Facial Features of Individuals Pictured in the News." *Journal of Communication* 54:88-104.

Omi, Michael and Howard Winant. 1994. *Racial Formation in the United States*. 2d ed. New York: Routledge.

Pager, Devah. 2004. "The Mark of a Criminal Record." *American Journal of Sociology* 108:937-975.

Palermo, George B., and Richard D. Knudten. 1994. "The Insanity Plea in the Case of a Serial Killer." *International Journal of Offender Therapy and Comparative Criminology* 38:3-16.

Pasewark, Richard A. 1986. "A Review of Research on the Insanity Defense." *The Annals of the American Academy of Political and Social Science* 484:100-114.

Perlin, Michael L. 1989-90. "Unpacking the Myths: The Symbolism Mythology of Insanity Defense Jurisprudence." *Case Western Reserve Law Review* 40:599-731.

_____. 1994. *Law and Mental Disability*. Charlottesville, VA: Michie.

_____. 2000. *The Hidden Prejudice: Mental Disability on Trial*. Washington, DC: American Psychological Association.

Petersilia, Joan and S. Turner. 1988 (June). "Minorities in Prison, Discrimination or Disparity?" *Corrections Today* 92-94.

Peterson, David. 2003. "Income Inroads Lure Women to Twin Cities." *Minneapolis Star Tribune*, June 15, p. 1A.

Phelan, Jo C. and Bruce G. Link. 1999. "The Labeling Theory of Mental Disorder: The Role of Social Contingencies in the Application of Psychiatric Labels." Pp. 139-149 in *A Handbook for the Study of Mental Health: Social Contexts, Theories and Symptoms*, edited by Allan V. Horwitz and Teresa L. Sheid. New York: Cambridge University Press.

Phelps, Edmund S. 1972. *Inflation Policy and Unemployment Theory: The Cost-Benefit Approach to Monetary Planning*. New York: W.W. Norton Company.

Plaut. V.L. 1983. "Punishment versus Treatment of the Guilty but Mentally Ill." *Journal of Criminal Law & Criminology* 74:428-456.

Potts, Marilyn K., M. Audrey Burnam, and Kenneth B. Wells. 1991. "Gender Differences in Depression Detection: A Comparison of Clinician

Diagnosis and Standardized Assessment." *Psychological Assessment* 3:609-615.

Quillian, Lincoln and Devah Pager. 2001. "Black Neighbors, Higher Crime? The Role of Racial Stereotypes in Evaluations of Neighborhood Crime." *American Journal of Sociology* 107:717-767.

Reisner, Ralph and Christopher Slobogin. 1990. *Law and the Mental Health System: Civil and Criminal Aspects.* St. Paul, MN: West Publishing Co.

Reskin, Barbara F. and Christy A. Visher. 1986. "The Impacts of Evidence and Extralegal Factors in Jurors' Decisions." *Law & Society Review* 20:423-438.

Resnik, Judith. 1996. "Asking about Gender in Courts." *Signs: Journal of Women in Culture and Society* 21:952-990.

Rice, Marnie E. and Grant T. Harris. 1990. "The Predictors of Insanity Acquittal." *International Journal of Law and Psychiatry* 16:217-224.

Roberts, Caton F. and Stephen L. Golding. 1991. "The Social Construction of Criminal Responsibility and Insanity." *Law & Human Behavior* 15:349-376.

Roberts, Dorothy. 2002. *Shattered Bonds: The Color of Child Welfare.* New York: Basic Civitas Books.

Robin, Gerald. 1997. "The Evolution of the Insanity Defense. Welcome to the Twilight Zone of Mental Illness, Psychiatry, and the Law." *Journal of Contemporary Criminal Justice* 13:224-235.

Robins, Lee N., J.E. Helzer, J. Croughan, and K.S. Ratcliff. 1981. "The NIMH Diagnostic Interview Schedule: Its History, Characteristics and Validity." *Archives of General Psychiatry* 28:381-9.

Robins, Lee N., B.Z. Locke, and Darrel A. Reiger. 1991. "An Overview of Psychiatric Disorders in America." Pp. 328-66 in *Psychiatric Disorders in America: The Epidemiological Catchment Area Study,* edited by Lee N. Robins and Darrel A. Reiger. New York: Free Press.

Roesch, Ronald, J.R. Ogloff, S.D. Hart, R.J. Dempster, P.A. Zapf, and K.E. Whittemore. 1997. "The Impact of Canadian Criminal Code Changes on Remands and Assessments of Fitness to Stand Trial and Criminal Responsibility in British Columbia." *Canadian Journal of Psychiatry* 42:509-514.

Rogers, Jeffrey L., Joseph D. Bloom, and Spero M. Manson. 1986. "Oregon's Psychiatric Security Review Board: A Comprehensive System for Managing Insanity Acquittees." *The Annals of the American Academy of Political and Social Science* 484:86-99.

Rogler, Lloyd H. 1997. "Making Sense of Historical Changes in the Diagnostic and Statistical Manual of Mental Disorders: Five Propositions." *Journal of Health and Social Behavior* 38:9-20.

Rosenfield, Sarah. 1982. "Sex Roles and Societal Reactions to Mental Illness: The Labelling of 'Deviant' Deviance." *Journal of Health and Social Behavior* 23:18-24. Beverly Hills, CA: Sage.

_____. 1989. "The Effects of Women's Employment: Personal Control and Sex Differences in Mental Health." *Journal of Health and Social Behavior* 30:77-91.

_____. 1992. "Factors Contributing to the Quality of Life of the Chronically Mentally Ill." *Journal of Health and Social Behavior* 33:229-315.

_____. 1997. "Labeling Mental Illness: The Effects of Received Services and Perceived Stigma on Life Satisfaction." *American Sociological Review* 62:660-72.

_____. 1999. "Gender and Mental Health: Do Women Have More Psychopathology, Men More, or Both the Same (and Why)?" Pp. 348-360 in *A Handbook for the Study of Mental Health: Social Contexts, Theories and Symptoms*, edited by Allan V. Horwitz and Teresa L. Sheid. New York: Cambridge University Press.

Rosenhan, D.L. 1973. "On Being Sane in Insane Places." *Science* 179:250-258.

Rothman, David J. 1980. *Conscience and Convenience. The Asylum and its Alternatives in Progressive America.* Boston, MA: Little, Brown and Company.

Rothman, Kenneth J. and Sander Greenland. 1998. *Modern Epidemiology.* 2d ed. Philadelphia, PA: Lippincot-Raven.

Rubin, Gayle. 1975. "The Traffic in Women." In *Toward an Anthology of Women*, edited by R. Reiter. New York, NY: Monthly Review Press.

Rubington, Earl and Martin S. Weinberg. 1987. *Deviance: The Interactionist Perspective.* New York: Macmillan.

Sacks, Valerie L. 1996. "An Indefensible Defense: On the Misuse of Culture in Criminal Law." *Arizona Journal of International and Comparative Law* 13:523.

Sampson, Robert and John Laub. 1993. *Crime in the Making: Pathways and Turning Points Through Life.* Cambridge, MA: Harvard University Press.

Sampson, Robert J. and Janet L. Lauritsen. 1997. "Racial and Ethnic Disparities in Crime and Criminal Justice in the United States." In *Ethnicity, Crime, and Immigration*, edited by M. Tonry. Chicago, IL: University of Chicago Press.

Scheff, Thomas J. 1963. "The Role of the Mentally Ill and the Dynamics of Mental Disorder: A Research Framework." *Sociometry* 26:436-53.

———. 1966. *Being Mentally Ill.* Chicago, IL: Aldine.

———. 1974. "The Labeling Theory of Mental Illness." *American Sociological Review* 39:444-52.

Schlesselman, James J. 1982. *Case-Control Studies: Design, Conduct, Analysis.* New York: Oxford University Press.

Schultz, Amy, David Williams, Barbara Israel, Adam Becker, Edith Parker, Sherman A. James, and James Jackson. 2000. "Unfair Treatment, Neighborhood Effects, and Mental Health in the Detroit Metropolitan Area." *Journal of Health and Social Behavior* 41:314-332.

Schultz, Alfred. 1970. *On Phenomenology and Social Relations.* Chicago, IL: University of Chicago Press.

Schur, Edwin M. 1984. *Labeling Women Deviant. Gender, Stigma, and Social Control.* New York: Random House.

Schwartz, Carol C., Jerome K. Myers, and Boris M. Astrachan. 1974. "Psychiatric Labeling and the Rehabilitation of Mental Patients." *Archives of General Psychiatry* 31:329-34.

Seig, Ann, Elissa Ball, and John A. Menninger. 1995. "A Comparison of Female Versus Male Insanity Acquittees in Colorado." *Bulletin of the American Academy of Psychiatry and Law* 23:523-532.

Shah, Pritesh J., William M .Greenberg, and Antonio Convit. 1994. "Hospitalized Insanity Acquittees' Level of Functioning." *Bulletin of the American Academy of Psychiatry and Law* 22:85-93.

Sharp, Susan F., Dennis Brewster, and Sharon RedHawk Love. 2005. "Disentangling Strain, Personal Attributes, Affective Response and Deviance: A Gendered Analysis." *Deviant Behavior* 26:133-157.

Shepherd, Jonathan and Mark Brickley. 1996. "The Relationship between Alcohol Intoxication, Stressors and Injury in Urban Violence." *British Journal of Criminology* 36:546-566.

Silver, Eric. 1995. "Punishment or Treatment? Comparing the Lengths of Confinement of Successful and Unsuccessful Insanity Defendants." *Law & Human Behavior* 19:375-388.

Silver, Eric, Carmen Cirincione, and Henry J. Steadman. 1994. "Demythologizing Inaccurate Perceptions of the Insanity Defense." *Law & Human Behavior* 18:63-70.

Silver, Eric and Brent Teasdale. 2005. "Mental Disorder and Violence: An Examination of Stressful Life Events and Impaired Social Support." *Social Problems* 52:62-78.

Simon, Rita and Jean Landis. 1991. *The Crimes Women Commit, the Punishments they Receive*. Lexington, MA: Lexington Books.

Simon, Rita. 1975. *Women and Crime*. Lexington, MA: Lexington Books.

Simpson, Sally. 1989. "Feminist Theory, Crime and Justice." *Criminology* 27:605-632.

Slovenko, Ralph. 1995. *Psychiatry and Criminal Culpability*. New York: John Wiley & Sons, Inc.

Smart, Carol. 1995. *Law, Crime and Sexuality. Essays in Feminism*. Thousand Oaks, CA: Sage Publications.

Smith, Roger. 1985. "Expertise and Causal Attribution in Deciding between Crime and Mental Disorder." *Social Studies of Science* 15:67-98.

Smith, Tom W. 1991. *What Americans Say About Jews*. New York: American Jewish Committee.

Sniderman, Paul M. and Thomas Piazza. 1993. *The Scar of Race*. Cambridge, MA: Harvard University Press.

Spohn, Cassia. 1990. "Decision Making in Sexual Assault Cases: Do Black and Female Judges Make a Difference?" *Women & Criminal Justice* 2:83-105.

Spohn, Cassia and David Holleran. 2000. "The Imprisonment Penalty Paid by Young, Unemployed Black and Hispanic Male Offenders." *Criminology* 38:281-306.

Spohn, Cassia and Jeffrey W. Spears. 1996. "The Effect of Offender and Victim Characteristics on Sexual Assault Case Processing Decisions." *Justice Quarterly* 13:649-679.

_____. 1997. "Gender and Case Processing Decisions: A Comparison of Case Outcomes for Male and Female Defendants Charged with Violent Felonies." *Women & Criminal Justice* 8:29-59.

Steadman, Henry J., Joseph J. Cocozza, and Bonita Veysey. 1999. "Comparing Outcomes for Diverted and Nondiverted Jail Detainees with Mental Illnesses." *Law & Human Behavior* 23:615-627.

Steadman, Henry J., Keitner, Braff, and Arvanites. 1983. "Factors Associated with a Successful Insanity Defense." *American Journal of Psychiatry* 140:401-404.

Steadman, Henry J., Margaret A. McGreevy, Joseph P. Morrissey, Lisa A. Callahan, Pamela Clark Robbins, and Carmen Cirincione. 1993. *Before and After Hinckley: Evaluating Insanity Defense Reform*. New York: Guilford Press.

Steadman, Henry J., John Monahan, Barbara Duffee, Eliot Hartstone, and Pamela Clark Robbins. 1984. "The Impact of State Mental Hospital

Deinstitutionalization on United States Prison populations, 1968-1978."
Journal of Criminal Law & Criminology 75:474-490.

Steffensmeier, Darrell and Emilie Allen. 1996. "Gender and Crime: Toward a
Gendered Theory of Female Offending." *Annual Review of Sociology*
22:459-487.

Steffensmeier, Darrell and Stephen DeMuth. 2000. "Ethnicity and Sentencing
Outcomes in U.S. Federal Courts: Who is Punished More Harshly?"
American Sociological Review 65:705-729.

Steffensmeier, Darrell, John Kramer, and Cathy Streifel. 1993. "Gender and
Imprisonment Decisions." *Criminology.* 31:411-446.

Steffensmeier, Darrell, Jeffery Ulmer, and John Kramer. 1998. "The Interaction
of Race, Gender and Age in Criminal Sentencing: The Punishment Cost of
Being Young, Black, and Male." *Criminology* 36:763-798.

Stepnick, Andrea and James D. Orcutt. 1996. "Conflicting Testimony: Judges'
and Attorneys' Perceptions of Gender Bias in Legal Settings." *Sex Roles*
34:567-579.

Sudnow, David. 1965. "Normal Crimes: Sociological Features of the Penal
Code in a Public Defender Office." *Social Problems* 12:255-276.

Szasz, Thomas. 1961. *The Myth of Mental Illness.* New York: Harper & Row.

Tausig, Mark, Janet Michello, and Sree Subedi. 1999. *A Sociology of Mental
Illness.* Upper Saddle River, NJ: Prentice Hall.

Teplin, Linda A. and Ecford S. Voit. 1996. "Criminalizing the Seriously
Mentally Ill: Putting the Problem in Perspective." Pp. 283-317 in *Mental
Health and Law: Research, Policy and Services*, edited by Bruce D. Sales
and Saleem A. Shah. Durham, NC: Carolina Academic Press.

Thoits, Peggy A. 1985. "Self-labeling Processes in Mental Illness: The Role of
Emotional Deviance." *American Journal of Sociology* 91:221-49.

_____. 1999. "Sociological Approaches to Mental Illness." Pp. 121-138 in *A
Handbook for the Study of Mental Health: Social Contexts, Theories and
Symptoms*, edited by Allan V. Horwitz and Teresa L. Sheid. New York:
Cambridge University Press.

Thomas, W.I. 1931. *The Unadjusted Girl.* Boston: Little, Brown.

Thurow, Lester C. 1980. *The Zero-sum Society: Distribution and the
Possibilities for Economic Change.* New York: Basic.

Torrey, E. Fuller, Joan Stieber, Jonathan Ezekiel, Sidney M. Wolfe, Joshua
Sharfstein, John H. Noble, and Laurie M. Flynn. 1992. "Criminalizing the
Seriously Mentally Ill: The Abuse of Jails as Mental Hospitals."
*Innovations and Research in Clinical Services, Community Support, and
Rehabilitation* 2:11-14.

Turner, R. Jay and Donald A. Lloyd. 1999. "The Stress Process and the Social Distribution of Depression." *Journal of Health and Social Behavior* 40:374-404.

Turner, R. Jay, Blair Wheaton, and Donald A. Lloyd. 1995. "The Epidemiology of Social Stress." *American Sociological Review*. 60:104-125.

Uggen, Christopher. 1999. "Ex-Offenders and the Conformist Alternative: A Job Quality Model of Work and Crime." *Social Problems* 46:127-151.

Umphrey, Martha Merrill. 1999. "The Dialogics of Legal Meaning: Spectacular Trials, the Unwritten Law, and Narratives of Criminal Responsibility." *Law & Society Review* 33:393-423.

U.S. Census Bureau. 2000. "States Ranked by Black Population, July 1, 1999." http://eire.census.gov/popest/archieves/state/rank/black.txt. Downloaded July 19, 2003.

_____. 2003a. http://eire.census.gov/popest/data/national/tables/asro/US-EST2001-ASRO-02.php. Downloaded May 29, 2003.

_____. 2003b. "Census 2000 Redistricting Data (Public Law 94-171) Summary File". http://factfinder.census.gov/servlet/BasicFactsTable .html. Downloaded July 19, 2003.

_____. 2003c. "State and County QuickFacts." http://quickfacts. census.gov/pfd/states/27/27053.html. Downloaded July 19, 2003.

U.S. Department of Justice. 1994. "Violence between Intimates." *National Institute of Justice*. Washington, DC: USGPO.

_____. 1997a. "Providing Services for Jail Inmates with Mental Disorders." *National Institute of Justice Research in Brief*. Washington, DC: USGPO.

_____. 1997b. "Lifetime Likelihood of Going to State or Federal Prison." *National Institute of Justice*. Washington, DC: USGPO.

_____. 1998a. *Homicide Trends in the U.S.* Washington, DC: USGPO.

_____. 1998b. *Women Offenders: Programming Needs and Promising Approaches*. Washington, DC: USGPO.

_____. 1998c. *The Women's Prison Association: Supporting Women Offenders and Their Families*. Washington, DC: USGPO.

_____. 1998d. "Prisoners Under State or Federal Jurisdiction, by Race, 1998." *Correctional Populations in the U.S.* Washington, DC: USGPO.

_____. 1999a. "Mental Health and Treatment of Inmates and Probationers." *Bureau of Justice Statistics Special Report*. Washington, DC: USGPO.

_____. 1999b. "Women Offenders." *Bureau of Justice Statistics Special Report*. Washington, DC: USGPO.

_____. 2001a. "Felony Defendants in Large Urban Counties, 1998." *Bureau of Justice Statistics*. Washington, DC: USGPO.

_____. 2001b. "Mental Health Treatment in State Prisons, 2000." *Bureau of Justice Statistics*. Washington, DC: USGPO.

_____. 2003. "Prisoner and Jail Inmates at Midyear 2002." *Bureau of Justice Statistics*. Washington, DC: USGPO.

_____. 2004. "Prisoners in 2003." *Bureau of Justice Statistics*. Washington, DC: USGPO.

U.S. Department of Labor. 2002. "Highlights of Women's Earnings in 2001" (Report 960). *Bureau of Labor Statistics*. Washington, DC: USGPO.

_____. 2003. "Labor Force Statistics from the Current Population Survey." http://data.bls.gov/. Downloaded July 19, 2003.

Ussher, Jane. 1991. *Women's Madness: Misogyny or Mental Illness?* Amherst, MA: The University of Massachusetts Press.

Walker, Nigel. 1968. *Crime and Insanity in England*. Chicago, IL: Aldine Publishing Company.

Walsh, Anthony. 1990. "Twice Labeled: The Effect of Psychiatric Labeling on the Sentencing of Sex Offenders." *Social Problems* 37:375-389.

Walters, Amy P. 1994. "Gender and the Role of Expert Witnesses in the Federal Courts." *Georgetown Law Journal* 83:635-663.

Warheit, George J., Charles E. Holzer III, and John J. Schwab. 1973. "An Analysis of Social Class and Racial Differences in Depressive Symptomatology: A Community Study." *Journal of Health and Social Behavior* 14:291-99.

Warheit, George J., Charles E. Holzer, and Sandra A. Avery. 1975. "Race and Mental Illness: An Epidemiologic Update." *Journal of Health and Social Behavior* 16:243-56.

Warren, Janet I., Barry Rosenfeld, and W. Lawrence Fitch. 1994. "Beyond Competence and Sanity: The Influence of Pretrial Evaluation on Case Disposition." *Bulletin of the American Academy of Psychiatry and Law* 22:379-388.

Wasyliw, Cavanaugh and Rogers. 1985. "Beyond the Scientific Limits of Expert Testimony." *Bulletin of the American Academy of Psychiatry and Law* 13:147-152.

Weiss, Marcia J. 1997. "A Legal Evaluation of Criminal Competency Standards: Competency to Stand Trial, Competency to Plead Guilty and Competency to Waive Counsel." *Journal of Contemporary Criminal Justice* 13:213-223.

Widom, Cathy Spatz, ed. 1984. *Sex Roles and Psychopathology*. New York: Plenum Press.

Wilbanks, William. 1987. *The Myth of a Racist Criminal Justice System*. Monterey, CA: Brooks/Cole.

Wilczynski, Ania. 1991. "Images of Women Who Kill Their Infants: The Mad and the Bad." *Women & Criminal Justice* 2:71-88.

Williams, David R. and Michelle Harris-Reid. 1999. "Race and Mental Health: Emerging Patterns and Promising Approaches." Chapter in *A Handbook for the Study of Mental Health*, edited by Allan V. Horwitz and Teresa L. Scheid. New York: Cambridge University Press.

Williams, David R., David T. Takeuchi, and Russell K. Adair. 1992. "Socioeconomic Status and Psychiatric Disorder Among Blacks and Whites." *Social Forces* 71:79-94.

Winship, Christopher and Robert D. Mare. 1992. "Models for Sample Selection Bias." *Annual Review of Sociology* 87:548-77.

Wonders, Nancy A. 1996. "Determinate Sentencing: A Feminist and Postmodern Story." *Justice Quarterly* 13:611-648.

Wooldredge, John D. 1998. "Analytical Rigor in Studies of Disparities in Criminal Case Processing." *Journal of Quantitative Criminology* 14:155-179.

Worrall, Anne. 1990. *Offending Women. Female Lawbreakers and the Criminal Justice System*. London: Routledge.

_____. 2002. "Rendering Women Punishable: The Making of a Penal Crisis." Pp. 47-66 in *Women and Punishment: The Struggle for Justice*, edited by Pat Carlen. Portland, OR: Willan Publishing.

Yeoman, Barry. 1999. "Bad Girls." *Psychology Today* 6:54-57&71.

Zedner, Lucia. 1991. *Women, Crime and Custody in Victorian England*. Oxford: Claredon Press.

CASES CITED

Addington v. Texas, 441 U.S. 418 (1979).

Anderson v. Grasberg, 247 Minn. 538, 78 N.W.2d. 450 (1956).

Drope v. Missouri, 420 U.S. 162 (1975).

Dusky v. United States, 362 U.S. 402 (1960).

Jackson v. Indiana, 406 U.S. 715 (1972).

O'Connor v. Donaldson, 422 U.S. 563 (1975).

Washington v. United States, 390 F.2d 444 (1967).

Youngberg v. Romeo, 457 U.S. 307 (1982).

INDEX

215